Praise for *The Art of*

Finalist for the 2018 Southern Book Prize

"In Berry's new book, *The Art of Loading Brush*, he is a frustrated advocate, speaking out against local wastefulness and distant idealism; he is a gentle friend, asserting as he always has, the hope possible in caring for the world, and your specific place in it . . . *The Art of Loading Brush* is singular in Berry's corpus."
— *The Paris Review*

"The cumulative force of these lyrical essays takes the reader's breath away, as if we have relearned something essential that contradicts the world all around us . . . Here is a man deeply rooted, wisely aware, offering a manifesto of weighty moral passion. He exposes the counterfeit quality of our dominant life and summons us to know and live differently."
— *The Christian Century*

"Berry has faithfully cultivated his given life within the limits of his marginal place in rural Kentucky, and . . . in the essays, stories, and single poem collected in his latest book, he distills his life's varied work into a coherent sense. And like Kentucky bourbon, it is a complex, mature sense, flavored by the fields and forests of his place."
— *Englewood Review of Books*

The Art of Loading Brush

The Art of Loading Brush

New Agrarian Writings

Wendell Berry

COUNTERPOINT
BERKELEY, CALIFORNIA

The Art of Loading Brush

The Library of Congress has cataloged the hardcover edition as follows:
Names: Berry, Wendell, 1934– author.
Title: The art of loading brush : new agrarian writings / Wendell Berry.
Description: Berkeley, CA : Counterpoint Press, [2017] | Includes
    bibliographical references and index.
Identifiers: LCCN 2017034645 | ISBN 9781619020382 (alk. paper)
Subjects: LCSH: Agriculture—United States. | Agriculture—Social
    aspects—United States.
Classification: LCC S441 .B46 2017 | DDC 338.10973—dc23
LC record available at https://lccn.loc.gov/2017034645

Paperback ISBN: 978-1-64009-158-0

Cover design by Nicole Caputo
Book design by Tabitha Lahr

COUNTERPOINT
2560 Ninth Street, Suite 318
Berkeley, CA 94710
www.counterpointpress.com

Printed in the United States of America

10 9 8 7 6 5 4 3

This book is indebted, as most of my books have been, to my conversation with my brother, John Marshall Berry, Jr. That conversation began in earnest half a century ago and ended just a few days before he died on October 27, 2016.

Our conversation remained from beginning to end under the influence of our father, of his devotion to farming, of his work in behalf of the small farmers of our region, and of our conversation with him.

That conversation was taken up many years ago between Tanya Berry and me. It continues between us and our children and their children.

This is the conversation of agrarians and agrarianism, far larger, older, and longer than our family or any family can remember, involving some people we know, and many we don't know.

I dedicate this book to that conversation and to all of its members, once, now, and to come.

You had to be here then to be able to don't see it and don't hear it now. But I was here then, and I don't see it now . . .

—ERNEST J. GAINES, *A Gathering of Old Men*

. . . our assumption that everything is provisional and soon to be superseded, that the attainment of goods we have never yet had, rather than the defence and conservation of those we have already, is the cardinal business of life . . .

—C. S. LEWIS, "De Descriptione Temporum," *Selected Literary Essays*

My view is that all artists, whether they know it or not, whether they would repudiate the notion or not, are in fact "showers forth" of things which tend to be impoverished, or misconceived, or altogether lost or willfully set aside in the preoccupations of our present intense technological phase, but which, none the less, belong to man.

So that when asked to what end does my work proceed I can do no more than answer . . . thus: Perhaps it is in the maintenance of some sort of single plank in some sort of bridge.

—DAVID JONES, *The Dying Gaul*

We are responsible for what we remember.

—JOHN LUKACS, talking with students at the University of Louisville, March 9, 2011

Contents

◈

The Art of Loading Brush

Preface[*]

by Maurice Telleen (in absentia)

Whatever agrarianism is, it is too important to be a mere movement.

· · ·

Movements, almost by definition, are compelled to be certain or "right." So it is not surprising that they tend to be self-righteous. In addition to being right they are convinced of both their inevitability and their superiority. The latter confers an aura of both practicality and pragmatism on them. Movements leave little room for meaningful dissent. They regard themselves as destiny. Movements are big on tunnel vision. Their tunnel. Their vision. So, let us agrarians give thanks that we are not part of a certified and accredited movement.

· · ·

Agrarianism's natural home is the field, the garden, the stable, the prairie, the forest, the tribe, or the village . . . and the cottage rather than

* Excerpts from "The Mind-Set of Agrarianism . . . New and Old" in *The Essential Agrarian Reader*, edited by Norman Wirzba, The University Press of Kentucky, Lexington, 2003.

the castle. So it is little wonder that most contemporary Americans are strangers to the term, the concept, and the geography.

. . .

One reason, I believe, for its being ignored is that agrarianism isn't just about money. It might get a more respectful hearing if it were. But it is about culture, just as agriculture was about culture. Before it got run into the ditch by agribusiness.

A funny thing about cultures is that they produce people who understand more than they know. Sort of like osmosis. So the old agrarians, to get back to our subject, knew a lot about local soil, local weather, local crops, animal behavior, and each other. They depended on each other. It almost defines that much abused word, provincial. It was very provincial and no doubt carried a load of both inertia and foolishness, along with wisdom.

But whatever the mix, it was rooted in places, communities, continuity, and people whose names and faces you knew. As a matrix, it worked reasonably well. Which is different from claiming that it was idyllic and completely satisfactory.

Introduction

I

This book, like several others I have written, is intended as a part of a public conversation about the relationship of our lives, and of our communal and economic life, to the lands we live from. That no such public conversation exists presently, or has existed for the last sixty or seventy years, has never been, and is not now, an obstacle to my "contribution."

Tanya Berry, my wife, says that my principal asset as a writer has been my knack for repeating myself. That insight has instructed and amused me very much, because she is right and so forthrightly right. It is true that my writings have often repeated certain movements of thought, which, as I must hope, have been made clearer by being repeated in changes of perception and context.

So far as I am able to name them, those habitual movements of thought, at least some of them, are as follows:

- From protest or public advocacy to work and to good work. This is akin to, sometimes the same as, the movement from universal to particular. Obviously, then, this is a movement from the public languages of commerce, politics, the media, and the news to a local, neighborly language, accurately referring to particular persons, places, and things, and to the acts by which they relate to one another.

- From the future, now for bad reasons the most fashionable of all times, to the present.
- From "job," the manna of the economists and the politicians, to "vocation," which is the authentic calling to the work that is properly one's own.
- From anywhere or everywhere to home, which is not a house for sale or a site for "development," but the place by which one is owned, year after year loved and known.
- From the global economy—which for five hundred years has plundered the land and exploited, enslaved, or murdered the people of the "foreign" or "rural" world—to a local economy that would care for and conserve all the goods of a place, including the membership of its living creatures.
- From my own depleted, disintegrated, and thus somewhat representative rural homeland to instances or thoughts by which its decline may be measured and understood.
- From reality as understood by materialism and industrialism to reality understood as divine creation, holy, whole, and beautiful.

As I look back over my work of several decades, I can see that the back-and-forth of my thoughts has hardly been graceful, as it is hardly graceful in these present pages. It will probably have to be seen as a struggle to find or recover the language necessary to speak, in the same breath, of work and love.

II

From my college years, when I first encountered the word, I have understood myself and my native culture as "agrarian." In my writing and conversation I have often used that word, assuming, no doubt too confidently, that others understood it more or less as I did. But political circumstances, a number of "opinion pieces" in newspapers and magazines, and my own recent work as represented here have put me under pressure to define "agrarianism" as fully and exactly as I can.

I was first alerted to the need for this by a young professor's article in a magazine of "ecocriticism," in which he questioned the "acceptability" of my writing in view of my avowed indebtedness to *I'll Take My Stand*, a collection of essays by "Twelve Southerners," sometimes known as "southern agrarians," which was published in 1930. My "ecocritic" assumed that any book published in 1930 by southerners would be necessarily a racist book, and that I and my writings, because of my acknowledgement of my debt, were necessarily racist as well. Those assumptions are fairly explicit. Others are implied: that agrarianism and racism are only southern; that only southerners were racists in 1930; that if a racist espouses agrarianism, then agrarianism is racist; that my own agrarianism could have come only from the "southern agrarians" and *I'll Take My Stand*.

The "ecocritical" charge of racism, though I would discount it as trivial, cannot be discounted as harmless. The problem with several of the isms now prominently condemned is what we might call flypaper justice: the impossibility, once accused of a categorical offense such as racism or sexism, of establishing one's categorical innocence. The Accuser, in these instances, is a subtler serpent than the Tempter. I am sure that some at least of the Twelve Southerners were born, as in fact I was, into a circumstance of racism that they merely accepted until the time when they were obliged consciously to deal with it. For example: Robert Penn Warren, one of the Twelve Southerners, later wrote two books conscientiously intended to be against racism. Not all the others were so penitent. Though the Accuser typically is self-exempted, an actual critic is obliged to take up the work of a particularizing judgment: Is there in the life and work of the person categorically condemned anything of positive worth that can be respected and salvaged? In the absence of the morally discriminating work of actual criticism, the Accuser sets a trap that finally catches us all. This is a variety of "liberal" zeal that falls exactly into the pattern of "conservative" zeal, condemning with ferocious righteousness the sins of *other* people.

In fact, I got my agrarianism by being born into an agrarian family in an agrarian community. And so I have naturally recognized it and been grateful for it wherever I have found it. I found it in *I'll Take My Stand*, which certainly can be associated with racism and contains some evidence of it, but it would be substantially the same book if those contaminants were removed. Its "Statement of Principles," to which I have given most praise, contains nothing of racism. Moreover, my closest agrarian friends and allies, beyond my family and neighbors here at home, have belonged to the Midwest, not the South.

I have found agrarianism in the conversation of living farmers, and as far back in the written record as Homer and the Bible. I am sure that it is about as old as farming, far older than writing. It would be reasonable to suppose that all professors of literature would know that Homer and the Bible cannot be competently read without granting a fundamental respect to swineherds and shepherds, planters of trees and sowers of seed. But it has been the business of both the liberals and the conservatives of our time to withhold that respect, as they have withheld it also from the lands of farming and grazing.

And so in defense of myself and of my own "side," I offer the following definition or characterization of agrarianism as I understand it:

1. An elated, loving interest in the use and care of the land, and in all the details of the good husbandry of plants and animals.

2. An informed and conscientious submission to nature, or to Nature, and her laws of conservation, frugality, fullness or completeness, and diversity.

3. The wish, the felt need, to have and to belong to a place of one's own as the only secure source of sustenance and independence. (The freed slaves who pled for "forty acres

and a mule" were more urgently and practically agrarian than the "Twelve [white] Southerners.")

4. From that to a persuasion in favor of economic democracy, a preference for *enough* over *too much*.

5. Fear and contempt of waste of every kind and its ultimate consequence in land exhaustion. Waste is understood as human folly, an insult to nature, a sin against the given world and its life.

6. From that to a preference for saving rather than spending as the basis of the economy of a household or a government.

7. An assumption of the need for a subsistence or household economy, so as to live so far as possible *from* one's place.

8. An acknowledged need for neighbors and a willingness to *be* a neighbor. This comes from proof by experience that no person or family or place can live alone.

9. A living sense of the need for continuity of family and community life *in place*, which is to say the need for the survival of local culture and thus of the safekeeping of local memory and local nature.

10. Respect for work and (as self-respect) for good work. This implies an understanding of one's life's work as a vocation and a privilege, as opposed to a "job" and a vacation.

11. A lively suspicion of anything new. This contradicts the ethos of consumerism and the cult of celebrity. It is not inherently cranky or unreasonable.

Those qualities describe a person distinctly of a kind. All of them, I am sure, were never fully and evenly present in any one person, any more than all the talents and virtues of an art would be fully and evenly present in one musician or one carpenter, but I am sure also that all of them are related and that in any several of agrarian farmers all of them would be present, recognized, and clearly spoken.

They do not of course describe a perfect human being. It certainly is possible, as the young professor of "ecocriticism" perceived, for agrarians to be racists. If that association were necessary or inescapable, then as a writer and advocate I would have been out of work all my life. But it seems to me, on the contrary, that the principles of community and neighborliness, inherent in agrarianism, contradict the principles of racism, just as the Declaration of Independence, written during slavery by a slave owner, contains an unqualified precept against slavery.

As several of the writings in this book testify, my knowledge of agrarianism and my respect for it have been confirmed by my reading, but they came to me by instruction and example from my own elders when I was a boy and a young man. It has become ever plainer to me that the great unchosen privilege of my life was the survival of a predominantly agricultural economy and an agrarian culture in my home country throughout my childhood, on into the 1970s, and continuing past then in some persons and households.

The reasons for this survival all seem peculiar to my region: a mostly sloping countryside, much divided by drains and streams, and thus, except in the bottomlands, impossible to divide into large, easily tillable fields, and so congenial to fairly small farms; a way of farming highly diverse in both crops and livestock; the long-standing economy and culture of tobacco, a crop traditionally grown in small acreages, requiring work for virtually the whole year, and dependent upon an extraordinary amount of skilled handwork; and, finally, our regional version of the federal tobacco program, the Burley Tobacco Growers Co-operative Association, which, by combining price supports with production control, assured a fair market value for a staple crop. For these reasons, the farms here were worked almost entirely by hand and by teams of mules and horses until the end of World War II. After that the tractors came, and the industrialization of farming began.

Suspicion of the new, of change, and a lively resistance thereto continued here until the end of the war. When daylight saving time was introduced as a part of "the war effort," the country people here just about unanimously refused to change their clocks. They balked, and with a principled passion. I remember the younger of my grandfathers, my mother's father (1881–1965), saying, "I would rather be a Republican than change my time." And I remember the 'fierce and somewhat heartbroken resentment of my father's father (1864–1946) against the coming of the tractors, which he lived barely long enough to see. He said the heavy rolling of their wheels would compact the soil. He was right about that, but I know he had also in mind the lightness over the ground of a good-moving team of mules, which had been his heart's love all his life. I think that agrarianism had, and where it survives it still has, a sort of summary existence as a *feeling*—an instinct, an excitement, a passion, a tenderness—for the living earth and its creatures.

After the war, the old resistance fell away. The old agrarianism could not survive, in the community and its economy, the coming and the ongoing development of the new "scientific" industrial agriculture. The problem that this book confronts is that agrarianism, though obviously defeatable by industrial technologies and cheap petroleum, is nonetheless necessary to the good health of the land and the people, and the forces that defeated it have not replaced it.

III

My native country, in which I have lived nearly all of my life, is ten or fifteen miles south of the Ohio River. By so substantial a margin I missed being a Yankee and an inheritor of Yankee virtues. I am a Kentuckian, a border-stater, which, to many people, means southerner. There are important historical and other differences between Kentucky and the South, but insofar as I am not a Yankee and am descended in part from slave owners, I am too handily classifiable as southern to protest, and so be it.

Anybody subjected to so broad a classification, however, will know how useless it is to the necessarily particular life's work of self-knowledge and local accountability. And there are the expectable liabilities. Though liberals do not have prejudices, they do sometimes deal in categorical judgments that they know to be absolutely just and true. A southern white man will learn about this without much research. That I am a southern agrarian white man accounts in part, I am very sure, for the "ecocritical" verdict that I am at least suspectably a deliberately racist southern agrarian white man.

Beyond that, and for a good many years, I have been classified in reviews of my books and in assortments of interesting facts as a "tobacco farmer." This comes apparently from some "site" on the Internet. According to the same source, I also grow wheat. So reliably informed, even some people who have visited this farm apparently assume that in a nook or hollow well out of sight among the slopes and the woods I have a tobacco patch and a field of wheat. So far, I have not received any blame for my implication in wheat-production—which in circumstances common enough, and especially in mine, would be sufficiently blamable. But the revelation that I am a tobacco farmer typically is accompanied by the suggestion I am, as such, an immoral man, and that my writings on agriculture are therefore to be held under suspicion, if not doubted altogether.

And so I know very well that the entitlement of everybody to "alternative facts" was not invented by apologists for Donald Trump. Perhaps I am now entitled to "equal time" to present my own alternative facts to the alternative facts mentioned above. This I need to do because tobacco and the federal tobacco program are prominent themes of this book.

I live in what has been one of the most prominent tobacco-producing counties in Kentucky, which has been one of the most prominent tobacco-producing states. Members of my family have been involved in growing tobacco and in various aspects of the tobacco economy as far back as I know anything about them. My father and my brother were actively involved in the Burley Tobacco Growers Co-operative Association. As I grew up, I played and then worked in tobacco crops (along with the other enterprises of our then highly diverse farming) on family and neighboring farms. Later, after my wife and children and I settled on our own small farm near Port Royal, I worked for thirty-some years, mainly at "setting" and "cutting," in the tobacco crops of my neighbors with whom I swapped work. But it has happened that I have never grown a tobacco crop of my own. During some of our early years here, when we were glad to have the money, I leased our "base" (the right, belonging to our place, to grow a small amount of tobacco) to neighbors. Later I swapped it for the use, not often, of a neighbor's tractor.

I am, then, not without complicity in tobacco production. But I can be called a tobacco farmer only by the same sort of categorical inference that from time to time has brought me under the suspicion or the allegation of racism. I understand very well the intellectual achievement of guilt by association. My intellect is entirely baffled and defeated, however, by the discovery that I grow wheat. On *this* farm?

Though I share fully, I believe, my people's love for tobacco (rightly grown, it is a beautiful and fascinating crop), though it was long a staple of my region's economy, and though a vital culture of family and neighborly work depended on it, I have never defended either the crop or its uses. The Surgeon General's Report on tobacco and cancer, which made defense of the crop morally impossible, was published in 1965, before my writing on agricultural problems began.

But I *have* defended the federal tobacco program, as represented here by the Burley Tobacco Growers Co-operative Association. The principles of the Burley Co-op—production control, price supports, service to small as to large producers—are not associated with tobacco necessarily, but are in themselves ethical, reputable, economically sound, and applicable to any agricultural commodity. I discussed this issue pretty fully in an essay, "The Problem of Tobacco," in 1991. In this book, I have attempted to see the Burley Co-op more clearly than before both in its geographic and historical context and in relation to what I take to be the necessity of its principles to the survival of the land and people of rural America.

It is wrong, I think, to deal with the past as if it can be simply departed from or "solved," or brought to "closure." It is discouraging to see the conservatives treat history as one of the "humanities" that can be dispensed with or ignored by hardheaded realists. It is both discouraging and amusing to be assured by the liberals that the past can be risen above by superior persons who, if *they* had been Thomas Jefferson, would have owned no slaves.

But the problems that belong to one's history, to one's place, and thus to one's life, cannot in any ready or simple way be solved, and some of them cannot be solved at all. Problems such as categorical judgments against kinds of people or the production of unhealthy commodities— or land abuse or pollution or social "mobility," to name some more— these are, for the willing, a life's work. They can be confronted, studied, struggled with, to some extent understood, and (always to the peril of truth and justice) judged. Such, anyhow, have been among the never-finished concerns of my writing.

As the author of such writing over a good many years, I know both that I cannot and that I should not expect agreement or approval from my critics. But I think that I rightly should expect them to acknowledge fairly the complexity of my subjects, and to be honest in their use of evidence.

IV

Readers will notice that the parts of this book, although they are related to one another and to my interest in the connection of land and people, are of different genres: essays, fictions, fictions partaking somewhat of the character of the essays, and, as epilogue, a poem congenial to the essays and participating in the fiction.

The most peculiar, and perhaps the most questionable of these mixtures, is in "The Order of Loving Care," in which one fictional character, Andy Catlett, from my novels and stories of Port William, encounters and learns from a number of my own "real life" friends and teachers. If my work had not been so incomplete in its parts, and there-fore continuous over so many years, such an expedient would not have been needed. But it happens that "The Order of Loving Care" is the third of a sequence of writings specifically about the "making" of Andy Catlett's mind, which, as it further happens, has been a theme of my Port William fiction since 1960.

With some significant differences, Andy Catlett's life is *like* my own. This likeness enables me, in fiction, to bear witness to my time and place. The differences between his life and mine make my testimony subject to imagination rather than merely to the factuality of my life, which, apart from imagination, would be a bore. As fiction, a story does not have to be submitted to the burdens of a tedious pursuit and gathering of facts, or to the risk of factual error and triviality, or to apology for forgetting facts.

However, in my fiction as in my essays, I have tried always to be true to the facts of history, natural history, work, tools, economy, and economic life. Once that condition is met, I see nothing inherently wrong in asking one genre to do the work of another.

V

Though conservative politicians and organizations were always opposed to the tobacco program of the New Deal, the small farms and small towns of what is now called "rural America" (meaning nearly all of our actual country) had substantial political support throughout the 1940s. My father and his friends who led the now-defunct Burley Tobacco Growers Co-operative Association had a significant influence in their region, and they could be heard and understood in Washington. My daughter, Mary, who continues my father's work in behalf of small farmers, has not one ally in state or national government.

President Eisenhower's Secretary of Agriculture, Ezra Taft Benson, proclaimed the official termination of favor to anything not "big." And now it has been a long time since an agrarian, or any advocate for the good economic and ecological health of rural America, could be listened to or understood or represented by either of the political parties.

To wakeful persons living in rural America, aware of the abuses of the land and the people, the presidential election of 2016 brought a too-familiar "choice." It was plain that neither Mr. Trump nor Mrs. Clinton would be much aware of the economic landscapes of farming, forestry, or mining, or of the people of the land-using economies. The corporations of food, timber, minerals, and energy would have the candidates' attention and regard, but not nearly so much the people who take the actual risks and do the actual work, and not at all the places where the work is done. The two candidates would either follow or not the long-time political custom of substituting the preservation of "wilderness areas" for conservation of nature, land, and people in the much larger portion of the country that is merely "rural." Neither candidate could have imagined or dared the economic revisions that would safekeep in good health the land and people of every place.

The best understanding of the election that I have seen so far came to me in a letter from my friend Mark Lawson, a church pastor and professor of religion in Liverpool, New York:

> It seems to me that the people who put Trump over the top were largely Rust Belt dwellers whose grandparents were forced to leave the farm for mind-numbing factory work, whose parents made a go of it with one generation of union-negotiated wages, but who were valued only as laborers and only until a cheaper means of production came along. The irony, of course, is that this segment of the population chose as the vehicle of their revenge a Manhattan real estate tycoon who got rich by exploiting bankruptcy laws and refusing to pay his own laborers (many of whom were undocumented workers). But . . . it requires no critical thinking skills to blame Muslims and Mexicans (or any other preferred scapegoats) rather than understand the long-term effects of unrestrained global capitalism.

I think that is accurate, fair, compassionate, and sufficiently critical of Mr. Trump's supporters.

For me, the ascent of Mr. Trump, a man who indulges his worst impulses and encourages the worst impulses of others, was immensely regrettable, but it was less a surprise than a clarification. His election and his choices of cabinet members (masked as "populism," whatever by now is meant by that) expose beyond doubt the nearly absolute ownership of our public life by the excessively wealthy, who are dedicated to freeing themselves and their corporate and of-course-Christian peers from any obligation to the natural and human commonwealth. Nothing could have made more clear the featherweight moral gravity, not of his voters, but of Mr. Trump's rich sponsors and his party.

But the gravitas of the liberals seems to me not much weightier. What did surprise me was the revelation, after the election, of the extent of their ignorance of their actual country and its economic history, and (surely because of that) the intensity of their animus against "rural America" and the "working class" people who voted for Mr. Trump. As a rural American, I was of course fully aware of the prejudice, equally conservative and liberal, against rural America and rural Americans. I knew that "rural" and "country" and "farmer" were still current as terms of insult. But I was not quite prepared for the venom, the contempt, and the stereotyping rhetoric that some liberal intellectuals (so proud of their solicitude for "the other") brought down upon their fellow humans.

As the fellow humans of their fellow humans, perhaps these liberals should be a little less eager to shake hands with themselves. It is hard not to see Mr. Trump as the personification, even the consummation, of the barely divergent "freedoms" espoused by the two sides: a man, by his own testimony, both sexually liberated and fiscally unregulated, the sovereign and autonomous American individual, the very puppet of his own desires. He, more than anybody else so far, is the incarnation of our long aspiration to do individually as we please.

Meanwhile, agrarianism as I have at least partly defined it has managed to survive, to maintain the loyalty and courage of a good many people, and to keep talking. It certainly is nothing like a third political party, or situated anywhere between the present two. At least, it provides a viewpoint from which to observe and measure the effects of those two and their contention upon the actual country. At most, it is an entirely different way of living, thinking, and speaking: the way of what I am obliged to call economic realism, indissolubly mated to ecology, to local ecosystems, and to the traditions of good husbandry and good neighborhood, starting at home and from the ground up.

VI

Finally, I need to say that the word "order," as in the title of one of the pieces of this book, now seems to me far preferable to "pattern," as used in my essay "Solving for Pattern" of 1980. "Pattern" signifies a rigidity of form and a mechanical repetitiousness that I don't see in nature or respect in human work. "Order," almost on the contrary, signifies the formal integrity by which a *kind* of creature or workmanship maintains its identity and remains recognizable even as it varies through time, adapting to difference and to change.

The order of loving care is of human making. It varies as it must from place to place, time to time, worker to worker, never definitive or final. It is measurable by the health, the happiness too, of the association of land and people. It is partly an ideal (remembering divine or natural order), partly a quest, always and inescapably a practice.

The Thought of Limits
in a Prodigal Age

Is there, at bottom, any real distinction between esthetics and economics?

—Aldo Leopold, *A Sand County Almanac & Other Writings*
on Ecology and Conservation

I want to say something about the decline, the virtual ruin, of rural life, and about the influence and effect of agricultural surpluses, which I believe are accountable for more destruction of land and people than any other economic "factor." This is a task that ought to be taken up by an economist, which I am not. But economists, even agricultural economists, farm-raised as many of them have been, do not live in rural communities, as I do, and they appear not to care, as I do, that rural communities like mine all over the country are either dying or dead. And so, only partly qualified as I am, I will undertake this writing in the hope that I am contributing to a conversation that will attract others better qualified.

I have at hand an article from the *Wall Street Journal* of February 22, 2016, entitled "The U.S. Economy Is in Good Shape." The article is by Martin Feldstein, "chairman of the Council of Economic Advisors under President Ronald Reagan . . . a professor at Harvard and a member of the Journal's board of contributors." Among economists Prof. Feldstein appears to be somewhere near the top of the pile. And yet his economic optimism is founded entirely upon current measures of "incomes," "unemployment," and "industrial production," all abstractions narrowly focused. Nowhere in his analysis does he mention the natural world, or the economies of land use by which the wealth of nature is made available to the "American economy." Mr. Feldstein believes that "the big uncertainties that now hang over our economy are political."

But from what I see here at home in the watershed of the Kentucky River, and from what I have seen and learned of other places, I know that industrial agriculture is in serious failure, which is to say that it is not sustainable. Projecting from the damages of the comparatively brief American histories of states such as Kentucky and Iowa, one must conclude that the present use of the farmland cannot be sustained for another hundred years: The rates of soil erosion are too high, the runoff is too toxic, the ecological impoverishment is too great, the surviving farmers are too few and too old. To anybody who knows these things, by witness of sight or by numerical measures, they would appear to qualify significantly the "good shape" of the economy. I conclude that Prof. Feldstein does not know these things, but is conventionally ignorant of them. Like other people of privilege for thousands of years, far more numerous now than ever before, he appears to take for granted the bounty of nature and the work that provides it to the human economy.

In remarkable contrast to the optimism of Prof. Feldstein, the *New York Times* of March 10, 2016, printed an article, "Who's Killing Global Growth?" by Steven Rattner, "a Wall Street executive and a contributing opinion writer." Mr. Rattner's downhearted assessment, like Prof. Feldstein's upbeat one, is based upon measures that are entirely economic or monetary, quantitative, and abstract: "financial markets," "projections for future growth," "wages," "consumer spending," "rising supply," "disappointing demand," etc. The "global growth" Mr. Rattner has in mind is purely financial and is without reference to the effect of such "growth" upon the health and the welfare of the globe's actual people and other creatures. Like Prof. Feldstein, Mr. Rattner appears to suppose, consciously or not, that the natural world and human workers will continue to supply their necessary goods without limit and to the allure simply of money.

I have at hand also a sentence from the *New York Review of Books*, September 24, 2015, by James Surowiecki, another highly credentialed economist. Mr. Surowiecki is reviewing among others a book by Joseph E. Stiglitz and Bruce C. Greenwald, *Creating a Learning Society: A New Approach to Growth, Development, and Social Progress.* This book, the reviewer says, "is dedicated to showing how developing countries can use government policy to become high-growth, knowledge-intensive economies, rather than remaining low-cost producers of commodities." I have kept this sentence in mind because of the problems it raises, all relating to my concern about the damages imposed by national and global "economies" upon land and people. Mr. Surowieki's sentence seems to be highly condensed and allusive, a sort of formula for increasing economic growth—or, as it actually says, for turning countries into economies. The sentence no doubt is clear to economists, but it has put me to some trouble. My interest is not in the analyses and theories of these economists, since they seem mainly to ignore the natural world and the human communities that are my concern. I am interested here in their public language, by which they reveal what they accept, and expect most others to accept, as axioms—what one might call their lore or more accurately their faith.

I assume, then, that by "low-cost producers of commodities" Mr. Surowiecki means "poorly paid producers of cheap commodities," that these commodities are material goods or raw materials produced from the land, that "knowledge-intensive economies" are based upon the abilities to exploit, trade, add value to, and market the cheaply produced commodities. Apparently it is taken for granted that this improving formula applies to *all* developing countries, their people, their land, and their natural resources, without regard to differences or distinctions among them. Such disregard of local and personal differences is a major article of this faith. It takes for granted furthermore that a knowledge-intensive economy, by causing growth, development, and social progress, will change a developing country into a developed country, and that this will be an all-around improvement. From the standpoint of industrial economists and their clients, this apparently is self-evident and unquestionable. It becomes immediately and urgently questionable from the standpoint of a dweller in a rural countryside who is bound to the land and the community by ties of history, family, and affection.

Here we arrive at a fundamental division of interest and allegiance, as probably also at the difference between two kinds of mind. The attention of these economists and others like them is directed as a matter of course to the monetary economy and to what, according to their abstract measurements, is good or bad for it. The attention of settled dwellers, at home in their chosen or hereditary places, is directed partially to the monetary economy, of course, and often in fear or sufferance, but their attention is directed also, out of natural affection and solicitude, to their places, the particular, unique, and irreplaceable patches of ground under their feet. Another difference involved here, if the settled dwellers are farmers, is that between people whose livelihoods are primarily dependent upon salaries and people whose livelihoods are primarily dependent upon the weather.

The settled dwellers, then, in their natural desire to remain settled, and facing the "promises" of development, certainly are going to have questions for the developers, and the first would be this: What is the net good that industrial economists, their employers, and their clients appear customarily to credit to growth, development, and "social progress"? In the United States, since at least the Civil War, and ever more rapidly after World War II, we have achieved industrial versions of all of those goals. But almost nobody is asking what is the worth of that achievement after we deduct its ecological and human costs. We have, in fact, been turning our country into an economy as fast as possible, and we have been doing so by an unaccounted squandering of its actual, its natural and its cultural, wealth.

As a second question, we should ask why commodities, the material goods that support our life, and the work of producing them, should be "low cost" or significantly cheaper than the goods and services of a "knowledge-intensive economy." There is no reason to believe that the present market values of technological (developmental) knowledge and of commodities are absolute or in any way permanent. Nor is there reason to believe that such issues of value are, or can be, reliably settled by the free market of our present economy, or by any market. The good health of the land economies is a value that a market as such cannot consider and cannot protect. Moreover, agribusiness in all of its aspects is a knowledge-intensive system, which uses knowledge ruthlessly to control and exploit land and people.

Apparently it is assumed that a country's economy of commodity-production, which could be as diverse as the country's climate and soils permit, can safely be replaced or further depreciated by an economy of knowledge only. And so, as a third question, we must ask how secure and how beneficent is a one-product economy. Is the market for knowledge infinite in its demand, or can it be over-supplied and depressed, as the one-product economy of coal in the Appalachian coal fields has often been? And it hardly needs to be said that in the Appalachian coal fields the benefits of the coal economy to a rich and distant few has never adequately been measured against its impoverishment of the local people and their land.

Perhaps no outsider—no visiting expert, no dispassionate observer, certainly no outside investor—will notice the inherent weakness and cruelty of a one-product economy in a region or a country. But the adverse effects will certainly be visible and acutely feelable to the resident insiders. Those who live and must make their lives within the boundary of such an economy experience daily the readiness of their political leaders to endorse and excuse the destructiveness of "the economy," as well as the public unwillingness to remedy or compensate the damages to the land and the people. The Appalachian coal economy has not only inflicted immeasurable and immeasurably lasting ecological and social damage to its region, but it has also distracted attention and care from the region's other assets: its forests, soils, streams, and the (too often exported) talents of its people.

And so a fourth question: How, even in a knowledge-intensive economy, even unendingly "growing" and wealthy, are the people's needs for food, clothing, and shelter to be met? Does the development of a highly lucrative knowledge economy entirely eliminate the need for the fundamental economies of subsistence? Do people eat and wear knowledge? Do they sleep warm in it? I know very well what the far-seeing economists will answer: People earning large salaries from "high-growth, knowledge-intensive economies" will *buy* their material subsistence from "low-cost producers of commodities" at home or, if not at home, then elsewhere. It is assumed that where there is a demand, and enough money, there will be unfailingly a supply, and this is another article of the industrial economic faith: The land and its "resources" will be always with us, and so will the poor who will dig, hack, and whittle an everlasting supply of low-cost commodities until they can be replaced by knowledge-intensive machines that will dig, hack, and whittle, no doubt on solar energy, faster and at a lower cost.

And so we come to question five: Do the economists of development ever attempt a fair assessment, or any assessment, of the value to a knowledge-intensive economy of a dependable local supply of life-supporting commodities? The answer, so far as I have learned, is that the developmental economists do no such thing. Their dream of human progress calls simply for the *replacement* of the commodity economy by the knowledge economy, and that is that. As evidence, let us consider a review of our economic past and future, "Moving On from Farm and Factory," by Eduardo Porter, in the *New York Times* of April 27, 2016.

Mr. Porter's premise is that the economies of farming and manufacturing, as a fixed and final consequence of historical trends, are now obsolete, or nearly so, and his statistics are sufficiently precipitous:

> Over the course of the 20th century, farm employment in the United States dropped to 2 percent of the work force from 41 percent, even as output soared. Since 1950, manufacturing's share has shrunk to 8.5 percent of nonfarm jobs, from 24 percent.

To this state of things Mr. Porter grants something like half an approval. Whereas nearly all of the "work force" once employed in farming have been "liberated . . . from their chains," he thinks that "The current transition, from manufacturing to services, is more problematic." Though for workers in the United States there are "options: health care, education and clean energy, just to name a few," these options "present big economic and political challenges." The principal challenges will be to get the politicians to abandon their promises of an increase of employment in manufacturing, and then to provide the government help necessary to make "the current transition from manufacturing to services" without too much rebellion by workers "against the changing tide." Mr. Porter's conclusion, despite these challenges, is optimistic:

> Yet just as the federal government once provided a critical push to move the economy from its agricultural past into its industrial future, so, too, could it help build a postindustrial tomorrow.

Mr. Porter's article, which clearly assumes the agreement or consent of a large number of his fellow economists and fellow citizens, rests upon the kind of assumptions that I have been calling articles of faith. Though it is certain that a lot of people, economists and others, are putting their faith in these assumptions, they are nonetheless entirely groundless. The assumptions, so far as I can trace them out, are as follows:

1. The economy of a country or a nation needs only to provide employment, it does not matter at what. And so of course no particular value can be assigned to the production of commodities.

2. So long as there is enough employment at work of some kind, a country or a nation can safely dispense with employment in sustainable farming and manufacturing, which is to say a sustainable dependence upon natural resources and the natural world.

3. Farming has little economic worth. It is of the past, and better so. Farm work involves no significant responsibilities, and requires no appreciable intelligence, knowledge, skill, or character. It is, as is often said, "mind-numbing," a servile condition from the "chains" of which all workers, even owners who work on their own farms, need to be "liberated."

4. The "output" of industrial agriculture will continue to "soar" without limit as ever more farmers are "liberated from their chains" by technology, and as technologies are continuously succeeded by more advanced technologies.

5. There is no economic or intrinsic difference between agriculture and industry: A farm is no more than a factory, a plant or an animal is no more than a machine or a substance.

6. The technological advances that have disemployed so many people from farming and manufacturing will never take away the jobs of service or postindustrial workers.

7. History, including economic history, is a forward motion, a progress, made up of irreversible changes. These changes can be established absolutely and forever in so little time as a century or two. Thus the great technological progress

since perhaps the steam engine—a progress enabled by the fossil fuels, war, internal combustion, external combustion, and a sequence of poisons—will carry us right on into the (climactic? everlasting?) "postindustrial tomorrow."

8. The need for "health care, education and clean energy, just to name a few," will go securely on and on, supplying without limit the need for jobs, whereas the need for food, clothing, shelter, and manufactured goods will be supplied by *what*?

Now I must tell why, as a comparatively prosperous and settled resident of my home country in the United States, I should be as troubled as I am by the faith or superstition or future-fantasy of the economists of so-called development. My family and I live, as we know and fear, in what the orthodox economists consider a backward, under-developed, and to-be-developed country. This is "rural America," the great domestic colony that we have made of our actual country, as opposed to the nation, the government, and the economy. This particular fragment of it is called "The Golden Triangle," a wedge of country bounded by the three interstate highways connecting Louisville, Lexington, and Cincinnati. The three are connected also by rail and by air. The Triangle is bounded on its northwest side also by the Ohio River. Because it is so fortunately located with respect to transportation and markets, this area is thought (by some) to be "Golden," which is to say eminently suited to (future) development.

The landscapes within the Triangle are topographically diverse—rolling uplands, steep valley sides, fairly level bottomlands—all, though varyingly, fragile and vulnerable to various established abuses. The soils are fertile, productive, responsive to good treatment, but much diminished by erosion and misuse in the years of "settlement," severely eroded in some places, still eroding in others. The native forest is predominantly hardwood, much diminished and fragmented, suffering from diseases and invasive species, largely undervalued, neglected or ill-used, but potentially of great economic worth if well used and cared for. The watercourses are numerous, often degraded, mostly polluted by silt or chemicals or both. There is, in most years, abundant rainfall.

The three cities seem generally to be prospering and expanding, but are expectably troubled by social disintegration, drugs, poverty, traffic congestion, and violence. The towns, including county seats, are in decay or dead, preyed upon by the cities and chain stores, diseased by urban and media culture, cheap energy, family disintegration, drugs, and the various electronic screens.

Especially during the early decades of the tobacco program, the farming here was highly diversified and, at its best, exemplary in its husbanding of the land. Because of the program, tobacco was the basis of a local agrarian culture that was both economically and socially stabilizing. The farms were mostly small, farmed by their resident families and neighborly exchanges of work. In addition to tobacco and provender for the households, they produced (collectively and often individually) corn, small grains, hogs, chickens and other poultry, eggs, cream, milk, and an abundance of pasture for herds of beef cattle and flocks of sheep.

The tobacco program with its benefits ended in 2004. Though it served growers of a crop that after the Surgeon General's report of 1965 could not be defended, the program itself was exemplary. Both the people and the land benefitted from it. By the combination of price supports with production control, limiting supply to anticipated demand, the program maintained the livelihoods of the small farms, and so maintained the livelihoods of shops and stores in the towns. It gave the same protection on the market to the small producer as to the large. By limiting the acreage of a high-paying crop, it provided a significant measure of soil conservation. Most important, it supported the traditional family and social structure of the region and its culture of husbandry.

For once and for a while, then, the farmers of this region stood together, stood up for themselves, and secured for themselves prices reasonably fair for one of their products. The tobacco program, once and for a while, gave them an asking price, with results in every way good. Before and after the program, which was *their* program, they have had simply to accept whatever the buyers have been pleased to offer. When producers of commodities have no asking price, the result is plunder of both land and people, as in any colony. By "asking price" I mean a fair price, as determined for example by "parity," which would enable farmers to prosper "on a par with" their urban counterparts; a fair price, then, supported by bargaining power.

After the demise of the tobacco program, and with it the economy and way of life it had preserved and stood for, this so-favored Triangle and its region have declined economically, agriculturally, and socially. The tobacco that is still grown here is grown mainly in large acreages under contracts written by the tobacco companies, and primarily with migrant labor. Most of the farms that are still working are mainly or ex-clusively producing beef cattle—which is good, insofar as it gives much of our vulnerable countryside the year-round protection of perennial pastures and hay crops, but it is a far cry from the old diversity of crops and livestock. Of much greater concern is the continuous planting of large acreages of soy beans and corn, a way of farming unsuited to our sloping land (or, in fact, to any land), erosive, toxic, requiring large ex-penditures of money for uncertain returns. For such cropping the fences are removed, making the land useless for grazing. Farms are being sub-divided and "developed," or cash-rented for corn and beans.

The land is no longer divided and owned in the long succession, by inheritance or purchase, of farmer after farmer. It has now become "real estate," ruled by the land market, owned increasingly by urban investors, or by urban escapees seeking the (typically short-lived) con-solation and relaxation of "a place in the country." The government now subsidizes land purchases by some young farmers, "helping" them by involving them in large long-term debts and in ways of farming that degrade the land they may, late in their lives, finally own. For many young people whose vocation once would have been farming, farming is no longer possible. You have to be too rich to farm before you can afford a farm in my county.

Only a few years ago, I received a letter from a man extraordinarily thoughtful, who described himself as an ex-addict whose early years were spent under the teaching and influence of a family elder, in the tobacco patches of a neighborhood of small farms. Caught up by the centrifugal force of a disintegrating community and way of life, he drifted into addiction, from which, with help, he got free. He wrote to me, I think, believing that I should know his story. People, he said, were wondering what comes after the tobacco program. He answered: drug addiction. He was right. Or he was partly right. His answer would have been complete if he had added screen addiction to drug addiction.

As long as the diverse economy of our small farms lasted, our communities were filled with people who needed one another and knew that they did. They needed one another's help in their work, and from that they needed one another's companionship. Most essentially, the grownups and the elders needed the help of the children, who thus learned the family's and the community's work and the entailed duties, pleasures, and loyalties. When that work disappears, when parents leave farm and household for town jobs, when the upbringing of the young is left largely to the schools, then the children, like their parents, live as individuals, particles, loved perhaps but not needed for any usefulness they may have or any help they might give. As the local influences weaken, the outside influences grow stronger.

And so the drugs and the screens are with us. The day is long past when most school-age children benefitted from work and instruction that gave them in turn a practical assurance of their worth. They have now mostly disappeared from the countryside and from the streets and houseyards of the towns. In this new absence and silence of the children, parents, teachers, church people, and public officials hold meetings to wonder what to do about the drug problem. The screen problem receives less attention, but it may be the worst of the two because it wears the aura of technological progress and social approval.

The old complex life, at once economic and social, was fairly coherent and self-sustaining because each community was focused upon its own local countryside and upon its own people, their needs, and their work. That life is now almost entirely gone. It has been replaced by the dispersed lives of dispersed individuals, commuting and consuming, scattering in every direction every morning, returning at night only to their screens and carryout meals. Meanwhile, in a country everywhere distressed and taxed by homelessness, once-used good farm buildings, built by local thrift and skill, rot to the ground. Good houses, that once sheltered respectable lives, stare out through sashless windows or have disappeared.

I have described briefly and I am sure inadequately my home country, a place dauntingly complex both in its natural history and in its human history, offering much that is good, much good also that is unappreciated or unrecognized. Outsiders passing through, unaware of its problems, are apt to think it very beautiful, which partly it still is. To me, and to others known to me, it is also a very needy place. When I am wishing, as I often do, I wish its children might be taught thoroughly and honestly its own history, and its history as a part of American history. I wish every one of its schools had enough biologists and ecologists to lead the students outdoors, to show them where they are in relation to drainages, soils, plants, and animals. I wish we had an economy wisely kind to the land and the people.

A good many years ago somebody, or several somebodies, named this parcel of land "The Golden Triangle." Like I assume most people here, I don't know who the somebodies were. I don't know how or what they were thinking or what their vision was. I know that the name "The Golden Triangle" is allied to other phrases or ideas, equally vague and doubtful, that have been hovering over us: the need for "job creation," the need to "bring in industry," the obligation (of apparently everybody) to "compete in the global economy," the need (of apparently everybody) for "a college education," the need for or the promises of "the service economy," and "the knowledge economy." None of these by now weary foretellings has anything in particular to do with anything that is presently here. They and the thinking they represent all gesture somewhat heroically toward "the Future," another phrase, obsessively repeated by the people out front in politics and education, signifying not much. Perhaps the most influential "future" right now is that of "the knowledge economy," as yet not here but surely expected. This means that in order to get jobs and to compete in the global economy, our eligible young people need to major in courses of science, technology, engineering, and mathematics while they are still in high school. This is the so-called STEM curriculum, dear to the hearts of our several too expensive, overadministered, underfunded, and ravenous state universities. And STEM is promoted by slurs, coming from the highest offices of state government, against such studies as literature and history.

The advantage of the STEM-emphasis to the education industry is fairly obvious. And if the great corporations of the global knowledge economy settle in the Golden Triangle or somewhere nearby, they surely will be glad to have a highly trained workforce readily available. But no supreme incarnation of the knowledge economy has yet arrived. If such an arrival is imminent or expected, that has not been announced to the natives. No doubt for that reason, the authorities have not predicted how many STEM graduates the future is going to need (and, as predicted, pay well). The possibility that the schools may turn out too many expensively educated, overspecialized STEM graduates evidently is not being considered. Nor evidently is the possibility that a surplus of such graduates, like their farming ancestors, will have no asking price, and so will come cheap to whomever may hire them. Maybe someday the people living here will have a fine, affluent Scientific, Technological, Engineered, and Mathematized Future to live in. Or, of course, maybe not.

That, anyhow, is development as we know it in The Golden Triangle. Meanwhile, our land is going to the devil, and too many of our people are addicted to drugs or screens or to mere distraction.

For a person living here, it is possible to imagine an economic project that would be locally appropriate and might actually help us. This likely is a project that could not be accomplished by economists only, but economists surely will be needed. The project would be to define a local or regional economy that, within the given limits, would be diverse, coherent, and lasting. If they were not so fad-ridden, economists might see that a knowledge economy, or any other single economy, cannot and should not occupy a whole region or a whole future. They might consider the possibility of a balance or parity of necessary occupations.

I am assuming a need for any locality, region, or nation to provide itself so far as possible with food, clothing, and shelter. Such fundamental economic provision, one would think, should be considered normal or fitting to human inhabitation of the earth. In addition to the economic benefits to local people of local supplies, a future-oriented society such as ours ought to consider the possibility that any locality might become stranded by lasting interruptions of long-distance transportation. Since for many years I have been trying to think as a pacifist, I feel a little strange in addressing issues of military strategy. But it seems preposterous to me that we should maintain an enormous, enormously expensive armory of weapons, including nuclear bombs, ready at every moment to defend a country in which most people live far from the sources of their food, clothing, and other necessities. Arguing from our leaders' own premises, then, the need for balanced local economies is obvious. From the recognition of local needs, both visible and supposable, the people of this or any region might reasonably proceed to a set of questions needing to be answered. Eventually, I think, there would be many such questions. I am sure that I don't know them all, but it is easy to foresee some of them:

1. After so long a history of diminishment and loss, what remains here, in the land and people of this place, that is valuable and worth keeping? Or: What that is here do the local people need for their own use and sustenance, and then, the local needs met, to market elsewhere?
2. What is the present use or value of the local land and its products to the local people?

3. How might we earn a sustainable income from the local land and its products? This would require adding value locally to the commodities—the goods!—coming from our farms and woodlands, but how might that be done?

4. What kinds of work are necessary to preserve and to live from the productivity of our land and people?

5. What do our people need to know, or learn and keep in mind, in order to accomplish the necessary work? The STEM courses might help, might be indispensable, but what else is needed? We are talking of course about education for livelihood, but also for responsible membership, citizenship, and stewardship.

6. What economic balances are necessary to reward adequately, and so to maintain indefinitely, the necessary work?

To answer those questions, close and patient study will be required of economists and others. The difficulty here is that, within the terms and conditions of the dominant economy over the last century and a half, the communities and economies of land use have been increasingly vulnerable. The effort to make them something like sustainable would have to begin with attention to the difference between the industrial economy of inert materials and monetary abstractions and an authentic land economy that must include the kindly husbandry of living creatures. This is the critical issue. As for many years, we are still hearing that almost any new technology will "transform farming." This implies an almost-general approval of the so far unrestrainable industrial prerogative to treat living creatures as comprising a sort of ore, and the food industry as a sort of foundry. If farming is no more than an industry to be unendingly transformed by technologies, as is still happening, then farmers can be replaced by engineers, and engineers finally by robots, in the progress toward our evident goal of human uselessness. If, on the contrary, because of the uniqueness and fragility of each one of the world's myriad of small places, the land economies must involve a creaturely affection and care, then we must look back fifty or sixty years and think again. If, as even some scientists have recognized, there are natural and human limits beyond which farming (and forestry) cannot be industrialized, then we need a more complex and particularizing language than the economists so far use.

The six questions I have proposed for my or any region do not derive from a wished-for or a predicted future. They have to do with what I would call "provision," which depends upon being attentively and responsibly present in the present. We do not, for example, love our children because of their potential to become well-trained workers in a future knowledge economy. We love them because we are alive to them in this present moment, which is the only time when we and they are alive. This love implicates us in a present need to *provide*: to be living a responsible life, which is to say a responsible economic life.

Provision, I think, is never more than caring properly for the good that you have, including your own life. As it relates to the future, provision does only what our oldest, longest experience tells us to do. We must continuously attend to our need for food, clothing, and shelter. We must care for the land, care for the forest, plant trees, plant gardens and crops, see that the brood animals are bred, keep the house and the household intact. We must teach the children. But provision does not foresee, predict, project, or theorize the future. Provision instructs us to renew the roof of our house, not to shelter us when we are old—we may die or the world may end before we are old—but so we may live under a sound roof now. Provision merely accepts the chances we must take with the weather, mortality, fallibility. Perhaps the wisest of the old sayings is "Don't count your chickens before they hatch." Provision accepts, next, the importance of diversity. Perhaps the next-wisest old saying is "Don't put all your eggs in one basket." When the bad, worse, or worst possibility presents itself, provision only continues to take the best possible care of what we have, or of what we have left.

The answers to my questions of course will affect the future. They might even bring about the "better future for our children" so famous with some politicians. But the answers will not come from the future. We must study what exists: what we know of the past, what we know now, what we can see now, if we look. It is likely that, if we look, we will see a need for the STEM disciplines, for we know already their capacity to serve some good purposes. But we will see that the need for them is limited by, for one thing, the need for other disciplines. And we will see a need also not to allow the value of highly technical knowledge to depress the value of the equally necessary and respectable knowledge of land use and land husbandry.

From its beginning, industrialism has depended on a general willingness to ignore everything that does not serve the cheapest possible production of merchandise and, therefore, the highest possible profit. And so to look back and think again, we must acknowledge real needs that have continued through the years to be real, though unacknowledged: the need to see and respect the inescapable dependence even of our present economy, as of our lives, upon nature and the natural world; and upon the need, just as important, to see and respect our inescapable dependence upon the economies—of farming, ranching, forestry, fishing, and mining—by which the goods of nature are made serviceable to human good.

And now, because it seems to be somewhat conventionally assumed that we are "moving on from farm and factory," we need to recognize again our inescapable dependence upon manufacturing. This does not imply that we must be dependent always and for every product upon large corporations and a global economy. If manufacturing as we have known it is in decline, then that gives room to the thought of a genuinely domestic and conserving economy of provision. This would be a national economy made up of local economies, which, to an extent naturally and reasonably possible, would be complete, self-sustaining, and local in scale. For example, in a town not far from where I am writing, we have recently gained a small, clean, well-equipped, federally inspected slaughtering plant, which completes locally the connection between local pastures and local kitchens, while providing work to local people. There is no reason for this connection and provision to be more extensive. To make the connection between pasture and kitchen by way of the industrial food system is to siphon livelihoods and life itself out of the rural communities.

We also have woodlands here that could even now produce a sustainable yield of valuable hardwoods. But trees cut here at present leave here as raw lumber or saw logs, at the most minimal benefit to the community. Other places and other people may prosper on the bounty of our forest, but not our place and, except minimally for the sellers and a few workers, not our people. It is not hard, considering this, to imagine a local forest economy, made up of small enterprises that would be, within the given limits, complete and coherent, yielding local livelihoods from the good use and care of the living forest to the production of lumber for buildings to finished cabinetry. The thought of such economies is of the nature of provision, not of projection, prediction, or contingency planning. The land and the people are here now. The *present* economic questions are about the work by which land and people might thrive mutually in the best health for the longest time, starting now.

To think well of such enterprises, and of the possibility of combining them in a diverse and coherent local economy, is to think of the need for sustaining all of the necessary occupations. Because a local, a *placed*, economy would be built in sequence from the ground up, from primary production to manufacturing to marketing, a variety of occupations would be necessary. Because all occupations would be necessary, all would be equally necessary. Because of the need to keep them all adequately staffed, it would be ruinous to prefer one above another by price, custom, or social prejudice. There must be a sustained economic parity among them.

In such an economic structure the land-using occupations are primary. We must be mindful of what is, or should be, the fundamental difference between agriculture or forestry and mining, but until the farmers, ranchers, foresters, and miners have done their work, nothing else that we count as economic can happen. And unless the land users do their work *well*—which is to say without depleting the fertility of the earth's surface—nothing we count as economic can happen for very long.

The land-using occupations, then, are of primary importance, but they are also the most vulnerable. We must notice, to begin with, that almost nobody in the supposedly "higher" occupational and social strata has ever recognized the estimable care, intelligence, knowledge, and artistry required to use the land without degrading or destroying it. It is as customary now as it was in the Middle Ages to regard farmers as churls—"mind-numbed," backward, laughable, and dispensable. Farmers may be the last minority that even liberals freely stereotype and insult. If farmers live and work in an economic squeeze between inflated purchases and depressed sales, if their earnings are severely depressed by surplus production, if they are priced out of the land market, it is assumed that they deserve no better: They need only to be "liberated from their chains."

The problem to be dealt with here is that the primary producers in agriculture and forestry do not work well inevitably. On the contrary, in our present economy there are constraints and even incentives that favor bad work, the result of which is waste of fertility and of the land itself. Good work in the use of the land is work that goes beyond production to maintenance. Production must not reduce productivity. Every mine eventually will be exhausted. But where the laws of nature are obeyed in use—as we know they can be, given sufficient care and skill—a farm, a ranch, or a forest will remain fertile and productive as long as nature lasts. Good work also is informed by traditional, locally adapted ways that must be passed down, taught and learned, generation after generation. The standard of such work, as the lineages of good farmers and of agrarian scientists have demonstrated, cannot be established only by "the market." The standard must be partly economic, for people have to live, but it must be equally ecological in order to sustain the possibility of life, and if it is to be ecological it must be cultural. The economies of agriculture and forestry are vulnerable also because they are exceptional, in this way, to the rule of industry.

To obtain the best work in the economies of land use, those who use the land must be enabled to afford the time and patience necessary to do the best work. They must know how, and must desire, to do it well. Owners and workers in the land economy who grow their own food will not likely be starved into mistreating their land. But they can be taxed and priced into mistreating it. And so the parity of necessary occupations must be supported by parity of income.

Parity in this sense is not a new thought, although new thinking may be required in applying it to the variety of crops and commodities produced in a variety of regions. But we do fortunately have some precedence for such thinking. The Agricultural Adjustment Act defines parity as "that gross income from agriculture which will provide the farm operator and his family with a standard of living equivalent to those afforded persons dependent upon other gainful occupation." Perhaps the idea of parity does not need much explanation or defense. If, as now and always, a sufficient staff of land-users is necessary to the health of the land and therefore to the lives of all of us, then they should be assured a decent livelihood. And this the so-called free market cannot provide except by accident.

The concept of parity, as fair-minded as it is necessary, addresses one of the problems of farming and farmers in the industrial economy. Another such problem, more fundamental and most in need of understanding, is that of overproduction. "Other gainful employment" in the cities escapes this problem because the large industrial corporations have not characteristically overproduced. Overproduction moreover is not a problem of subsistence farming, or of those enterprises of any farm that are devoted to the subsistence of the farm family. The aim of the traditional economy of the farm household—a garden, poultry, family milk cow, meat animals, vines, fruit trees—was *plenty*, enough for the family to eat in season and to preserve, plus some to share or to sell. Surpluses and scraps were fed to the dogs or the livestock. There were no leftovers.

Surplus production is a risk native to commercial agriculture. This is because farmers individually and collectively do not know, and cannot learn ahead of time, the extent either of public need or of market demand. Given the right weather and the "progressive" application of technologies, their failure to control production, even in their own interest, is thus inevitable. This is not so much because they won't, but because, on their own, they can't. Either because the market is good and they are encouraged, or because the market is bad and they are desperate, farmers tend to produce as much as they can. They tend logically, and almost by nature, toward overproduction. In the absence of imposed limits, overproduction will fairly predictably occur in agriculture as long as farmers and the land remain productive. It has only to be allowed by a political indifference prescribed by evangels of the "free market." For the corporate purchasers the low price attendant upon overproduction is the greatest benefit, as for farmers it is the singular cruelty, of the current agricultural economy. Farm subsidies without production controls further encourage overproduction. In times of high costs and low prices, such subsidies are paid ultimately, and quickly, to the corporations.

This version of a farm economy pushes farmers off their farms. By increasing the wealth of urban investors and shoppers for "country places," it increases the price of farmland, making it impossible especially for small farmers, or would-be small farmers, to compete on the land market. The free market lays down the rule: Good land for investors and escapists, poor land or none for farmers. Young people wishing to farm are crowded to the economic margins and to the poorest land, or to no land at all. Meanwhile overproduction of farm commodities always implies overuse and abuse of the land.

The traditional home economies of subsistence, while they lasted, gave farmers some hope of surviving their hard times. This was true especially when the chief energy source was the sun, and the dependence on purchased supplies was minimal. As farming became less and less subsistent and more and more commercial, it was exposed ever more nakedly to the vagaries and the predation of an economy fundamentally alien to it. When farming is large in scale, is highly specialized, and all needs and supplies are purchased, the farmer's exposure to "the economy" is total.

It ought to be obvious that an economy that works against its sources will finally undercut the law of supply and demand in the most fatal way, that is, by destroying the supply. A food economy staffed by producers who are always fewer and older, whose increasing dependence on industrial technologies puts them and their land at ever greater risk, obviously cannot feed without limit an increasing population. But the reality of such an increasing scarcity is unaccounted for by the doctrine of the free market as applied to agriculture. Even less can this version of freedom comprehend the need for strict limits upon land use in order to preserve for an unlimited time the land's ability to produce. In a natural ecosystem, even on a conservatively managed farm, the fertility cycle may turn from life to death to life again to no foreseeable limit. By opposing to this cycle the delusion of a limitlessness exclusively economic and industrial, the supposedly free market overthrows the limits of nature and the land, thus imposing a mortal danger upon the land's capacity to produce.

When agricultural production is not controlled by a marketing cooperative such as the tobacco program, the market becomes, from the standpoint of the farmers, a sort of limitless commons, the inevitable tragedy of which is inherent in its limitlessness. In the absence of any imposed limit that they collectively agree to and abide by, all producers may have as large a share of the market as they want or can take. Only in this sense is the market, to them, "free." To limit production as a way of assuring an equitable return to producers is assuredly an abridgement of freedom. But freedom for what? For producers, it is the freedom to produce themselves into bankruptcy—to fail, that is, by succeeding. For the purchaser, it is the freedom to destroy the producers as a normal and acceptable expense. The only solution to the tragedy of the limitless market is for the producers to divide their side, the selling side, of the market into limited fair shares by limiting production, which is exactly what the tobacco program accomplished here in my region. By preventing the farmers' overuse of the market, it prevented as well the overuse of the land.

Agribusiness corporations of course don't openly advocate overproduction. They don't have to assume visibly the moral burden of their bad motive. All they have to do is stand by, praising American agriculture's record-breaking harvests, while either hope or despair drives the remaining farmers to produce as much as they can. The agribusinesses then are glad to sell the very expensive surplus of seeds, chemicals, and machines needed for surplus production.

The agricultural tragedy of the market is in part political. And how was the by-now entirely dominant political position on the agricultural free market defined? In the middle of the twentieth century, think tanks containing corporate and academic experts laid down the decree that there were too many farmers. They decreed further that the excess should be removed as rapidly as possible, and that the instrument of this removal should be the free market, with all price supports and production controls eliminated. The assumption evidently was that the removed farmers would be replaced by industrial technologies, recommended by the land-grant universities, and supplied by the corporations. The surplus farmers would increase the industrial labor force, and they and their families would enlarge the population of consumers of industrial products. It was proposed of course that all of society, including the displaced farm families and farm workers, would benefit from this. There would be no costs, social or agricultural, no problems, no debits, nothing at all to subtract from the accrued economic and social assets. This would institute an evolutionary process that would unerringly eliminate "the least efficient producers." Only the fittest would survive.

In short, by granting a limitless permission and scope to the free market and technological progress—which is assumed to work invariably for the best—politicians, by doing merely nothing, could rid themselves of any concern for farmers or farmland. The representatives of the people and the guardians of the common good were thus able to "free" the market to promote the (allegedly) inefficient farmers to (supposedly) the suburbs while subjecting the countryside to limitless progress and modernization. Against this heartless determinism, it is useful to remember that it was the aim of the program for burley tobacco in my region to include and help every farmer, even the smallest, who wanted to grow the crop. The difference was in the minds of the people whose work during four decades at last shaped an effective program. Those people, unlike the experts of the midcentury think tanks, were thoughtful of the needs of farming and farmers as opposed to the needs of the corporate free market known as the economy. The doctrine of "too many farmers" has never been revoked. No limit to the attrition has been proposed.

As evidence of the persistence of this doctrine, here is a passage from a letter of October 3, 2016, from John Logan Brent, Judge Executive of Henry County, Kentucky:

> I have taken a couple of afternoons to work on the accounting for farming cattle under the current terms. Enclosed you will find that product based upon a real example, which is our 100 acre farm . . . and its approximately 25 cow herd. . . . The good news is that for a young man wishing to earn a middle, to slightly below middle class annual salary of $45,000 farming cattle full-time, he only has to have $3,281,000 in capital to get started. If he can find 780 acres to rent, he only has to have $551,000 for used cows and equipment. I say this is the good news, because the reality is that this was based on a weaned calf price of $850 from June of this year. According to today's sales reports, that same calf is now $650 at best.

That alone, forgetting other adverse agricultural markets, would be an excellent recipe for the elimination of farmers. And conservationists should take note, as mostly they have not done, that in the absence of the eliminated farmers and with the consequent increase of agricultural dependence on the fossil fuels and toxic chemicals, there will be more pollution of water and air.

The related problems of low prices and overproduction of a single but significant crop were solved for about sixty years, in my part of the country and in others, in the only way they could be solved: by a combination of price supports and production controls. This was the purpose and the work of the tobacco program. I want now to look more closely at the Burley Tobacco Growers Co-operative Association, not this time as the brightest public occurrence in the history of my home countryside, but in terms of the suitability of its economic strategy to farming everywhere.

Here I must acknowledge that this organization and, more important, its economic principles have had the allegiance and the service of members of my family for three generations. Beginning in the winter of 1941, when the "Burley Association" renewed its work under the New Deal, my father, John M. Berry, Sr., served as vice president for sixteen and as president for eighteen years, retiring in 1975 but serving as an advisor until a few years before his death in 1991. My brother, John M. Berry, Jr., served as president from 1987 to 1993. My daughter, Mary Berry, started the Berry Center in New Castle, Kentucky, in 2011 for the purpose mainly of remembering, advocating, and applying the Association's proven economic strategy and its purpose of assuring a decent livelihood for small farmers. My son serves on the Berry Center board.

Under this program, support prices for the various grades of tobacco were set according to a formula for assuring a fair return on the cost of production. Production was controlled by allotting to each farm, according to its history of production, at first an acreage, and later a poundage, that would be eligible for price supports under the program. The total of the allotments for each year was determined by the supply, worldwide, that was available for manufacture. The rule was that the supply on hand should be sufficient for 2.4 years. If the supply was less than the predicted demand for 2.4 years, allotments would be increased; if more, allotments would be reduced. I don't know why the factor was set at 2.4. Its significance, however, is that production was limited according to an established measure of expected demand.

To buy a crop or a portion of a crop protected by the program, a purchaser had to bid a penny a pound above the support price. The government's assistance to the program consisted of a loan, made annually "against the crop," which permitted the program to purchase, store, and resell the portion of any year's crop that did not earn the extra penny a pound—which, thanks to the loan, would be purchased by the Association and the grower paid at the warehouse. The cost to the government was only administrative until, in response to protests, this cost was charged to the farmers, and the program then operated on the basis of "no net cost" to the government. This program succeeded remarkably well in doing what it was designed to do, and a part of its success is that it still provides a pattern for the thought and hope of those who are working for the survival of land and people.

The tobacco program is an example of a necessary service that government can provide to people who cannot provide it to themselves. The point most needing to be made now is that parity of pricing under the tobacco program was in no sense a subsidy. It did not involve a grant of money, a government giveaway, or a public charity. The concept of parity was used, by intention, to *prevent* government subsidation. Its purpose was to achieve fair prices, fairly determined, and with minimal help from the government. My father defended parity as an appropriate incentive: "It accords with our way of life, and it gives real and tangible meaning to the philosophy of 'equal opportunity.'" He thought of "direct subsidy payments" as virtually opposite to parity and an "abominable form of regimentation."

The tobacco program in all of its versions was finally defeated and destroyed in 2004 by the political free marketers who had always opposed it, and who had resented it in proportion to its success. During the six decades of its life, the Burley Tobacco Growers Co-operative Association helped keep farm families on their farms and gainfully employed in Kentucky, Missouri, Indiana, Ohio, and West Virginia. One measure of its success was the decrease of farm tenancy among the growers from 33 percent in 1940 to 9 percent in 1970. During those years some of the population of tenant farmers undoubtedly died, and some left farming, but most of them ceased to be tenant farmers by becoming owners of farms. This was a defining event in the lives of a considerable number of worthy people whom I knew. The farmer-members of the Association overwhelmingly renewed their support in referendum after referendum.

The Burley Association was thus truly a commons and a common good, based not only upon correct political and economic principles, but also upon the common history and culture, and thus upon the understanding consent of its sharers. So complete was the understanding of the members that in 1955, because of an oversupply of tobacco in storage, they voted for a 25 percent reduction of their allotments. On April 8, 2016, my neighbor Thomas Grissom, by far the best historian of the Association, wrote in a personal letter to me:

> After years of research, I have concluded that the most distinctive characteristic of the Kentucky [Burley] Tobacco Program is its design and application of an industrial agriculture commodity program to the cultivation and production of an agrarian crop indigenous to an agrarian society.

I think that Tom's perception is exactly right and that he found the right and necessary terms to describe it.

Burley tobacco, despite the dire health problems that it was found to cause and the consequent disfavor, was very much an agrarian crop. It was characteristically and mainly the product of small family farms, produced mainly by family labor and exchanges of work among neighbors. It was for a long time the staple crop in a highly diversified way of farming on landscapes that typically required considerate and affectionate care. As long as the market paid highly for high quality (which it finally ceased to do), the production of burley tobacco demanded, and from its many highly competent producers it received, both conscientious land husbandry and a fine artistry.

Industrialism and agrarianism are almost exactly opposite and opposed. Industrialism regards mechanical or technical functions as ideal. It rates its accomplishments by quantitative measures. Though it values the prestige of public charity, it is motivated necessarily by the antisocial traits that assure success in competition. Agrarianism, by contrast, arises from the primal wish for a home land or home place—the wish, in the terms of our tradition, for the freedom and independence that come with dependence on a parcel of land, however small, that one owns and is owned by or has at least the use of. Agrarianism grants its highest practical value to the good husbandry of the land. It is motivated, to an extent effective and significant, by neighborliness, family loyalty, and devotion to the coherence and longevity of communities.

As long as it has a sufficiency of "natural resources" and remains free of imposed political or economic restraint, an industrial economy will dominate and destroy an agrarian economy—no matter that the agrarian economy is indispensable for a continuing supply of resources. This defines precisely the need for the "design and application of an industrial agricultural commodity program to the cultivation and production of an agrarian crop indigenous to an agrarian society." For a while the Burley Tobacco Growers Co-operative Association—never mind the deserved infamy of tobacco—did preserve a sort of balance between the interests of industrialism and agrarianism, which prevented their inherent difference and opposition from becoming absolute, and thus absolutely destructive of the agrarian society. This balance was fair enough to the industry and it permitted the growers to prosper. The program worked in fact to the best interest of both economies.

From the perspective of this balance during the decades when it worked as it should have, it is possible to see that a step too far toward industrialism was probably taken by the Burley Association itself when, in 1971, it permitted the "lease and transfer" of production quotas away from the farms to which they had been assigned. This change, made under pressure from industrializing members, permitted the accumulation of allotments finally into very large acreages dependent upon more extensive technology and migrant labor. The program then was obliged to "balance" a reduced agrarianism against an increased industrialism.

With the demise of the program in 2004, the region's indigenous agrarianism could survive only as a history, a memory, and a set of vital principles that someday may be revived and reincarnated in reaction against the damages of industrialism.

For the past six decades, except for such a remnant of the New Deal, the government has done nothing for farmers except to quiet them down by subsidizing uncontrolled production, which really is worse than nothing. But this "policy," in the minds of the dominant politicians, signified that they were "doing something for agriculture" and so relieved them of thinking or knowing about agriculture's actual requirements. For example, the Democratic platform preceding President Clinton's first term initially contained no agricultural plank. My brother, John M. Berry, Jr., who was on the platform committee, was dismayed by this innovation, and he said so. He was then told that a plank was being drafted. When he saw the result, he laughed. He asked if he might draft a more meaningful plank. After much resistance, he was allowed to do so. He then "spent the next six hours redrafting the amendment so as to satisfy the Clinton staff." I am quoting his letter of June 29, 1992, to Dr. Grady Stumbo, chair of the Kentucky Democratic Party. The letter goes on to say that Clinton's staff refused to permit any reference to

"supply management," "price support" or any government guarantee of a fair price for farmers. They also refused to permit any reference to agribusiness control of farm policy or the level of agribusiness profits. They also refused to permit any language that could be construed as a commitment . . . to anything specific for agriculture or the rural community. . . .

I had already been advised that Chairman Ron Brown had

formed an agriculture task force and sold seats to its members for $15,000* contributions to the Democratic National Committee.

Those seats went to representatives of agribusiness and other interests that have traditionally written farm policy for the Republicans.

The doctrine of "too many farmers" thus had become the established orthodoxy of the leaders of both parties. My brother was then president of the Burley Tobacco Growers Co-operative Association, which was still a major life support of our state's small farmers. By 1992 tobacco had become indefensible as a product, and it bore too great a public stigma to be touchable by a national candidate. My brother understood that, and he did not expect approval specifically of the tobacco program. But he knew that the working principles of that program would protect farmers who produced commodities other than tobacco everywhere in the country—and would also protect our own farmers when they no longer produced tobacco. He knew that Mr. Clinton, if he wanted to, could endorse the program's principles without endorsing its product. The agricultural plank of the 1992 Democratic platform, as published, gave a general approval to "family farmers receiving a fair price," to "a sufficient and sustainable agricultural economy . . . achieved through fiscally responsible programs," and to "the private–public partnership to ensure that family farmers get a fair return for their labor and investment." And of course it condemned "Republican farm policy." It committed Mr. Clinton and his party to do nothing. And nothing was what they did.

In 1995 President Clinton spoke to an audience of farmers and farm leaders in Billings, Montana. He acknowledged that the farm population by then was "dramatically lower . . . than it was a generation ago." But, he said, "that was inevitable because of the increasing productivity of agriculture." Nevertheless, he wanted to save the family farm, which he held to be "alive and well" in Montana. He believed we had "bot-

---

* My brother told me not long before his death in 2016 that the "contributions" actually were $30,000.

tomed out in the shrinking of the farm sector." He said he wanted to help young farmers. He spoke of the need to make American agriculture "competitive with people around the world." And so on.

He could not have meant what he said, because he was speaking without benefit of thought. And why should he have thought when he was not expected to do so? He was speaking forty or fifty years after politicians and their consulting experts had abandoned any effort to think about agriculture. "Inevitable" is a word much favored by people in positions of authority who do not wish to think about problems. When and why did Mr. Clinton in 1995 think that the inevitable "shrinking of the farm sector" had ceased? In fact, "the farm sector" had not bottomed out in 1995; there is no good reason to think that it has bottomed out, at less than 1 percent of the population, in 2016. And how could he have helped young farmers except by giving them the protections against the free market that my brother had recommended three years before? Mr. Clinton was talking nonsense in Billings in 1995 because he did not have, and could not have had from his advisers, the means to think about what he thought he was talking about. The means of actual thought about the use and care of the land had been intentionally discounted and forgotten by people such as themselves.

It appears to be widely assumed by politicians, executives, academics, public intellectuals, industrial economists, and the like that they have a competent understanding of agriculture because their grandparents were farmers, or they have met some farmers, or they worked on a farm when they were young. But they invoke their understanding, which they do not have, only to excuse themselves from actual thought about actual issues of agriculture. These people have found "inevitability" a sufficient explanation for the deplorable history of industrial agriculture. They see the reason for the present discontent of "blue collar" voters as low or "stagnant" wages. They don't see, in back of that, the dispossession that made many of them wage-workers in the first place. The loss everywhere of small farms and small towns and the respectable livelihoods that they provided was ruled "inevitable" and thus easily explained and forgotten. In their perceived worthlessness and dispensability, at least, the people of the farms and small towns were in effect racially equal. If, for instance, black small farmers were helped to prosper, as some liberals would have liked, then white small farmers would have had to be helped to prosper, which would have pleased neither liberals nor conservatives.

It was, then, "inevitable" that the independent livelihoods in the old economies of the countryside and the small towns should be replaced by the mainly subservient livelihoods in industry, or by unemployment. But if the "working class" counted for nothing and were dispensable as small farmers or farmhands or as small independent keepers of shops and stores or as independent tradespeople and craftspeople, why then should they count for something and be more than dispensable as "blue-collar workers"? In the corporate and urban economy the blue-collar workers were just as "inevitably" replaceable by technologies as they had been before. They were then notified that they were losing out because they were "uneducated." They needed "a college education," in default of which they were offered "retraining" and "job creation." But these were only political baits, which left the blue-collared ones to their "inevitable" fate of low or stagnant wages or unemployment.

This doctrine of inevitability, also known as technological progress, is in fact a poor excuse for an economic and technological determinism, as heartless as it is ignorant, which has belonged about equally to the political establishment of both parties. Realizing that they were the broken eggs of an omelet that others would eat, the blue-collar workers became angry. Their anger turned them to Donald Trump, who at least recognized their existence and the political usefulness of their anger.

In the pre-Trump version of the history of progress, determinism and inevitability overruled any need for actual knowledge and actual thought. But with the ascendancy of Mr. Trump, at least some of the determinists seem to be reverting to free will. While the conservatives, who have strained at a gnat and swallowed a camel, endeavor to digest their dinner, the liberals talk of "connecting" with the blue-collar workers of rural America, to whom they have given not a substantive thought since Ezra Taft Benson, Eisenhower's secretary of agriculture, pronounced to their grandparents the political death sentence, "Get big or get out."

Let us remember also the workers, white and black, who in their thousands became simply obsolete at the instant when "efficient" machines were brought into the coal mines, the factories, and the fields of sugarcane and cotton. I thought of them when I read in a column by Roger Cohen in the *New York Times* of November 19, 2016, that "the very essence of the modern world" is "the movement of people and ever greater interconnectedness, driven by technology." Mr. Cohen approves of this "essence" and is afraid that Mr. Trump will stop it. What he has in mind surely must be the *voluntary* movement of people. The movements of people *actually* "driven by technology" are outside Mr. Cohen's field of vision, surely only because of his political panic. Millions of people, as we know, have been driven away from their homes in the modern world by the similarly imperative technologies of industrial production and industrial war.

I am uncertain what value Mr. Cohen assigns to "interconnectedness," but he cannot be referring to the interconnectedness of families in their home places, or of neighbors in their neighborhoods. How the loss of those things can be compensated by movement, driven or not, is far from clear. The same obscurity clouds over any massive "movement of peoples," as over the arguments by which these movements are excused or justified. It does not require a great refinement of intellect to see the harm that is in all of them.

The experts who decided in the middle of the twentieth century that there were too many farmers had in fact no agricultural knowledge or competence upon which to base such a judgment. They and their successors certainly had not the competence to assume any responsibility for, or in any way to mitigate, the totalitarian displacement of about twenty million farmers.

• • •

Farming is one of the major enactments of the connection between the human economy and the natural world. In the industrial age farming also enacts the connection, far more complicated and perilous than industrialists admit, between industrial technologies and living creatures. Some science certainly needs to be involved, also more and better accounting. But good farming is first and last an art, a way of doing and making that involves human histories, cultures, minds, hearts, and souls. It is not the application by dullards of methods and technologies under the direction of a corporate-academic intelligentsia.

If we should want to revive, or begin, in a public way the actual thinking about agriculture that has actually taken place in some cultures, that is still taking place in some small organizations and on some farms, what would we have to do? We would have to begin, I think, by giving the most careful attention to issues of carrying capacity, scale, and form, to issues of production, of course, but also and just as necessarily to issues of maintenance or conservation. The indispensable issue of conservation would apply, not just to the farm's agricultural "resources," but also to the ecosystem that includes the farm and to the waterways that drain it. I think, moreover, that this attention to issues must be paid always outdoors in the presence of examples. The thing of greatest importance is to think about the land with the land's people in the presence of the land. Every theory, calculation, graph, diagram, idea, study, model, method, scheme, plan, and hope must be caught firmly by the ear and led out into the weather, onto the ground.

It is obvious that this effort of thinking has to confront everywhere the limits both of nature and of human nature, limits imposed by the ecosphere and ecosystems, limits of human intelligence, human cultures, and the capacities of human persons. Such thought is authenticated by its compatibility with limits, its willingness to accept limits and to limit itself. This will not be easy in a time overridden by fantasies of limitlessness. A market limitlessly usable by sellers and limitlessly exploitable by buyers is merely normal in such a time. And limitlessness is the common denominator of the dominant political sides, both of which tend to refer to limitlessness as "freedom."

We have the liberal freedom of unrestrained personal behavior, and the conservative freedom of unrestrained economic behavior. These two freedoms are more alike, more allied, and more collaborative than either side would like to admit. Opposition to the industrial economy's ravaging of the landscapes of farming and forestry now comes from a small and scattered alliance of agrarians, not from liberals or conservatives.

Conservatives and liberals disagree passionately about climate change, for example, yet liberal protests against climate change far exceed protests against the waste and pollution that occur locally in industrial agriculture and are its reputed causes. And neither the conservatives who esteem the fossil fuels nor the liberals who deplore them have advocated rationing their use, either to make them last or to reduce their harm. For these people the old ideals of *enough* and *plenty* have been overruled by the ideals of *all you want* and *all you can get*. They cannot imagine that for farmers a limitless market share, like a limitless appetite, can lead only to the related diseases of *too much* and *too little*.

Science, apart from moral limits in scientists, seems to be limitless, for it has produced nuclear and chemical abominations that humans, with their very limited intelligence, can neither limit nor safely live with. "Anything goes" and "Stop at nothing" are the moral principles that some scientists have borrowed apparently from the greediest of conservatives and the most libertine of liberals. The faith that limitless technological progress will finally solve the problems of limitless contamination seems to depend upon some sort of neo-religion.

The good care of land and people, on the contrary, depends primarily upon arts, ways of making and doing. One cannot be, above all, a good neighbor without such ways. And the arts, all of them, are limited. Apart from limits they cannot exist. The making of any good work of art depends, first, upon limits of purpose and attention, and then upon limits specific to the kind of art and its means.

It is a formidable paradox that in order to achieve the sort of limitlessness we have begun to call "sustainability," whether in human life or the life of the ecosphere, strict limits must be observed. Enduring structures of household and family life, or the life of a community or the life of a country, cannot be formed except within limits. We must not outdistance local knowledge and affection, or the capacities of local persons to pay attention to details, to the "minute particulars" *only* by which, William Blake thought, we can do good to one another. Within limits, we can think of rightness of scale. When the scale is right, we can imagine completeness of form.

The first limit to be encountered in making a farm—or a regional or national economy—is carrying capacity: How much can we ask of *this* land, this field or this pasture or this woodland, without diminishing the land's response? And then we come to other limits, perhaps many of them, each one addressing directly our imagination, sympathy, affection, forbearance, knowledge, and skill. And now I must call to mind Aldo Leopold, who, unlike most conservationists since John Muir, could think beyond wilderness conservation to conservation of the country's economic landscapes of farming and forestry. His conception of humanity's relation to the natural world was eminently practical, and this must have come from his experience as a hunter and fisherman, his study of game management, and his and his family's restoration of their once-exhausted Sand County farm. He knew that land-destruction is easy, for it requires only ignorance and violence. But the obligation to restore the land and conserve it requires humanity in its highest, completest sense. The Leopold family renewed the fertility and health of their land by their work, their pleasure, and their love for their place and for one another.

Aldo Leopold thought carefully about farming and forestry because he knew that far more land would be put to those uses than ever could be safeguarded in wilderness preserves. In an essay of 1945, "The Outlook for Farm Wildlife," he laid side by side "two opposing philosophies of farm life" (the italics being his):

1. *The farm is a food-factory*, and the criterion of its success is salable products.

2. *The farm is a place to live.* The criterion of success is a harmonious balance between plants, animals, and people;
   between the domestic and the wild; between utility and
   beauty.

This is a statement about form, contrasting a form that is too simple
and too exclusive with a form that may be complex enough to accom-
modate the interest of what is actually involved. Under the rule of the
first form, "the trend of the landscape is toward a monotype." This form
can be adequately described as the straightest, shortest line between
input and income. All else is left out or denied. Such a form concedes
nothing to its whereabouts. It is placed upon whatever landscape merely
by imposition, as a cookie cutter is imposed upon dough. In its simplic-
ity and rigidity, such a form is bad art, but also, as Leopold knew and as
we now know better than he could have, it is bad science.

The second form is described as "a harmonious balance" among a
diversity of interests. On such a farm, made whole by the high artistry
of farming, every part is both limited and enabled by the others. This
harmonious balance, I should not need to say, cannot be prefabricated.
It can be realized only uniquely within the boundary of any given farm,
according to the natures and demands of its indwelling plants and animals, and according to the abilities, needs, and wishes of its resident
human family. Wherever this is fully accomplished, it is a grand masterpiece to behold.

Leaving the Future Behind:
A Letter to a Scientific Friend

Take therefore no thought for the morrow: for the morrow shall take thought for the things of itself. Sufficient unto the day is the evil thereof.

—MATTHEW 6:34 (KJV)

Man has lost Dante's vision of that "love which moves the sun and the other stars," and in so doing he has lost the power to find meaning in his world. . . . He has lost all conviction that he knows where he is going and what he is doing, unless he can manage to plunge into some collective delusion which promises happiness (sometime in the future) . . .

—THOMAS MERTON, *Disputed Questions*

Dear ———,

By your continuing generosity and friendly nudging, you have invited me into "further conversation about the utility of using scientific studies of the past and the present to reduce the uncertainty about predicting the future health of individuals and populations." And you have sent me a copy of *A World of Propensities* by Karl Popper as a point of reference. In short, you have asked me again to consider "the future," though you know I won't grant it much standing, and "prediction," though you know I won't grant it much respect.

Well, I will grant the future enough standing to speak of it as a problem. The future is a time and a world not yet in existence. We can say, not very usefully, that we are now living in the future of the past, which is to some small extent knowable. The future of the present we do not know. But, obviously, we humans wish to have a future: We want to continue to live, and we desire life for our children and our children's children. We know that in some circumstances some of us have wished to die, but we don't like that wish, we fear it and hope to avoid it. We also should remember that for at least two thousand years some of us have been predicting, expecting, fearing, or desiring the end of the world, which we know is bound to come, though we don't know when. Perhaps we should ask if the dissatisfaction with the present, and the longing for quitting time, the weekend, vacation, and retirement—all by now customary in the industrial world—is not a "death wish." I think it is.

Because we wish instinctively for life to continue, and we suppose the future will arrive, we place theoretically in front of ourselves a time and a world we call "the future." Because of our love and fear of the future, we have invented several ways of thinking about it or preparing for it. The conventional ways (excluding dreams and visions) are clearly profitable to some of us, and so they are always in agitation. The future includes every envisionable happiness and calamity, and so the (profitable) ways of preparing for it may be virtually infinite, all being subject to change. But let us see.

The amateurs of the future are the fortune tellers, the self-employed visionaries, the determined or deterministic optimists and pessimists, the religiously faithful, and the general run of wishers and hopers. Any of these can lead or mislead us into the future, in which the inevitable fulfillments or disappointments may be construed, without sustaining evidence, as proofs. ("See! I prayed for rain, and it rained!")

The only context of hope, I suppose, is the future, but that is a dangerous business. Native to our character and condition as it may be, experience teaches us not to rely on hope, and there is always the considerable danger that we will hope for the wrong things.

As for the future, it extends from the next second to the end of the world. In the very short term, it may be that prediction is even more native to our character and condition than hope. It seems plain enough to me that we could not walk without predicting that our next step will alight firmly on solid footing. But nothing more than walking has persuaded me of the embarrassment of prediction. I know that others are more fortunate, but I am an awkward person. All of my life I have been falling down—not regularly, which might have made me a predictor—but frequently, surprisingly, and ungracefully, so that even before getting up I always look about for witnesses. Always unexpectedly, a hole or a stick or my other foot will trip me and I will be precipitated to the ground like a handful of jackstraws. Almost all my days likewise have led to surprises that could not have been predicted.

Professionally, the future seems to belong to the more or less scientific experts. We want, sometimes desperately, to know what is going to happen. We want a prognosis, a projection, a prediction, a contingency plan, a posture of military readiness. For this clairvoyance, in the modern world, we turn to the scientists who supply the answers as professional services, usually paid for "up front." These services cannot be properly valued until the future has become the past. What could be better business than selling at a set price an article of unknown value?

There is, then, nothing in our dealings with the future that is substantive enough to justify our fevered obsession with it, which has made it a "time" more important to us than either the past or the present.

In preparing us for the future, projection and prediction have the limited validity of reasoning or deducing the future from the past. We "project" by assuming that if traffic at the airport has increased at the rate of 5 percent a year for five years, it will increase by 5 percent next year and the next and the next (therefore we need to be building a bigger airport). Sometimes projections are useful, sometimes not. Finally every projection will run into absurdity, as Mark Twain demonstrated some time ago in *Life on the Mississippi*:

> In the space of one hundred and seventy-six years the Lower Mississippi has shortened itself two hundred and forty-two miles . . . [A]ny person can see that seven hundred and forty-two years from now the Lower Mississippi will be only a mile and three quarters long . . .

Projection becomes absurd, apparently, when an unconsidered limit falls upon it from ambush. Projection moves toward certainty or "truth" by counting repetitions and by further processes of reasoning. Because the sun has come up on millions of mornings, we can confidently expect it in the morning; if the same experiment produces the same result a certain number of times, we assume that it would produce the same result an endless number of times, and the result to the extent of that assumption is true. But again we have the limit-in-ambush: The sun is burning and so it will burn out, though we don't know when.

Maybe all predictions ultimately are projections and have the limited rationality of projections, which is to say that our every effort to predict will finally meet either unforeseen circumstantial limits or simply the limits of our knowledge and intelligence. As you (and Popper) point out, the degree of predictability probably changes with context. A chemical "proven" to be safe in a laboratory may be provably unsafe, or beyond such provability, in a river.

I believe—and you, with scientific authority, know—that predictability applies much more securely to machines than to creatures (organisms, ecosystems, worlds). Something was, and is, not predictable from nothing. Living organisms could not have been predicted from the lifelessness that preceded them. I don't think it could have been predicted that some reptiles would evolve into birds. If you see a squirrel in the middle of the road, you can't predict whether it will run to the right or the left (therefore you should slow down). Our friend Wes Jackson points out that an "emergent quality cannot be predicted before it has been seen."

A machine runs by repeating the same motions predictably over and over again. It does not alter its running by any sensitive response to any outward circumstances—whereas the human heart (as I once heard Brian Goodwin tell a class of medical students at the University of Michigan) never makes two beats that are exactly identical, because it is alive and must respond livingly to the changing circumstances of a living body in a living world.

It may be said that a thermostat "responds sensitively" to the changing circumstance of temperature and so "controls" the circumstance, much like the heart. But that is speaking figuratively. A thermostat is a highly specialized machine that responds only to temperature. It will never evolve as or into an organ. The circumstances of the heart, moreover, are not predictable and are no doubt too numerous and various to be definitively catalogued. By a curious paradox, a thermostat, which is in no sense human, nevertheless has a human limit: It is capable of doing only what humans have designed it to do. By inversion of the same paradox, a healthy heart, which is entirely human but not a human invention, has limits that are natural but not specifically human. You have warned me that "it is true that every single heartbeat is unique, but at a larger time scale it is very predictable." But here we meet again the limit-in-ambush: At a yet larger time scale the heartbeat will (uniquely) cease, but we don't know when.

I will venture further to suggest that vices are more predictable than virtues. Given the continuation of technological progress and the persistence of greed, the next advances in hospital care are fairly predictable: The robotic bedpan is on the horizon. The advances that come of effective kindness or compassion might, even in present circumstances, be surprising. Technological advances are made for average or theoretical patients and are justified by accounting, whereas kindness or compassion occur only in transactions between living individuals and are justified by need. (See the parable of the Good Samaritan).

At this point I ought to take notice of a self-consciously scientific treatment of prediction and predictability. In their book of 2010, *The Grand Design*, Stephen Hawking and Leonard Mlodinow neatly wipe out my distinction between creatures and machines by proposing that the newest science is the best science, and that, according to this science, "it seems that we are no more than biological machines and that free will is just an illusion."

But this seemingly leads directly to a problem: "While conceding that human behavior is indeed determined by the laws of nature, it also seems reasonable to conclude that the outcome is determined in such a complicated way and with so many variables as to make it impossible in practice to predict." To answer this impossibility, the authors produce what they call "an effective theory": "[S]ince we cannot solve the equations that determine our behavior, we use the effective theory that people have free will." But: "That effective theory is only moderately successful in predicting behavior because . . . decisions are often not rational or are based on a defective analysis of the consequences of the choice."

That certainly is darkening counsel. To what point does one construct an "only moderately successful" theory to affirm an idea that one has already declared to be false? What now are we to do? And how successful is "moderately successful"?

Hawking and Mlodinow lapse at one point into the (to them) discouraging prospect that we may *not* discover "an ultimate theory of the universe," though we may "continue forever finding better theories, but never one that cannot be improved upon." Still, many scientists continue to predict or assume that their (extremely expensive) researches will show the universe to be an entirely predictable machine with an entirely predictable future. There is much talk of the (predicted) "theory of everything." I am assuming that the scientific prophets mean their language strictly and exactly. The "theory of everything," if it refers dependably to everything, will show everything to have been predetermined—and not by a mysteriously preexisting mind or will, but rather by a (mysteriously) preexisting physical or natural law. A universe entirely predetermined would be entirely predictable. The predictable future would be a perfect, unlimited projection.

It is easy (if one has contemplated the third chapter of Genesis) to understand the allure of such an immense and perfect knowledge, bringing an end at last to all the disorder of unpredictability and surprise. But after such success, after the fulfillment of such knowledge, what then? Would we be "as gods" then? Or would we have the ultimate humiliation of knowing ourselves to be the helpless and hopeless parts of an entirely predictable, determined, and determining machine? This looks remarkably like another version of the "religious" longing to be free of problems, which may be another version of the death wish.

Once a perfectly predictable universe, a perfect machine of a universe, is proposed, we must ask how the existence of a perfectly predictable universe might have been predicted. Hawking and Mlodinow dispose of this question with breathtaking confidence:

> M-theory predicts that a great many universes were created out of nothing. Their creation does not require the intervention of some supernatural being or god. Rather, these universes arise naturally from physical law.

This proposes (with religion) that nothing preceded creation, but also (*more* religiously?) that nature and physical law preceded nothing. This clearly is a kind of faith, and a faith moreover that is here earnestly recommended by two scientists who are aggressively contemptuous of faith.

Hawking and Mlodinow believe in cosmic, evolutionary, and historical progress. The history of the universe (or universes) is a record of continuous improvement, culminating in the history of science, which likewise has continuously improved. How are we to account for this? By "a series of startling coincidences in the precise details of physical law" that are the result, in turn, of "luck in the precise form and nature of physical law," which is ultimately explainable as "spontaneous creation." This explanation appears to be founded almost entirely upon a "scientific" language that is vague and presumptuous without limit.

It is impossible for me to take seriously such language and such thought. But I know I had better not brush it aside as of no importance, and that is because I see a considerable danger in it. This letter, by your invitation, is my part of a discussion in which we don't altogether agree. But our discussion is possible because we are friends, and we agree somewhat. There is a partial convergence. We converge when you tell me and I agree that "the physical world is more predictable than the biological world." We then diverge somewhat when you, as a scientist, speak of "biological organisms" and I, following my culture tradition, speak of "living creatures." But we immediately converge again in our mutual good will toward the life, human and other, of this world. And that, I think, makes us mutually aware of the dire misfit between the merely physical or mechanical world of Hawking and Mlodinow, assumed to be perfectly predictable, and the less predictable living world that, as you and I agree, we may choose to treat with loving care.

The future now being so full of scientific pessimism, determinism, heroism, and gobbledygook, I believe that you sent me *A World of Propensities* as a sort of life raft. Whereas the scientific predestinarians offer only the "hope" that the universe and all its parts and events will be proven to be predictable and free will "just an illusion," Karl Popper's vision of the world, its history, and its creatures is meant to serve a genuine hope. Popper was a man of good will, better tempered, better humored, more generous, and better company than Hawking and Mlodinow. Popper's book, *A World of Propensities*, published in 1990, may be read as an attempt to head off the bleak (and flimsy) determinism of *The Grand Design*, published twenty years later. Both books refer to Heisenberg, Hawking and Mlodinow's with the assurance that the progress of modern science will carry us beyond his "uncertainty principle" into the certainties of the entirely predictable universe, Popper's with evident welcome to the realization that Heisenberg's "indeterminacies" give scope to change, change to probabilities, probabilities to "weighted possibilities" or "propensities."

Propensities are inclinations or preferences that, in given situations, cause changes. In the first of the two lectures that compose his book, having established to his satisfaction the reality of propensity as a force of change, Popper makes it the basis of a validation of free will:

> [I]n our real changing world, the situation and, with it, the possibilities, and thus the propensities, change all the time. They certainly may change if we, or any other organisms, *prefer* one possibility to another; or if we *discover* a possibility where we have not seen one before. . . . All this amounts to the fact that *determinism is simply mistaken*: all its traditional arguments have withered away and indeterminism and free will have become part of the physical and biological sciences. [The italics are Popper's.]

A few paragraphs later Popper says:

> These tendencies and propensities have led to the emergence of life. . . . And the evolution of life has led to better conditions for life on earth and thus to new possibilities and propensities; and to new forms of life . . . All this means that possibilities . . . have a kind of reality. . . . And in so far as these possibilities can, and partly will, realize themselves in time, the open future is, in some way, already present, with its many competing possibilities, almost as a promise, as a temptation, as a lure.

And then near the end of this lecture, Popper says that, in the course of evolution, "the organisms were in search of a better world." Such a remarkably humorous statement, I think, can have come only from warmth of heart, a kind of indulgent fellow-feeling for "the or-ganisms" as they pick their way slowly through the millennia toward Karl Popper and his doctrine of propensities and free will. I like Pop-per's argument, but I am not as convinced by it as I would like to be. In his second lecture he supplies three sentences that are convincing in themselves because they represent the organisms as finders of solutions to specific practical problems—not as idealists "in search of a better world":

> All organisms are problem finders and problem solvers. And all problem solving involves evaluations and, with it [*sic*], values. Only with life do problems and values enter the world.

Like Hawking and Mlodinow, though to opposite purpose, Pop-per seems to conflate or confuse evolution with an ameliorative sense of progress, every change producing something better. It seems to me that Popper's argument depends too much on his figures of speech, which are more "interpretative" than scientific. As living creatures, I suppose, we may be permitted to regard life as better than non-life. But by what propensity or choice could non-life have solved the problem (to continue Popper's metaphor) of becoming life? And by what standard of "better" other than self-interest (if capable of that) could organisms have solved their problems? And how could even innumerable sequences of self-interested solutions produce, by "evaluations," the communal good of "better conditions for life on earth"?

Those questions, and such questions, are important and ought to be asked. Even more important, I think, is the question of how to re-spond. And the possible responses appear to be limited. We can say that events have occurred in the long reaches of time that were mysterious or miraculous. Or to explain them, using our small knowledge and small intelligence, we can develop theories that will inevitably mix science with conjecture (however reasonable or logical), and they will look thin when stood against the great phenomena that they explain. Or we can assume, as many apparently do, that science finally, and perhaps soon, will command the full and final Truth—which of course makes of science a kind of religion, or at least a superstition. But it seems to me that science is badly corrupted when scientists depart from their responsibly limited and limiting ways of testing or proving comparatively small truths.

The future, anyhow, is unlikely to be in any simple way a continuation of the past. And the present, if we include subtraction as one of our means of thinking about time, is not in an easily measurable way an improvement upon the past. Like many other people, I cherish hope for the success of compassion, mercy, forgiveness, neighborly love, responsible freedom, and the loving care of the earth that all of those goods imply, but the success of that hope is only endangered by ignoring our record of costs and losses. Projections, predictions, futurological visions, contingency plans, like our dearest hopes, are continuously fretted and crumbled as the possible futures shrink through the needle's eye of the present into the singular past.

The past, Popper says, "is fixed." But our knowledge of it is incomplete and imperfect. We verify it to some extent by records and numbers, which may remain subject to revision and which also are subject to shifts in perspective as time passes. The present is too brief and fleeting to be captured for study. The future is predictable or foreseeable only by a kind of faith and within narrow limits. This, I think, is a fair description of our condition, our life in time, our tragedy.

Earlier in this discussion of ours, countering your scientific learning and long practice only with my own imperfect reading and experience, I said to you that of all our means of preparing for the future I respected only provision, and I stand by that. Provision is the sum of our ways of securing from the earth our food, clothing, and shelter—and of taking proper care of the sources of these things in nature and in human culture. It rests upon no guarantees, and it does not pretend to know the future. In a recent fall, for example, we had a small flock of twenty-two bred ewes. That was provision. Attacks by predators quickly eliminated six of the ewes. That was of the nature of provision. We responded by folding the remaining ewes every night, and so brought them safely through the winter to lambing time. That was provision. We will continue the nighttime folding, with what success we cannot know. That is of the nature of provision.

I don't believe we can escape the necessity of provision and providing. Except for that, I think we need to restrain and reduce our presumptions upon the future, which, in our age of industrial technologies, are producing grotesque and dangerous results. We need, for example, neither the expense nor the risk of our huge arsenal of nuclear weapons. We should never have made ourselves willing to destroy the world and ourselves in order to "win" a future war. We built the interstate highway system, thus destroying the rail passenger service, at enormous economic and ecological costs, supposedly in preparation for an invasion at some time in the future. (There is no chance that these highways could be used by the future invaders?) We spy on everybody, fearing that anybody may sometime be an enemy. Privately, we humans often prepare for the future, often badly, on the basis of hopes and dreams. But collectively our preparations seem to be motivated mainly by fear. Businesses and industries thrive upon our popular fears of attack, defeat, enslavement (by foreigners), sickness, age, death, and the weather. There is big money in "knowing" the future, especially if it is "known" to be bad. But we capitalize also on our ignorance of the future by bequeathing to more fortunate times—when people will be smarter, science more perfect, technologies more miraculous—an enormous legacy of poisons and depletions.

And so we have made of the future, not a coming time, but a limitless vacuity in which we elaborate our fears and fantasies, to which we defer payment of our perhaps unpayable ecological debts, and where we store our most lethal and enduring "wastes." This cynical and, finally, addictive dependence on the future also works to disguise present problems and to delay solutions. Waste and pollution are everyday problems to which all of us contribute in daily and ordinary ways. To collect them under the heading of "climate change" sensationalizes and enlarges them, assigns the remedies to governments and corporations, and to the future. To sell digital technology, as a solver of problems but not a cause of problems, as it was and is sold, abuses the future in order to abuse the present.

The most dangerous attribute of the future, as we have been more and more inclined to need and to use it, is its limitlessness. There are no deadlines in the future, when all problems may be solved, when the whole Truth of the universe may be learned, when the world may end in apocalypse or another Bang—or when, because of our dreadful "creative destructions" now, we will all be healthy and happy. Because the future is limitless, we can project without limit into it. It is limitless, to us, because we know nothing about it. Because we know nothing about it, we are free to talk endlessly about it. It is hard to imagine why we do this except to distract ourselves from the difficult things we do know about and ought urgently to be talking about. We give up the incarnate life of our living souls, in the only moment we are alive, in order to live in dreams and nightmares of the future of a world we have already diminished and made ill, in no small part by our often mistaken preparations for the future. Why, living now and only now, should we afflict ourselves with predictions of a hellish future in which we are not alive and perhaps will never live? Or why should we delude ourselves with visions of a future technological heaven-on-earth in which we certainly will never live?

By withdrawing our false, speculative, wishful, and fearful claims upon the future, we would significantly and properly reduce the circumstance or context within which we live and think. This would place us within our right definition, our right *limits*, as earthly creatures and human beings. It is only within those limits that we can think practically, usefully, and so with hope, of our history, of what we have been and who we are, of our sustaining connections and relationships.

As we both know, the most famous and influential future-fear at present is of climate change. Of all the competing future catastrophes, climate change is number one. A multitude of people, including scientists and other experts, have devoted themselves exclusively to the threat of climate change. It is a great "movement." I am not a climate change denier. If a lot of scientists are worried about climate change, I think we all should worry about it. But I certainly am a critic of the climate change movement, and for what I consider good reasons.

My foremost reason is that when so many people are devoted so exclusively to a single fear, the movement ceases to have the quality of prudence or provision, and takes on the character of a fad. To anyone privileged, as I have been, to live into old age, the faddishness of the climate change movement is not new. I was a young husband and father when the fear of nuclear holocaust was blown into a fad. That was the age of Civil Defense, escape routes, bomb shelters, stockpiles of food, weapons, and ammunition, all for the sake of surviving a nuclear attack that might come at any moment. Clearly the cheap and sensible alternative to panic and its preparations was resignation. Since my little family and I could not afford the preparations, I pretty well resigned myself to whatever might be our fate, and I took a limited pleasure in feeling sensible, frugal, simplified, and relieved.

Well, the nuclear holocaust was too long delayed to remain a fad. The *threat* very much remains, but for the time being most people seem not much interested and not much afraid. Overpopulation—the population "bomb"—likewise had its panic and its fad. Though the *threat* remains, the obsession for the time being has died. It is significant that neither fad produced a remedy.

The great question now needing to be asked is how to get from protest, or fear or anger or guilt, to the actual accomplishment of good work. By good work I mean work that is necessary, enduringly valuable, pleasing to the worker, and not infected with the insanity of such a concept as "creative destruction." Our movements of protest are typically addressed to political leaders, demanding correction or improvement in the future. They always involve crowds in public places, the display of signs and banners, the shouting of slogans, a sort of T-shirt oratory, but never a suggestion of good work that the participants can go home and do.

The problem with prediction, no matter how scientifically respectable it may be, is its power to bring on first a fear and then a movement that can be popularized into a fad. But of all bad motives none may be worse or more hopeless than fear. Nobody, I think, has ever done good work because of fear. Good work is done by knowing how and by love. Love requires faith, courage, patience, and steadiness, none of which can come from fear. Also it appears to be impossible to sustain for very long even the most reasonable fear of a future catastrophe. It seems likely, moreover, that the larger and more complete the anticipated catastrophe, the more *boring* it is. The coming of Doomsday or the death of the planet or the end of life as we know it or the extinction of our species does not invite thought or even much attention. Modern Americans seem well able to abide or ignore the possibility of their own extinction as well as that of other creatures, though they would be greatly anguished by the threatened extinction of the automobile. The complete catastrophe will end all of our fears and even the worst of our problems. Atheists at least should anticipate it with some pleasure. But I don't think anybody is going to dwell on any version of The End for very long. Though a nuclear "device" may explode or the world end at any moment, finally people must go about their daily business. And then they can return to the really pertinent questions about the goodness or badness of their daily business and their happiness or unhappiness in doing it.

What is truly interesting is the possibility that in spite of some very big difficulties mostly caused by themselves, humans may continue to live on this Earth for a time unpredictably long—*and* that there may be unsensational, unrevolutionary, not very high-technological ways of thinking and working already available that could make them reasonably safe, comfortable, and happy while they live.

To get to such ways of thinking and working, I believe we have got to understand how the great one-cause, fear-motivated climate change movement, for example, can become a major distraction, not only from

better ways of problem solving and better ways of thinking and working, but also from the local causes of climate change—which has, after
all, only local causes.

But this letter so far has been too general and theoretical, too far up in
the air for a queasy old acrophobe like me. It is time to bring it down
to some ground-level, actual places where the future has arrived and
become the past, and where the still-awaited future will have to be dealt
with when it arrives, as likely it will.

Let us consider the instance of a Kentucky county for which I am
not authorized to speak, and so I will call it Rural County. Since Mr.
Trump's election with the help of many votes from "white blue-collar
rural Americans," the urban liberals and Democrats have discovered
Rural America, the country itself, which apparently is as new to them
as it was to Columbus, and whose inhabitants are as inferior as he
thought the Indians to be. To these discoverers, Rural America is all
one place, everywhere the same. And so Rural County, Kentucky, can
be taken as representative of Rural America. Less than half of the Rural
Countians "believe in climate change," and nearly three-quarters voted
for Mr. Trump. If a liberal inquirer goes there, as inevitably one will do,
she will find some of the expected rural people—backward, provincial,
ignorant—who offend on both accounts. To its liberal discoverers and
explorers, this pretty adequately describes Rural County and the rest
of Rural America. To them every detail is a general truth, every individual a type. The Rural Americans are a sin-ridden people. Whatever
one wants to accuse them of, they are probably guilty of: racism and
sexism, of course, old-fashioned vices that Urban America long ago got
clean rid of. The urban liberals and Democrats forget or don't know that
the people of Rural America became obsolete as small farmers, small
merchants, and trades-people in the country towns, and then became
obsolete again as "blue-collar workers."

As a Rural Person, I happen to know a number of further particulars about Rural County. I know that if the liberal inquirer should

stay a few days longer, talk more, and look all around, she would find that the human inhabitants of Rural County fit as comfortably into the definition of their species as the liberals of the cities and universities, that they may be sorted into a variety of kinds, even that they may be somewhat known as individuals. Some of them she might find interesting, some she might even like. She would certainly discover that Rural County was once predominantly a farming county, in which the care of crops and orchards was performed by family members and neighbors working together, and with their children. She would find that the county's farm economy, which is now badly weakened, was once supported by the federal tobacco program, which is now dead. She would learn that most of the people, instead of living from their farms and the farms' sustaining stores, shops, and trades in the small towns, now commute to "jobs" in the corporate economy—that, in short, Rural County is largely a "bedroom community," in which the people sleep but do not work. She would learn that for want of a strong local economy the young people mostly go away after high school and don't come back. She would find that there is a drug problem, and other problems also fairly new. Perhaps most interesting with respect to our subjects of the future and climate change, many of the people of Rural County are employed at three coal-fired power plants, one in the county and two nearby, and so Rural County is in part coal-dependent. Insofar as these plants are causes of climate change, this county may be said to be climate-change-dependent. Whether or not the people "believe" in climate change, they *know* of the presence of the power plants and their dependence on them; they *know* that air pollution is a problem because they see, smell, and suffer from it.

I have now said enough about Rural County to show that it can be to some extent known, to some extent sympathized with, and to some extent thought about. Thought about it is possible, necessary, possibly effective, and I know that some people who live there are thinking about it. The local realization that local people, one's family and neighbors, oneself also, are suffering from an economy they are dependent on—as in every rural county, as in every city—is a useful sort of crisis. It invites

thought. It invites competent, exacting, affectionate, and therefore interesting local thought that is entirely unlike the fearful thought that
is excited by the prediction of global catastrophe—although the local
thought is pertinent to the global problem because it addresses its local
causes. However global may be the problem of climate change, it has
no global solution to be applied only by global politicians as a result of
global protest. The critical problem, again thought-inviting and truly interesting, is how to get from a public "position" to effective work, which
will have to be good local work. Where else can one begin actually to
work except at home? Protest is directed at the top: Get the *leaders* to
stop carbon emissions or whatever else is wrong. Actual work can start
only at the bottom, at home and underfoot, where the causes and the
effects actually reside.

I feel no discomfort in saying that to require people to "believe in climate
change" as a test of their human worth is both a pointless snobbery and
a meaningless distraction. The language of this curious imperative rests
implicitly upon the idea of an authoritarian society of scientific hier-
archs who *know* and underlings who *believe*. It is assumed furthermore
that the underlings *must* believe *because* the anointed knowers know.
Disbelievers are charged with "distrusting science."

But this brings reasonable nonscientists to ask on what basis they
should trust science. The reasonable answer is that they should trust
science on the same basis on which scientists properly trust science.
They trust it to be, so far, true: What has proved to be predictable in
the past remains, for now, predictable. The prescription to the general
public that they should unconditionally "trust science" and "believe in
climate change" comes from no authority at all, but is only the application of a naïve or cynical double standard: For scientists, skepticism
is right—it is their habit of mind and their mode of work—but for all
others it is wrong. This offends reason. It offends good sense. Skepticism can come from and lead to error, of course. But it is reasonable
and proper insofar as it resists or distrusts any authority that is merely

assumed or supposed. Speaking at Harvard in 1955, Edwin Muir said that "the great ascendency of science has brought a superstitious reverence for authority, the authority of those who are in the secret." But mere citizens by now are likely to know that scientific authority is open to question, if only because of the public mind-changing about what fats in food make people fat. But they know too the proclivity of grant-hungry scientists to sensationalize "news" of discoveries of things that "may" exist or "may" be true. And they can hardly escape the thunders of old, great, famous scientists who issue pronouncements, predictions, and prophecies on the basis of nothing but their prizes and positions. The conflation, or the confusion of biological evolution and technological progress, seems to me another reason to distrust science.

And so I think we will endanger nothing valued by either of us if we bypass the would-be orthodoxy of belief in science, along with the future that it claims as its own, and get on to present problems that humans are competent to deal with and to work that they are competent to do. Our time's great wrongs of waste and pollution are wrong in themselves. They would be wrong whether or not they cause climate change. They are wrong according to the economic measure of thrift. They are wrong according to the measure of the sanctity of the living world, and because of their immediate practical harms to nature and to human nature. Their first damage is to the character of the perpetrators.

A case very much in point is that of a large coal-fired power plant that was planned not long ago for western Kansas. Its construction was successfully opposed by appealing to people's intuitive and inherited disapproval of waste and pollution. The plant's potential contribution to climate change was intentionally never mentioned, because there was no reason to do so and a very good reason not to do so: To do so would have divided the otherwise undivided opposition to the plant. For those aware of the local particulars, the problem declared itself this way: Both the believers and the disbelievers in climate change believed in conservation, in doing "the right thing." Their agreement on conservation defeated the power plant. Their disagreement on climate change was irrelevant.

And let us notice that the Kansas power plant was stopped mainly by local opposition, not by a national or a global protest movement. In my own experience local opposition to a local threat has been effective in itself, and *more* effective because only local opposition can legitimate opposition from elsewhere. The coal industry's flagrant abuses of the land and people of the Appalachian coal fields has been permitted not only by political collusion, though there has been enough of that, but also, perhaps mainly, by the absence of concerted local opposition. The region's almost exclusive dependence upon the coal industry for jobs, few as they came to be, has understandably stifled the opposition that would be most effective.

There is no effective opposition in the coal counties because those counties are entirely dependent upon *one* economy: the economy of coal. There is no alternative to the self-interest and the fate of the one industry. Effective opposition could have come only from the existence of at least one other economy, preferably a local economy based upon the local people's control and use of the local landscape.

In the 1970s, for example, my own county of Henry was one of several threatened by a projected Louisville International Jetport that would have destroyed 50,000 acres of productive farmland, and of course completely overturned the life, human and otherwise, of a much larger area of small farms and small towns. It would have imposed an alien and heedless economy upon a home country and its people. The problem for the developers was that the farming economy already in place was at that time still lively, diverse, decently prosperous, and coherent. Rumors of unheard-of land prices were cast about to attract and divide the farmers, who spurned the lure and held together. They, with their friends in the towns and in Louisville, defeated the airport, which, as they knew, offered them nothing that they needed or wanted, and much that they disliked and reasonably feared. There was a living alternative, preferred by the local people, to the glorious future offered by the developers. The people *chose* what they preferred, and they prevailed by their own resistance, with little or no official help. This was not the sort of choice that state or national governments help people to make.

I have kept that story of the great airport in mind because it seems to me to authenticate and support Thomas Jefferson's advocacy for an agrarian democracy of small land owners. Our farmers here took a stand that was formidable and successful, not just because it was reasonable and honorable, but also because they were standing on their own ground.

The further point is that if we want to stop an evil, we are unlikely to do so by meeting it with our shouts of protest somewhere in the air over the capitols. We have got to meet it on the ground in unglamorous and overlooked places such as Rural America or Rural County, where it is rooted.

I know that because of my emphasis on locality and local economy, you and other fore-fearers of global disasters will accuse me of being "against" efforts for policy change. But that is not so. A bad policy ought obviously to be replaced by a good one, or at least a better one, and I have advocated, demonstrated, and protested for changes in land-use policy for half a century. But problems that are initially local and primarily cultural are not going to be much helped by policy.

Rural County and Rural America are damaged and suffering now because the policy (so to speak) since the middle of the twentieth century has been to abandon the actual country and its actual people to the determinism of "market forces" and Ezra Taft Benson's decree, "Get big or get out." The consequence, as you know as well as I do, and as anybody who looks can see, is that Rural America is a colony belonging to the corporations, and its economy is a colonial economy. If you compute the difference between what a thousand pounds of beef pays into Rural County when it is sold and what Rural Countians pay to buy it back as hamburger or steak, you will have described the action of a siphon that takes everything—the produce of the land, the work of the people, the young people—and gives back as near as possible to nothing. And this computation leaves out the "side effects" of land loss, soil erosion, forest degradation, toxic contamination of soil and water, bad health, etc.

The hard truth is that if policy changes should put a stop entirely and at once to the emission of all the greenhouse gases, and the climate thereupon reverted to whatever is considered normal, the decline of Rural America, its land and its people, would continue and grow worse.

A further hard truth is that under the rule of "Get big or get out" and the so-called free market, a lot of people, inevitably if not calculatedly, have become dispossessed and poor: jobless, homeless, hopeless, and unhealthy. Industrial systems, technologies, and values remaining in place, small farmers can't compete with big farmers, who can't compete with bigger farmers; small locally owned stores can't compete with chain stores; small tradespeople can't compete with corporate "services." This is undemocratic, sacrilegious, and inhuman, which has not mattered a tinker's damn to the makers of policies, Democrat or Republican, liberal or conservative.

Perhaps nobody should be surprised, but to a Rural American who for decades has witnessed, suffered, and protested the pillage of Rural America by "the right," it is at least disgusting to see it now condemned as backward by "the left."

A land and a people so long exploited and so far depleted will not foreseeably be much improved by the government's current programs to "solve" a few oversimplified or misdefined problems. To develop a policy to correct, for example, the ongoing abuses of farmland and farmers, politicians would have to recognize, understand, and oppose those abuses, which at present is not expectable. What we have instead, to answer dispossession and unemployment, are distant, abstract, uncomprehending, concerned-sounding schemes such as "job creation." But when job creation comes in at the door, vocation long ago has flown out the window.

"Vocation" and "calling" are the names of the obsolete idea that for all persons there are specific kinds of work to which they are summoned by God or by their natural gifts or talents. The kind of work may be cabinet-making or music-making, cooking or forestry, medicine or mechanics, science or law or philosophy or farming—any kind of work that is whole in the sense that its tasks can be started and completed by the same person. People who are doing the work they are called to do are happy in doing it. For them there is no distinction between work and pleasure. A "job," by contrast, is understood as any work whatever that one can earn money by doing, for the completion and quality of which one is not responsible, and which one would prefer not to do. A high-paying profession, in fact, is only a job and a drudgery to a person who has no vocation for it.

Once any idea of vocation has been disvalued and forgotten, it becomes easy and therefore apparently inevitable for politicians to propose that a county's or a region's need for "jobs" should be answered by "bringing in industry," and to educate the children to be ready-made for jobs in the brought-in industry—as soon as the future can bring it in. This is the policy for my part of Rural America, as evidently for many other parts. And now, wishing to come forward myself (for a change) as a predictor, I offer this as a sure thing: No industry is going to allow itself to be brought in to any place in order to make a better future for that place's children. It will come in only if it sees in that place (and its children) a better future for its executives and shareholders. If we can look past or away from the "policy" of the brought-in solution, and thus can see our actual place and its actual people, then I think the idea of vocation will more or less naturally return to mind.

The primary vocation probably is the call to go home, to go where one's gifts and one's work can be offered to one's family and neighbors, to one's home place—to "what is actually loved and known," to borrow a necessary phrase from the poet and painter David Jones. Even in our generally rootless society, there are people who would testify to this. But over the millennia so would (and have) innumerable exiles, forced migrants, and sold slaves.

The concern of policy is not and will never be vocation or "the actually loved and known." Policy certainly may be good or bad, and good policies certainly should be chosen and worked for. But a policy, except in the minds of those who apply it at home, inevitably will slide toward solutions universally applicable, to be enacted by average people for the sake of average results. Some Rural Countians, on the contrary, would like to make Rural County a place for people loved and known, its own children above all, to come home to or to stay at home in, because it would offer them satisfying, healthful, and sustaining work that they would be pleased to do all their lives.

And so, my friend, I have headed where, knowing me, you may have anticipated that I would head: toward the idea, the possibility, and the hope of a conserving and caring local economy. When I think of the great problems of the present world, including of course climate change, I think of local economy. As soon as I know that you and the other predictors are securely stowed away in the future with your computers, computer models, statistics, and projections, fearing now the fearfulness yet to come, I light out for home, where everything I love is suffering a long-established, still-continuing damage *right now*. This damage, as I have said, as you know, is among the cited causes of climate change. In order to improve the future, you predictors will have to come back into the present and to this damage here and now.

I know that local economies of a sort have existed, and thus perhaps can exist, in cities, for I observed the neighborhood centers of small shops and stores when I lived in New York City in the early 1960s; they were then in decline at about the same rate and for the same reasons as the rural small towns. But I am a Rural American, and so I have thought best and most often about the need for local economies of the farm and forest lands.

Unlike the large protest movements, the attention of a local economy cannot be focused upon some single threat or problem. Rather than the singular *issue*, a good or conserving local economy would have a *subject*, which would be the health (the wholeness, the holiness) of the local land and the local people. Like a protest movement, a good local economy would be defensive of a perceived good, but its defense would be necessarily broad and diverse, for its purpose would be to defend, by caring responsibly for, everything belonging to it that it needs and values. It would always be trying to defend all of its goods, natural and human, against the great evil of waste.

If you have stayed with me so far, you are asking me, as I am always asking myself: Who will do the work? About this I am not fooling myself. I can't for a minute believe that, excepting the Amish communities, any locality in Rural America could count more than a few people who are willing, and who know how, to do the mental and physical work required. No machine will ever take loving care of the living membership of the living world. That requires self-employment at work that is responsible, plentifully rewarding, beautiful in its ways and ends, diverse, difficult, tiring, surprising, frustrating, messy, bloody, muddy, and dusty. Except for professional sports, work involving the use of the body has rarely been enough respected among us, or decently paid. We have typically assigned it to "inferior" people such as racial minorities or farmers. Escape from it is a large component of "the American Dream," accounting not a little for the popularity of "higher education." It accounts also for our alleged problem with Mexican immigrants, for we have always despised people we depend on to do the work that we are too good (and too ignorant) to do for ourselves.

The *New York Times* of April 4, 2017, reported on a manufacturing boom in south-central Idaho, a prosperity somewhat anomalous in "non-metro America." As the *Times* thinks and we are expected to agree, this is wonderful and highly recommendable to the rest of non-metro America. But:

> Much of southern Idaho's growth . . . has been linked to dairy products. And most of the workers in the dairies . . . are foreign-born, mostly from Mexico. "You can't talk about success in Idaho without talking about foreign-born labor," said Bob Naerebout, the executive director of the Idaho Dairymen's Association.

There could hardly be a balder confession of the hypocrisy of the political animus against immigrants who "take our jobs"—or of the fundamental hopelessness of a "success" dependent on brought-in industry and brought-in workers (whose children will likely become too educated and too good for the work of their parents).

But to do the real work of an economy authentically local, I am thinking of the knowing and willing few, a saving remnant perhaps, who I know are well-scattered throughout Rural America. They will do for a start.

Thinking of Rural County, I have imagined first that we are flying over it, which is the way modern Americans typically have seen such places, if they have seen them at all. And then I have imagined coming in for a landing, descending from the ethereal zones of the universal, the official, the commercial, the fashionable, the mechanistic, the futuristic, the public, the ideal—the zones and forms of non-being. As we descend, the topographical features seem to rise up out of their maplike flatness and become three-dimensional and distinct: steeps and levels, swales and swells, forests and fields, hollows and valleys of streams, the waters shining. Once we set foot on it and move in it, if we look with some feeling and care, the place reveals itself with an almost facial expressiveness, and we see its aspects, prospects, uses, abuses, beauties, and problems. As we walk among them, the people emerge from classification and preconception. We see them severally in their unique looks and gazes, postures and gaits. We hear in their voices the influence of the place and its history as they speak sometimes for themselves among the clichés of the media and the public. As we look at them, we remember seeing from above their almost deserted farms and town lots, the power plants and factories where jobs are now to be found and most of the work is done. We remember the veil of polluted air over it all.

I have said properly that "we" have seen this, or have seen it if we have looked. We have seen too, for it is plain enough, that these people are suffering from what they are dependent on, and that this is a lethal addiction. But now I must forego the authority of "we" and speak for myself.

If Rural Countians are suffering from what they are dependent on, they are in that way like all Rural Americans. We all are living from, and living always less well from, a colonial or predatory economy, run by plutocrats, to whom we and our land are "resources" to be used or used up at their pleasure. Since probably the beginning of oceanic navigation, but becoming especially and increasingly dominant since the end of World War II, the reigning assumption has been that anything we don't have in one place we can get from some other place and, therefore, that any lesser place may be depleted or destroyed for the (supposed) betterment of any (supposedly) greater place.

All my thoughts, my friend, come down finally to this: If a place— a family farm, a country town and its neighboring countryside, a city and its tributary region—does not keep and care for and use enough of its natural and human goods for its own maintenance and its people's thriving, the result is destruction, *permanent* damage—even, as I will dare to say, climate change.

And this, for Rural County and Rural America, is the result of nearly seven decades under the rule of "efficiency" and "profitability" in "production," which was the rule of "too many farmers" as determined by corporate and academic experts after World War II, which was the rule of "Get big or get out" as decreed by Secretary of Agriculture Ezra Taft Benson in the 1950s. This became and it remains farm policy, accepted by both political parties. For liberals and Democrats it is a policy of neglect, of not-thinking, of faith in technology. For the conservative Republican corporate Christian capitalists, it is a policy of laissez-faire, which is to say the "freedom" to take as much as possible from Rural America and Rural Americans and leave as little as possible. For the consequent human loss and suffering, the liberals, after waiting for "the inevitable" to happen, have offered the non-solutions of government programs and safety nets. The conservative Republican corporate Christian capitalists have offered democratically to the poor, the sick, and the hungry an equal opportunity on the "free market," and the sturdy conviction that nothing builds moral character like dispossession, displacement, sickness, hunger, and early death. (Eventually, surely, it will be revealed how the conservative Republican corporate Christian capitalists can have forgiven Jesus for healing the sick and feeding the hungry at no charge. They devoutly believe, no doubt, that charity was his hobby. But then what was his job?)

So far as I can see, and I have been looking hard for a long time, the only defense of land and people against a predatory or colonial economy, which has been global really for as long as humans have traveled the globe, is a reasonably coherent, reasonably self-sufficient and self-determining local economy. This would have to be consciously and conscientiously a counter-economy. A counter-culture would be necessary also, but it had better come as a part or a consequence of the effort to make and continue a counter-economy. A local economy, if pretty fully realized, would be solid and lasting. It would be an economy truly economic, not like the present industrial economy enriching the rich by consuming and making waste of goods from anywhere, but living by the mutual thriving of neighbors and taking proper care of all the goods that are its own. It would make itself lasting by valuing its sources and making them last.

To such a possibility—or, if we wish, such a work of provision—the future offers no help. Hope may, in a sense, run to the future, but the *ground* of hope cannot be found there. The future is groundless. Insofar as it is the future, it is forever airborne, unlanded. Because the future, also by definition, is limitless, it is not a context or a circumstance, let alone a place or an ecosystem. Because it is limitless, it can tell us nothing about the limits of nature or human nature, nothing of what is natural or normal or native. There are no natives in the future.

The present obviously is where we should look first, and the present provides us most generously and valuably the Amish example. The Amish settlement in Holmes County, Ohio, is the largest and one of the oldest in the United States. I have had friends there and have been their student for more than forty years. To put it as briefly as possible, the Amish have made themselves different from the rest of us by their obedience to the Gospel's imperative to love their neighbors as themselves. This means, in practical terms, that they do not compete with their neighbors but instead depend upon them for help, that they do not think of replacing their neighbors with industrial technologies, that their farms are small and powered mainly by teams of (very good) draft horses, that in Holmes County their farms range in size probably between 80 and 125 acres, that they practice the radical neighborliness of the Gospels, and that they live close to their neighbors.

To maintain their difference, which essentially is a difference of religious practice, the Amish communities must be more than ordinarily self-determining and self-sufficient. And so, to maintain their difference, the Amish have had consciously to learn and teach and observe the principles and practices by which communities are kept alive. As a result, the good Amish communities such as those of Holmes County are the most self-aware and intact of any that I have known. To a considerable extent, this is because they do not make the distinction, common in the larger society, between a community and its economy. In Holmes County there can be no such thing as an Amish "bedroom community" or an Amish community that consumes but does not produce.

Perhaps because their community life is so consciously and conscientiously a local economic practice, granting them the freedom and the means to be generous, the Amish, though different, are not isolated or isolationist. Their relationship to the surrounding society is complex, and it involves a considerable, if carefully limited, interdependence. So far as I have seen, the Amish extend their neighborliness to all their neighbors. You don't have to be Amish to receive Amish kindness.

A thoughtful observer of such a community, so necessarily and so consciously sustained by its local economy, will understand soon enough that it is not afflicted by unemployment, human obsolescence, homelessness, and the cult of "job creation." Where the land is so democratically divided and lovingly cared for (because it is God's own and God's gift), and where neighbors are always needed and always cared for, nobody can be unemployed. There are many kinds of productive work needing to be done. And so an economic life and a cultural standing are provided to vocation, neighborliness, thrift, generosity, and true charity. I think the Amish are far less captive to the future than the rest of us, and that is because their lives are so complexly serviceable to their land and their neighbors in the present. And so they are providing for the future as fully and effectively as humans possibly can.

If we are addicts in an addictive society, dependent on what we are suffering from, we need a live example of something better, and the Amish of Holmes County offer us that. I don't see how one can disparage their accomplishment, or ignore it, unless one is opposed to so general a distribution of small farms, shops, and trades, so much self-employment, so little "management," such an absence of stockholders.

The Amish example has the great advantage of having continued from the seventeenth century right on into the present. It is, so to speak, the living proof of its history. Most of Rural America, on the contrary, is living proof of the decline and decay that have come with its subjugation to an economy always sacrificing the presently living land and people for the sake of "a better future."

But we have to be careful. Sometimes the past even of mainstream Rural America can show us ways of living and working that once belonged to us and so belong to us still, and for a time these were authenticated by a kind of success, not the kind of success offered by the schools in 2017, but nonetheless a success native to a place and a time.

I want now to offer an example from my own history and experience. For this I am indebted, as I often am, to the research and the conversation of my friend and neighbor, Thomas Grissom. Tom has shown me an advertisement placed in the *Henry County Local* of September 27, 1946, by the town of New Castle, the county seat of Henry County, Kentucky. In those days New Castle was self-assured, as no small rural town can be today. It was advertising itself as a place to come to for needed goods and services. Here is what it had to offer: 4 grocery stores, 2 dry goods stores, 2 jewelry stores, 1 hardware store, 1 hardware and novelty store, 5 garages and filling stations, 1 seed store, 2 coal dealers who also offered livestock feed and general hauling, 1 shoe repair shop, 2 cream stations (where farmers sold their cream), 1 appliance shop, 2 barber shops, 2 beauty shops, 1 hatchery, 5 doctors (who made house calls), 1 veterinarian, 1 drugstore, 1 restaurant, 1 hotel, 1 tourist court ("modern log cabins"), 2 funeral homes, 2 blacksmith shops, 1 newspaper and job printing shop, 1 pool parlor, 5 lawyers, 1 bank, 6 insurance agents. That is 55 stores, shops, trades, and services. From my own memory I can add a grain mill run by the owner of one of the blacksmith shops; also a "locker plant" where people rented large drawers for the storage of frozen food, and where they could have home-produced meat cut and wrapped for freezing. Additionally there was the courthouse with its several offices, and the government agricultural offices. New Castle then had, within the town limits, a population of about 650.

I am a native of Henry Country and have lived in it for most of my life. I did much of my growing up in New Castle. I remember the names of most of the owners and workers in the listed places of business, and most of the professional people. New Castle was a lively place in 1946, commercially and socially. Its Saturday nights were crowded. In the stores and shops and work places, loafers were expected and accommodated. People stood before counters and showcases and passed the time of day with proprietors and clerks. In some places men stood and loafed, in others they sat and loafed. In some places the two races loafed apart, in others together. The most thoroughly integrated place around may have been the big stove in Wilson Ricketts's garage. Where the loafers were, conversation was, jokes also, and teasings of boys. A boy, a white boy anyhow, pretty much had the freedom of the town. I was familiar with all of its public interiors, where I visited, looked, watched, listened, and answered questions such as "Boy, whose daddy are you?" I can still see the linotypist at work and the busy presses at the *Local* office. We boys would sometimes take broken bicycles or other jobs of work into one of the garages or shops to use the tools. When my brother and I were carpentering, we would mark our boards and carry them to one of the blacksmith shops where the handsaws were dependably sharp. I liked best to be in the blacksmith shops because of the work with hot metal. Of all the workmen I knew, the blacksmiths were the ones who *could* not be lazy or unskilled or slow or inexact. In a place so diversely busy, a boy who wanted to was often able to get himself hired. A good many boys had regular before-school or after-school jobs. And odd jobs would turn up. One of the storekeepers hired me for a while to trap rats at fifty cents a head. If there had been enough rats and I a better trapper, I would surely have become a boy of wealth, but I believe my earnings came to a dollar and a half, plus a lot of conversation with the storekeeper, plus a rare intimacy with the innards of the store. The town was at least as educational as the school.

I digress, of course. But the town's generosity to a growing boy is not foreign to my main point, which is that New Castle was then a farm town. Virtually all of its varied and thriving economic life in 1946 rested upon the farms and farm households that surrounded it.

I know, from another *Henry County Local* article discovered by Tom Grissom, that on October 15, 1947, a Henry County Field Day took place on a farm near Pleasureville. "Between three and four thousand people" gathered that day to see demonstrations of new farm machinery, several kinds of field work, and techniques of soil conservation. The crowd was addressed by a local member of the United States House of Representatives, the president of the University of Kentucky, and the editor of the former Louisville *Times*. One of the sponsors of the event was the "recently organized" Henry County Soil Conservation District. The signal event of the day most likely was the construction of six miles of contour terraces, which were recommended and widely used, then and for perhaps a decade afterward, for the control of soil erosion. I remember the *general* interest at that time in soil conservation. I remember a church service on a "Stewardship Sunday" that featured a talk by the county Soil Conservation Agent on the stewardship not of the church but of the farmland.

• • •

I have been presenting evidence from an era of Rural American history about as over and done with and about as irrecoverable as the era of Daniel Boone. Because it is the county seat, New Castle still has a full complement of lawyers and all the county offices, employing more people now than in the 1940s. But the agricultural bureaucracy, including the Extension Service, have displaced themselves into new buildings well outside of town, while usable spaces *in* town go unused. There is a Dollar Store and a gas station, both outside the town. One of the old garage buildings is still in use as a garage. There is a drug store, a doctor, a welding shop, two restaurants, two beauty shops, a used-car lot, and a store selling used stuff (a fixture apparently of every dying country town), and so forth, but no longer a grocery store.

A county agricultural field day like the one at Pleasureville in 1947 is now unimaginable. If one were held now and widely advertised, it would not attract a tenth of the 1947 crowd. A politician or two might come to speak, but certainly not the president of what is now called our "flagship university," and certainly not the editor of Louisville's so-far-surviving *Courier-Journal*. And now the main attraction would be the display of technologies; few if any would be interested in soil conservation. From the retrospect of seventy years, the 1947 event may be the most remarkable for its cross purposes. *Something* at least of the past was there in the manifest interest in soil conservation. In Henry and its neighboring counties at that time, any gathering of farmers would have included many who knew by inheritance and firsthand the tragedy of soil erosion.

But the future was there also as represented by the demonstration of new tractors and other farm technologies, which represented the unspent impetus of the war industries now needing to live on and prosper by the manufacture of machines, fertilizers, and poisons for use in farming. The future of soil conservation eventually would collide pretty much head-on with the future of "agri-technology." Agri-technology would triumph overwhelmingly, and the history of Rural America would curve round again to the tragedy of soil erosion and would add further abuses.

The farmers at the 1947 field day could balance evenly enough their interest in the new equipment with their interest in soil conservation for just one reason: Though they were then hurrying to buy tractors, for some years yet they would be using two-row equipment for plowing, planting, and cultivating. The problem, the limit-in-ambush, was that if terraces are built true to the contour, they cannot be kept a uniform distance apart, and if they are not built fairly true to the contour, there is no point in building them. As a result, some crop rows will "point off" against a terrace before they reach the edge of the field. This is manage-able with two-row equipment. With even four-row equipment, it be-comes intolerably awkward and costly. As the farm people, especially the farmers' children, left farming, there was no denying the need for ever-larger equipment. When they bought their first tractor, the farm-ers, without knowing it, had put themselves onto the ratcheted single track of technological progress, which would lead millions of them into failure and out of farming. Meanwhile the survivors were ignoring the old terraces, and were cropping slopes and waterways as if they were flat.

On many of the small farms of Henry County or Rural County, the first tractors were small, not significantly "better," which is to say faster or more powerful, than the teams of mules or horses that they replaced. They were merely more fashionable and in some ways more convenient. And yet the difference the tractors made was profound and without limit. Before, the farm's working energy came freely from the sun, and cheaply from homegrown pasture, hay, and grain; now it had to be purchased from a corporation at a cost determined by the corporate economy; fuel, parts, and depreciation the farmers now paid as a kind of rent for the use of their own property. Before, the scale and speed of work was subject to biological limits; now it was subject to the mechanical logic of industrial progress, which doomed the small tractor to be replaced by a big one that was doomed to be replaced by a bigger one, and so on and on. By the same logic, the life of the farmer became always less creaturely and more mechanical. As the ever-newer technology replaced the work teams, so it replaced the help of neighbors, so it replaced the help of the farmers' children. By the same logic, farming became subject to a sequence of specializations as the farm animals and crops were drawn apart into separate "food factories," and the culture of farming, as it survived in the minds of the "modern farmers," lost its ancient diversity and complexity.

This as yet barely describable, barely accountable replacement or subjection of creatures by machines takes us right to the heart of the history of our country since World War II—though few historians are likely to think so. Once begun, it was, and it so far remains, unstoppable. But because it is exhausting everything it depends on, it cannot be inexhaustible. That it will finally meet with a limit still in ambush is, I suppose, predictable enough.

But the future of this so-called agriculture is important mainly as a distraction. The relevant issue is that this so-called agriculture is wrong right now. The signs of its failure, to the few (apparently) who can recognize them, are everywhere and are obvious. Even to urban journalists and intellectuals, a plain sign of failure ought to be the decline of New Castle, or of Rural County or of Rural America. And to a historian, supposing one exists who can read the signs, a most remarkable fact would be the absence, in Henry County or in Rural County, of any effective resistance to their decline. Those places and such places were not perfect by a long shot. But they were reasonably decent places to live in, reasonably prosperous, coherent, and self-knowing, in some ways neighborly, imaginably capable of becoming better.

But there seems to have been nothing in them—no principle, no affection, no conscious local loyalty—to resist their decline, nothing to head off the ruin of the land and the people. The people in and around New Castle in 1946 did not think of the need for a fairly adequate local economy, and that was because they had one, but they had no standard by which to judge its usefulness or its worth. Nothing about local economy would or could have been taught then in the schools. The churches, as I remember, were fairly active, fairly well attended, but interested mainly in the future of souls and economically forceless. There was nobody to tell you to love your neighbor as yourself if you would rather have a tractor.

And so in Henry County, Rural County, and most of the rest of Rural America, farm life and home life and community life are now at the lower end of a decline that started in 1945. The Amish communities of Holmes County, on the contrary, are still about as coherent, self-sufficient, and self-determining as they were. That is because they did have the living principles they needed to survive. Against the allure of technological progress, they chose the prosperity of their neighbors and their land. They took literally and seriously the instruction, the *law*, that they should love their neighbors as themselves. That apparently cleared their eyes, and they could see the signs. When they were offered something "better," they asked, "What will this do to our community?" Their standards were right. Ours, such as they were, were wrong.

The truth of it and the hell of it is that the rural communities familiar to me and to you, from V-J Day until now, have been under the spell and under the sway of the future, a.k.a. "a better future for our children." The farmers I knew who sold their work teams and bought their first little tractors did so on the best advice. They had behind them not just the "best science" but *all* the science of official agriculture from the loftiest bureaucrat to the least-published professors, all predicting, upon the basis of their experiments and studies, the great gains to be realized from labor-saving and increased efficiency. They were, in short, blinded by the future and could not read the present signs. This was a scientific consensus probably more complete than the consensus of climate science, and it was wrong.

Here, my friend and fellow worrier, I can summon you as my witness. Unlike probably most of the younger members of the school of prediction, but like many of the urban and academic members of our generation, you got your start as a Rural American, a smart farm kid from a county near mine, who went to college and then entered the Tenure Track from which there is no return. But, like me, you remember what was here in our homeland when we were boys, you have recognized (in going by) what is here now, and you know how to subtract.

I think we have to see that Science has become conglomerated into an allegorical figure, a giant or a god, who supposedly looks all around like a great owl from its highest perch, seeing "objectively" everything involved. But of course it does no such thing, and it never has. If we stand outside the sanctuary where its believers have gathered to offer it their trust, we see that this Science is a much smaller figure, merely human, humanly capable of being wrong, of directing its efforts toward the most money and the highest bidder, of "proving" and approving the new against the old. Its great enterprise of discovering and proving facts has freely involved or allowed the division and isolation of facts. No fact need confront a competing fact. No fact of technological innovation need ever associate with the facts of community or ecological life.

Against the new pressure to "trust science" now coming from my liberal friends and allies, I am forced to realize more clearly than before that I have never granted such a trust. In my boyhood I sided passionately with the agrarian way of farming that I had been taught, that I had learned in part and entirely loved, against the "scientific" agriculture that opposed it. For a while as a teenager I lapsed into an infatuation with internal combustion, and for a while, under the influence of universities, I lapsed into the limited attraction of an academic career. But after I came home to live, even as a sometime professor, I began an argument against the scientific-corporate-political orthodoxy of agriculture that I have kept up for fifty-three years. The success of that orthodoxy, that great consensus of the higher learning, has been manifested to my own study and witness by enormous damage, much of it permanent, to the land and people of Rural America. If I should live to twice my present age, I think that I still would not be counted among the trusters of Science.

Now to take a final look at our subject of the future and the need for prediction, I want to step back to the economy of this region, that once was ours and still is mine, as it was in 1946 and 1947. A very significant reason for our prosperity at that time was the work of the Burley

Tobacco Growers Co-operative Association, which then had been in place since January 1941.

The aim of the Association was to secure for the farmers of our region a return for their work equivalent to, or "on a par with," that of their urban counterparts. The history and economy of burley tobacco, like the culture of the crop, are dauntingly complex. I won't attempt a full description, but will say only that the crucial problem the Association needed to solve was that of surplus production. This is a problem that has accompanied farming for many centuries. It remains unsolved, and almost entirely unacknowledged, to this day. The problem is succinctly defined by Gary Snyder in *The Great Clod: Notes and Memoirs on Nature and History in East Asia*:

> In primitive society, surpluses are exchanged directly among groups or members of groups; peasants, however, are rural cultivators whose surpluses are transferred to a dominant group that uses the surpluses both to underwrite its own standard of living and to distribute the remainder to groups in society that do not farm but must be fed for their specific goods and services to turn. . . . The rulers become persons who are alienated from direct contact with soil, growth, manure, sweat, craft— their own bodies' powers. The peasants become alienated from the very land they used to assume belonged to Mother Earth herself, and not to a Duke or King.

The accumulative power, then, resides not in the adequate supply, in what the living provide for themselves in order to continue living, but in the surplus. And the economically powerful are not those who produce the surplus, but the ones who gather it up and control it. Eventually, according to Mr. Snyder, there appeared in China the inevitable traders or businessmen who "made fortunes by buying low and selling high, gambling on surplus and dearth." For the buyer, buying low is made possible by the availability on the market of a surplus, the more than enough of a product that more than satisfies the demand for it, and so depresses its price to the producer.

In earlier times, peasants were particularly useful because only they could produce the surplus coveted by their "betters," but they were not particularly valued. There were plenty of them, and so they were granted no respect or fairness. The name of "peasant" has no doubt always been a belittlement. In the "developed" countries, the producer of surpluses is no longer a peasant but a farmer, and "farmer" is likewise a term of belittlement. In the fairly recent past, farmers, unlike peasants, have been variously forced or lured into "mobility," and by now their decline approaches extinction—which may somewhat worry their "betters" as soon as they hear of it.

Surplus production, which once kept peasants dependably and profitably poor, became in modern times a major impoverisher and bankrupter of farmers. Tobacco, for a long time the "staple crop" of my region, readily lends itself to overproduction. It is a foliage crop which, under the right conditions, can be kept in storage or "stockpiled" for years. It thus grants to buyers on the "free market" a formidable bargaining power against farmers. That a long-term supply of a product requires a long-term supply of producers is a fact that seems mostly to have escaped the notice of the corporate purchasers of agricultural products, an error that somewhat dims the luster (among the business class) of "business acumen."

The tobacco-producing farmers in Kentucky, as elsewhere, suffered, and their land suffered from their economic powerlessness in the first decade of the twentieth century, and again in the 1920s and 1930s, when it was possible for a year's work to earn them too little or next to nothing or nothing. In those decades there were repeated attempts at cooperative marketing—efforts, that is, to withhold an entire year's crop from the market in order to enforce acceptable prices. These were desperate measures, sometimes violent, and they repeatedly failed. Unanimity was impossible to maintain among the producers when, for instance, some would *have* to have the money from their crop even if the money was too little. This effort of cooperative marketing was able to succeed only as the New Deal's tobacco program, when a government loan "against the crop" made it possible for the regional growers' association to buy, store, and resell any tobacco that did not bring the support price, and to pay the grower at the warehouse. The Burley Tobacco Growers Co-operative Association dealt effectively with the problem of surplus production in my part of the country, keeping many thousands of farmers at work and decently paid for more than sixty years.

This program worked to the benefit of farmers, large and small, because it was a necessary federal enablement that was applied in the affected region by local leaders. The leaders of the Burley Association knew their people, whose fate they shared, and knew their economic situation. They worked for, and offered to the Association's members, no more than a solution, possible and practical, to their biggest problem.

Year after year for a long time, as you may remember, this program supplied a large practical benefit to a lot of people, a benefit that they fully earned and deserved by their work. It had much to do with the ongoing, ordinary dutifulness that I am calling provision, very little to do with prediction. There were no foretellings, triumphal or dreadful, of the future. The aim of the program was first to stop and then to prevent a present and ever-threatening wrong. The aim was not a future prosperity but a fair price in the present year, and by 1941 this was immediately attainable.

My father, John Marshall Berry, Sr., became conscious of the suffering of farm families, from his own experience and observation, when he was a child. From his college years on, he understood the economic issues and was involved in the effort for cooperative marketing. He became a board member and then vice president of the Burley Association in 1941. He served as president from 1957 until 1975. From the much that I remember of him and from what I remember and have learned about his senior colleagues, I believe I know pretty well the motives that made the Burley Association. The leaders all belonged to the region and the people they served, and so they served under the discipline of local affection and loyalty. They shared fully in the most defining experience of their people in their time: the years, as my father remembered, "of six-cent tobacco, farm foreclosures, unpaid tax bills, scarcely enough of anything except fear, and . . . when a farm program was merely the subject of elaborate planks in party platforms." Their work, moreover, was informed by Christian ethics, and by Jeffersonian democracy, which gave them, at that time, some standing in the Democratic Party.

The character of the people who led this cooperative effort is suggested by a tribute to John W. Jones, banker of North Middletown, who was president of the Association from 1941 until his death in 1957. The tribute was co-written by my father and W. L. Staton, who was secretary-treasurer. They said that in his work for the organization Mr. Jones had "applied the tenets of the Christian faith as the measurements of men's rights and duties . . ." And (a sentence that in its syntax and cadence is distinctly my father's): "He was great at the level where the many individually benefitted; and he was great at the level where the Great were guided by his counsel." And in the days when the Louisville *Courier-Journal* still had a competent interest in agriculture, its editors wrote of Mr. Jones that "his main interest in life always was the people around him" and "he believed people mattered more than any business or product."

Those qualities had their natural and reasonable effect in the Association's principle that the smallest producer was entitled to membership and to the same protection on the market as the largest producer, and this was made explicit in the establishment of minimum allotments. Production control was implemented by the assignment to every farm, according to its history of production, a quota or allotment, at first a limited acreage, later a poundage, that was eligible for price supports under the program. But there was a minimum below which the allotment could not be reduced, no matter the size or history of the farm. This minimum "stood for protection of tenants and share croppers, and safeguarded the rights of small growers." That purpose may be instructively compared to the postwar doctrines of "too many farmers" and "Get big or get out."

My father's own steady conviction was that a family owning and farming well a farm of a decent size ought by right to be able to earn a decent living. I knew well several married couples he kept in mind, whose worth and example embodied and justified his conviction.

Looking back, then, it seems to me that my father and his friends did the work of provision, which was simply to do the right thing as it became possible in their time. When the motives, the standards, and the character of the people are right, then the work of provision will be right. By that provision the future receives all the assurance that it can reasonably be given.

It is impossible to believe that the minds that made the Burley Association could have offered to "new farmers" in 1941 the following advice from Zippy Duvall, president of the American Farm Bureau, in 2017:

> The best days of agriculture are ahead of us. My word of advice to them is to be patient. Help get through this difficult time we are in and start making plans for the future. Agriculture is like a rollercoaster ride; you just need to put the seatbelt on and hang on for the ride.

That is either cynical or cowardly, and it is heartlessly deterministic. It seems to me characteristic of an age when thought is dominated by a reflexive deference to the future and to expert advice. It requires only a vocabulary of clichés and the posture of a vine. The Farm Bureau, being ever of the conservative Republican corporate Christian capitalist state of mind, was opposed of course to the tobacco program, though its tobacco-growing members were willing (gritting their teeth) to accept its benefits.

For many years, maybe always, American agriculture has been darkly overshadowed by something or other. At first it was the ignorance and presumption of the farmers themselves, their failure to be careful enough of what preceded them, their squandering of the forest and then of the prairie. Later it was the "conservative" use of their success, their own surplus production, to drive out the supposed surplus of farmers, the "too many" and the too small.

And for all the years since the end of World War II, our agriculture has been overhung by industrial visions and working models of "farms of the future." First it was the technology of "factories in the fields," and then came the "animal factories." These advertised and then realized futures bore the trademark of the land-grant colleges of agriculture, which granted the land, the people, and the ecosystems freely to the dominance of industrial technologies and methods. Their most "revolutionary" and revealing "farms of the future" would enclose the whole enterprise within walls and under a roof, inside a dome or a skyscraper, with all the "work" automated and robotized. These future farms perfect the misanthropy that is at the heart of industrialism, as well as the industrial bias against nature. They embody the death wish of complete control, an economic and technological totalitarianism excluding all the vagaries and irregularities of nature and humanity. If this should be the future, it will be the triumph, the very Eden, of predictability, the new heaven and earth of the conservative corporate capitalist mind and the liberal corporate capitalist mind.

But even as visions or dreams, the "farms of the future" belong to the reality of our time, and they deliver a verdict of real force against the values of neighborly love and the small farm that informed the minds that made the Burley Tobacco Growers Co-operative Association. Such predictions, whether or not they are realizable in the future, advise us at least of a present ambition strongly antipathetic to the idea that the land might be owned by people who are not rich, or that a human family might own and live and thrive upon a small farm that they and other creatures consider to be their *home*.

It is obvious that we would have no privilege from living in an entirely predictable world. On the contrary, our privilege, if we will accept it, is that we live in a world that finally is not predictable at all. Speaking of the superlative workmanship of the Shakers, Thomas Merton said that if you truly understand, as the Shakers did, that the world may end at any moment, you know that there is no reason to be in a hurry: You take your time and do your work well. In what to the Shakers was the future and is now so soon our past, knowledgeable people such as Merton have praised and given thanks for their artistry, which did the world no harm but added to it work unendingly beautiful. If we do now the work we are called to do, on a scale appropriate to our limited knowledge and intelligence, thus permitting ourselves to do the best possible work, and thus limiting the effects of any badness in our work, then we have to assume that the future will not complain of us.

The Christianity of Merton and the Shakers is hardly the only religion that counsels us to "take no thought for the morrow." This is because thinking of the future is an escape. And despite our frantic claims upon Christianity as our more or less national religion, we are an escapist society. Our country was "settled" largely by escapees, people leaving behind a past or a place in some manner used up, heading off for a "new" place where the future was expected to be brighter. As a people, we have escaped to the West from the East, from the country to the city, from the city to the suburbs, from the suburbs back to the country or back to the city. And because we have never known well enough, or worked well enough, where we were, this has almost always been a movement from old damage to new destruction, and always with the aim of "a better future for our children."

In fact, actual work that is actually good requires us to give our minds entirely to the present. If one is to build a fine chair or a fine house, one must give one's whole thought to the work as the work requires it, moment to moment. To be distracted by the thought even of finishing the work, or by the thought of the clock or a deadline, is to work badly, and often to be in danger. And this is far more important than we modern Americans, in our age of what Merton called "collective delusion," have been able to learn, for we have removed ourselves further and further from the significance of vocation and good work. David Jones, the artist I quoted earlier, left us a sentence that points straight into the heart of our problem:

> [T]he workman must be dead to himself while engaged upon the work, otherwise we have that sort of "self-expression" which

is as undesirable in the painter or the writer as in the carpenter, the cantor, the half-back, or the cook.

To be dead to oneself is to be alive to the work. It is to be alive in the present, the only time we are alive, and to continue to live there, so long as we don't look at the clock.

To be, instead, alive primarily to ourselves, to the infernal importance of "being myself," and to the centrality of the future to this peripheral self, is to withhold ourselves from the present, and from everything that is present with us: our families, our neighbors, our places. Above all, I am going to say at the end of this letter, it is to withhold ourselves from our places, as we Americans undeniably have done. "The land was ours before we were the land's," Robert Frost wrote seventy-five years ago of a problem he thought by then corrected, but he was wrong. As I have demonstrated in this letter (and a number of times before), we are more alienated from our land now than when Frost's poem was written, and there is much evidence that we did not then know well where we were.

As a nation, we have never ceased to rush into the future and the more of everything that the future so easily promises or threatens. Our supreme selfishness, leading to a supreme ignorance, has been in asking our land to adapt to the wishes of our ephemeral selves. Because of the ease and seeming cheapness of long-distance transportation, we have deferred, already at an immense cost, the finally inescapable need to adapt ourselves, our economies, and our work to the places where we live.

Now, my old friend, I would like to leave the future behind. When you asked me to write more about it, and I took the bait, I must still have had some hankering toward it, but I have now talked myself out of any interest I may have had. You and I will have more to say, I hope, but of other things. I grant you that the future (probably) is coming, but I am not setting out to meet it somewhere between now and then. I will wait and let it come to me. From here the future looks to me like an unhappy time filled with a lot of disappointed people: optimists who thought it would be better and pessimists who thought it would be worse.

Now I am heading back to the present, where I am at home with other people and other creatures I actually love and know, and where I have work and pleasure waiting to offer me the ordinary luxury of being dead to myself, alive to the present world.

The Presence of Nature in
the Natural World:
A Long Conversation

The great trouble of our age, involving the whole human economy from agriculture to warfare, is in our relationship to the natural world—to what we call "nature" or even, still, "Nature" or "Mother Nature." The old usage persists even seriously, among at least some humans, no matter how "objectivity" weighs upon us. "Of all the pantheon," C. S. Lewis wrote, "Great Mother Nature has . . . been the hardest to kill."[1] With Nature we have, properly speaking, a relationship, for the responses go both ways: Nature is fully as capable of responding to us as we are of responding to her. In the age of industrialism, this relationship has been radically brought down to a pair of hopeless assumptions: that the natural world is passively subject either to unlimited pillage as a "natural resource," or to partial and selective protection as "the environment."

We seem to have forgotten that there might be, or that there ever were, mutually sustaining relationships between resident humans and their home places in the world of Nature. We seem to have no idea that the absence of such relationships, almost everywhere in our country and the world, might be the cause of our trouble. Our trouble nonetheless exists, is severe, and is getting worse. Instead of settled husbanders of cherished home places, we have become the willing parasites of any and every place, destroying the source and substance of our lives, as parasites invariably do.

This critical state of things has not always been explicitly the subject of my writing, but it has been constantly the circumstance in which I have written, for I have had constantly and consciously in sight the progressive decline of my home countryside and community. I have been perforce aware that this is a local manifestation of a decline that is now worldwide, affecting not only every place but also the oceans and the air, and I have of course felt a need to understand, and to oppose so far as I have been able, this downslope of all creation. In this effort of thought, I have been always in need of teachers, friends, and allies among the living and the dead. The mercy or the generosity accompanying this effort has been that I have found perhaps not all but many of the teachers, friends, and allies I have needed, often when I have needed them most.

By that I do not mean to suggest that my looking for help has been easy or carefree. To begin with, I never trusted, and after a while I rejected, the hope that many people have invested in what we might call the industrial formula: Science + Technology + Political Will = The Solution. This assumes that the science is adequate or soon will be, that the technology is adequate or soon will be, and therefore that the only essential task is to increase political pressure favoring the right science and the right technology.

An outstanding example of the industrial formula in action is the present campaign against global warming. If the scientific calculations and predictions about global warming are correct (which I am willing to assume that they are, though I have no science of my own by which to know), then its causes are waste and pollution. But "global warming" is a ravenously oversimplifying phrase that gobbles up and obscures all the myriad local instances of waste and pollution, for which local solutions will have to be worked out if waste and pollution are ever to be stopped. The phrase "global warming" suggests no such thing. Global warming, the language insists, is a *global* emergency: a global problem requiring a global solution. To solve it we have the science, we have the technology, and now we have only to prevail upon the world's politicians to enforce the recommended solution: burning less fossil fuel.

But from where I live and watch, I see the countryside and the country communities being wrecked by industrial violences: a heartless gigantism of scale and power, massive and irreparable soil erosion, pollution by toxic chemicals, ecological and social disintegration—and of course an immense burning of fossil fuels, making in turn an immense contribution, as alleged by scientists, to global warming.

I have no doubt at all that even if the global climate were getting better, our abuses of the land would still be the disaster most seriously threatening to the survival of humans and other creatures. Land abuse, I know, is pretty much a global phenomenon. But it is not happening in the whole world as climate change happens in the whole sky. It is happening, because it can happen, only locally, in small places, where the people who commit the abuses also live. And so my question has been, and continues to be, What can cause people to destroy the places where they live, the humans and other creatures who are their neighbors, and ultimately themselves? How can humans willingly turn against the earth, of which they are made, from which they live? To treat that as a scientific and technological or political question is not enough, is even misleading. The question immediately and at least is economic: What is wrong with the way we are keeping house, the way we make our living, the way we live? (What is wrong with our minds?) And to take the economic question seriously enough is right away to ask another that is also but not only economic: What is happening to our souls?

There is no industrial answer to such questions. Industrialism has never provided a standard by which such questions can be answered. I long ago hatched out of the egg in which I could believe that industrialism is capable of competent judgments of its effects, let alone competent solutions to the problems it has caused. Its "solutions," on the contrary, tend to increase the problems, as in the desperate example of industrial war, in which more never produces less; or the example, equally desperate, of agricultural pesticides, which must become more toxic and diverse as immunities develop among the pests. Since industry has no language with which to speak to us as living souls and children of Nature, but only as interchangeable employees, customers, or victims, by what language can we, in the fullness of our being, speak back to industrialism?

Seeing that my need for help was defined by that question, I have faced another difficulty: I am inescapably a product of "Western" culture, first as I was born and grew up in it, and then as I, by my work, have made myself able to know it and more responsibly to inherit it. The difficulty was that Western culture, especially when it is understood as Christian culture, however decayed, has been for many years in disfavor among writers and intellectuals, some of whom have seen it as the very origin of our unkindness toward "the environment." At its best, this disfavor has produced useful criticism, for professedly Christian institutions, nations, and armies have much cruelty and violence to answer for. At its worst, it is fashionably attitudinal and dismissive, so that we now have "Shakespeare scholars" who cannot recognize Shakespeare's frequent references to the Gospels.

For some, it has been possible and useful to turn away from the Western or Christian inheritance to find instruction and sustenance in, mainly, oriental or tribal cultures. I am glad to acknowledge my own considerable indebtedness to the little I have managed to learn of oriental, American Indian, and other cultures, which have been often confirming and sometimes clarifying of the cultural lineage and faith that I consider my own. From Gary Snyder's Buddhism, for instance, I understood more clearly than from any other source that the practice of a religion is necessarily economic: how we live on and from the earth.

But I am too completely involved in western culture by the history of my mind, my people, and my place to be capable of a new start in another tradition. My need to make as much sense as I could of my history and experience, as I began fifty years ago to think of my task, clearly depended on my willingness to do so, not only as a native of a small patch of country in Henry County, Kentucky, but also as an heir and inevitably a legator of Western culture. If I hoped to make sense, my culture would have to be always, at least implicitly, my subject, and I would have to be its critic. If I was troubled by our epidemic mistreatment of the natural or given world, especially in the economic landscapes that we live from, then I would have to search among the artifacts and records of my culture, in the time I had and so far as I was able, to find probable causes, appropriate standards, and possible corrections. This search began, as I would later realize, in my school years, before I could have explained, even to myself, my need and purpose.

Eventually, provoked by attacks on Western culture as founded upon a supposedly biblical permission to humans to use the earth and its creatures in any way they might please, I read through the Bible to see how far it might support any such permission, or if, on the contrary, it might impose on humans the obligation to take good care of a world both given to them as a dwelling place, as to the other creatures, and to which they had been given as caretakers.

I found of course Genesis 1:28 ("Be fruitful and multiply, and replenish the earth, and subdue it: and have dominion over the fish of the sea, and over the fowl of the air, and over every living thing that moveth upon the earth"), which is the verse the detractors have found, and is pretty much the sum of their finding. But I also found that the Bible as a whole is a context that very sternly qualifies even the "dominion" given in Genesis 1:28. And I found many verses and passages that, even out of context, require humans to take the best possible care of the earth and its creatures. To speak to Genesis 1:28, for instance, there is the first verse of Psalm 24: "The earth is the Lord's, and the fullness thereof: the world and they that dwell therein." To that verse, singly and without context, if one takes it seriously, there are only two sane responses: (1) fear and trembling, and (2) a human economy that would conserve and revere the natural world on which it obviously depends. But it is possible for materialist environmentalists (as for many professing Christians) to read and not see, even to memorize a passage of language and not know what it says. It is easy, even intellectually

108 J The Art of Loading Brush

permissible, to quote from a book that one has not read. And now most people are too distracted automotively and electronically to know what world they are in, let alone what the Bible might say about it.

In a world allegedly endangered by biblical religion, it is dangerous to be ignorant of the Bible. I must say, now, that I am not an uncritical reader of the Bible. There are parts of it that I dislike, but there are parts of it also in which I place my faith. From those parts, or some of them, I gather an old belief that God is not merely above this world, or behind it, but is *in* it, and it lives by sharing His life and breathing His breath. "If he gather unto himself his spirit and his breath," Elihu says to Job, "All flesh shall perish together, and man shall turn again unto dust" (Job 34:14–15). Like Psalm 24, these fearful verses clearly imply a mandate for the good care of all creation, and this becomes explicit in the Gospels' paramount moral commandment (Matthew 22:39) that we must love our neighbors as ourselves, even when our neighbors happen to be our enemies. This neighborly love cannot be a merely human transaction, for you cannot love your neighbor while you destroy the earth and its community of creatures on which you and your neighbor mutually depend.

The Bible, then, is not defined by misreading, or Western culture by economic violence, any more than a body is defined by a disease.

Over the years, for my soul's sake and for the sake of my work, I have returned many times to the Bible, testing it and myself by such understanding, never enough, as I have been able to bring to it.

I have also returned repeatedly to the pages of several English poets, who lived and worked of course under the influence of the Bible, and whose interest in the natural world and the magisterial figure of Nature has been instructive and sustaining to me.

Both Chaucer and Spenser testify that "this noble goddesse Nature" or "great dame Nature" comes to them from a Latin allegory written in about the seventh decade of the twelfth century by Alanus De Insulis, or Alan of Lille. This book, *De Planctu Naturae* (*Plaint of Na-*

ture), is composed of alternating chapters of verse and prose. It tells the story of Alan's dream-vision in which he converses with Nature, whom he recognizes both as his "kinswoman" and as the Vicar of God. The Latin original apparently is extremely hard to translate. According to James J. Sheridan, whose translation I have used,

> The author revels in every device of rhetoric. . . . He so inter-
> weaves the ordinary, etymological and technical signification
> of words that, when one extracts the meaning of many a sec-
> tion, one despairs of approximating a satisfactory translation.[2]

Despite its intricacy even in English, and the strangeness in our time of Alan's leisurely pleasure in rhetorical devices—he elaborates, for example, a sexual symbolism of grammar—this is a book extraordinarily useful to a reader interested in the history of our thought about the natural world as well as the history of conservation.

At the beginning of his book, Alan's happiness has been overcome by grief because of humanity's abandonment of Nature's laws. His own immediate complaint is against homosexuality, which seems to have been widespread and fairly openly practiced and acknowledged in his time. This he understands as a consequence that comes "when Venus wars with Venus."[3] For my own sake in my own time, I am sorry that he begins this way, for I am much troubled by our current politics of private life. Some of us now may reasonably object to Alan's view of homosexuality as unnatural, or anti-natural, but it would be a mistake to dismiss him on that account at the end of his first sentence.

As Alan continues the story of his vision, his objection to homosex-uality becomes incidental to his, and Nature's, objection to lust, which is one of the whole set of sins that are opposed both to the integrity of Nature and to the integrity of human nature. The two Venuses that are at war are the Venus of lust or mere instinct and the Venus of respon-sible human love. This duality is analogous to, and dependent upon, the double nature of humankind. In the order of things, as in the Chain of Being, humans are placed between the angels and the animals. Strongly attracted in two conflicting directions, they have the hardship of a moral obligation to keep themselves in their rightful place.

Nature, then, as "faithful Vicar of heaven's prince," makes two requirements of us. She requires us to be natural in the general sense that, like other animals, we are born into physical embodiment, we reproduce, and we die. But she most sternly conditions her first requirement by requiring us also to be natural in the sense of being true to our specifically human nature. This means that we must practice the virtues—chastity, temperance, generosity, and humility, as they are named, their procession led by Hymenaeus,* in the *Plaint*—that keep us in our rightful place in the order of things. We must not be prompted by lust, avarice, arrogance, pride, envy, and the other sins, prodigality being the sum of them all, either to claim the prerogatives of gods or to lapse into bestiality and monstrosity. This is Nature's requirement because her own integrity and survival depend upon it, but she herself is unable to enforce it. She very properly acknowledges the limit of her power when she explains to Alan that although "man is born by my work, he is reborn by the power of God; through me he is called from non-being into being, through Him he is led from being into higher being."[4]

To put it another way: Humanity as an animal species—"the only extant species of the primate family Hominidae," says *The American Heritage Dictionary*—is a limitless category in which anything we may do can be explained, even justified, as "natural." But the necessity of our communal life as fellow humans, as well as our shared and interdepending life as a species among species, imposes limits, defining, for the sake of our survival and that of the living world, a higher or moral human nature, specified by Nature herself in her conversation with Alan. The nature of every species is uniquely specific to itself. Human nature in its fullest sense is the most complex of all, for it involves standards and choices.

---

* Hymenaeus was once, until forsaken by her, the husband of Venus. The son of that marriage is Desire. In Alan's mythology, Hymenaeus is "closely related" to Nature and has "the honor of her right hand." He represents the sanctity, and the bad history, of marriage.

To speak of this from the perspective of our own time and the fashionable environmentalist prejudice against "anthropocentrism," it is our mandated human nature that allows us, by understanding the legitimacy of our own self-interest, or self-love as in Matthew 22:39, to understand the self-interest of other humans and other creatures. A human-centered and even a self-centered point of view is inevitable— What other point of view can a human have?—but by imagination, sympathy, and charity *only* are we able to recognize the actuality and necessity of other points of view.

It is impossible to speak of such things in a positivist or "objective" language, pruned of its upper branches and presided over by professional or specialist consciences embarrassed by faith, hope, and charity. And so it is a relief to resume the freedom and completeness of the language in which we can say that Nature, the Vicar of God, is the maker or materializer of a good world, as affirmed by Genesis 1:31, entrusted to the keeping of humans who must prove worthy of it by keeping true to their own, specifically human, nature, which is defined by that worthiness, which they must choose.

According to Alan's great instructor, the integrity of the natural world depends upon the maintenance by humans of *their* integrity by the practice of the virtues. The two integrities are interdependent. They cannot be separated and they must not be separately thought about. This is the moral framework of *Plaint of Nature*, and I would argue that it persists in a lineage of English poets from Chaucer to Pope, whether or not they can be shown to have read Alan. The same set of traditional assumptions can be shown also to support the work of a lineage of agricultural writers and scientists of about the last hundred years, as I will later demonstrate. So far as my reading, observation, and experience have informed me, I believe that Nature's imperative as set forth in the *Plaint* is correct, not just for the sake of morality or for the sake of Heaven, but in its conformity to the practical terms and demands of human life in the natural world. The high standards of Nature and of specifically human nature obviously will not be comforting to humans of the industrial age, among whom I certainly must include myself, and they are not in fashion, but that hardly proves them false.

As Alan grieves over the degeneracy of humankind, Nature appears to him. She is "a woman" whose hair shines with "a native luster surpassing the natural."[5] He proceeds to describe in patient detail her hair, her face, and her neck. He devotes seven fairly substantial paragraphs, in Sheridan's translation, to her crown, the jewels of which are elaborately allusive and symbolic. He describes with the same attention to detail and reference her dress, on which is depicted "a packed convention"[6] of all the birds; her mantle, which displays "in pictures . . . an account of the nature of aquatic animals,"[7] mainly fish; and her embroidered tunic, a part of which has been damaged by man's abuse of his reason, but on the remainder of which "a kind of magic picture makes the land animals come alive."[8] He discreetly refrains from looking at her shoetops and her undergarments, but is "inclined to think that a smiling picture made merry there in the realms of herbs and trees"[9]—which he then describes.

The presence of Nature is so numinous and exalted, of such "starlike beauty,"[10] that Alan faints and falls facedown. Though my interest is fully invested in this book, my own reaction here is much less excited, and I doubt that any reader now could find much excitement in this exhaustive portraiture, though I agree with C. S. Lewis that "the decorations do not completely obscure the note of delight."[11] The problem is that Alan's description of Nature is too distracted by his rhetorical extravagances to give us anything like a picture of her.

We get a better sense of her, I think, in his later invocation, in which he describes Nature's character rather than her appearance:

O child of God, mother of creation, bond of the universe and its stable link . . . you, who by your reins guide the universe, unite all things in a stable and harmonious bond and wed heaven to earth in a union of peace; who, working on the pure ideas of [Divine Wisdom], mould the species of all created things, clothing matter with form . . .[12]

It is no doubt wrong, or at least pointless, to ask Alan for a "realistic" portrait, as if he were dealing merely with a personification. His effort to describe Nature's appearance, exaggerated as it is, failing as it does, speaks nonetheless of his need to realize her, not merely as an allegorical person, but as a presence actually felt or known.

The really useful question, it seems to me, is not how Alan's Nature functions in a medieval allegory, but what she means historically as a figure very old and long-lasting, of whom people have needed, of whom some people need even now, to speak. How might one explain this need? My reading is sufficient only to assure me that Alan's vision of Nature draws upon a variety of sources, classical and Christian. She came to him as a figure of attested standing and power, he did imagine her, she did appear to him in something like a vision.

In Alan's *Plaint of Nature* and in Christian poems much later, the classical deities continue to appear, still needed by imagination, no longer perhaps as vital gods and goddesses, but at least as allegorical figures standing for their qualities or powers. That Nature takes her place prominently among them in the work of later poets appears to be owing largely to Alan. Sheridan says, "It is in Alan of Lille that she reaches full stature."[13] And according to Sheridan it was Alan who "theorized that God first created the world and then appointed Natura as His substitute and vice-regent . . . in particular to ensure that by like producing like all living creatures should increase and multiply . . ."[14]

And so Nature comes into the plot of Alan's Christian allegory reasonably enough, to keep company with Venus, Cupid, Genius, and a cast of personified vices and virtues. But if allegory tends toward simplification and a kind of shallowness—Truth is going to be purely true, and Greed purely greedy—Alan's representation of Nature tends in virtually the opposite direction: She is complex, vulnerable, mysterious, somewhat ghostly, less a personification than the presence, felt or intuited, of the natural world's artificer. She comes from an intuition of order and harmony in creation that is old and independent of empirical proofs. That we have personified her for so long testifies that we know her as an active, purposeful, and demanding force. Her domain, in the *Plaint* and elsewhere, is both natural and supernatural. As Vicar of God, she joins Heaven and Earth, resolving the duality of spirit and matter.

To say, as I just did, that we know her is obviously to raise the question of what we mean, and what we ever have meant, by saying that we "know." In our time an ideological tide has been carrying us toward a sort of apex at which none of us will claim to know anything that has not been proved and certified by scientists. But to read Alan of Lille is to realize that there was a time, a *long* time, when such knowledge was neither available nor wanted, but when many necessary things were nonetheless known. Thomas Carlyle, writing from his own perch in the modern world about the twelfth-century monk Jocelin of Brakelond, had to confront this very question: "Does it never give thee pause . . . that men then had a *soul*, not by hearsay alone, and as a figure of speech; but as a truth that they *knew* . . ."[15]

A century and a half later in the same darkening age, I asked my friend Maurice Telleen, who had much experience of livestock shows: "Does a good judge measure every individual by the breed standards, or does he go by intuition and use the breed standards to check himself?" In reply Maury said something remarkable: "He goes by intuition! A slow judge is always wrong." I thought his reply remarkable, of course, because it confirmed my belief that, among people still interested in the qualities of things, intuition still maintains its place and its standing as a way to know.

Intuition tells us, and has told us maybe as long as we have been human, that the nature of the world is a great being, the one being in which all other beings, living and not-living, are joined. And for a long time, in our tradition, we have called this being "Natura" or "Kind" or "Nature." And if we forget, our language remembers for us the relation of "natural" (by way of "kind") to "kindness" and "kin," and to "natal," "native," "nativity," and "nation." Moreover, as understood by Alan of Lille and the poets who descend from him, the being and the name of "Nature" also implicates the history of human responsibility toward the being of all things, and Nature's continuing requirement of that responsibility.

Contrast "Nature," then, with the merely clever poeticism "Gaia" used by some scientists to name the idea of the unity of earthly life, and perhaps to warm up and make congenial the term "biosphere." "Gaia" is the name of the Greek goddess of the earth, in whom no modern humans, let alone modern scientists, have even pretended to believe. Her name was used, no doubt, because, unlike "Nature," it had no familiar or traditional use, could attract no intuitive belief, or appeal at all to imagination.

By name Nature familiarly belongs to us, and she has so belonged to us for many hundreds of years, but considered from a viewpoint strictly biblical and doctrinal, she still may seem an intruder. Like the other classical deities, she joins the biblical tradition somewhat brazenly. The writers needed her perhaps because she has persisted in oral tradition, and because there remained not a Christian only but a general human need for her. That she usurps or threatens the roles of all three persons of the Trinity suggests that there was also a felt need for her to some degree in spite or because of them. Speaking only for myself, I will say that for me it has always been easy to be of two minds about the Trinity. The Father, the Son, and the Holy Spirit, as they appear in their places, as "characters" so to speak, in the Gospels, I have found simply recognizable or imaginable as such, but I think of them as members of "the Trinity" only deliberately and without so much interest. As an idea, the Trinity, the three-in-one, the three-part godhead, seems to me austerely abstract, complicated, and cold. The more it is explained, the less believable it becomes.

Perhaps it is this aloofness of the Trinity that calls into being and causes us to need this other, more lowly presence, holy yet familiar, matronly, practical, concerned, and eager to teach: Nature, the mother of creatures as the Virgin is the mother of God. And here I remember that Thomas Merton, in his prose poem "Hagia Sophia," sees both Nature and the Virgin as sharing in the identity or person of Holy Wisdom: "There is in all visible things an invisible fecundity, a dimmed light, a meek namelessness, a hidden wholeness. This mysterious Unity and Integrity is Wisdom, the Mother of all, *Natura naturans*." And later: "*Natura* in Mary becomes pure Mother."[16] In Merton's treatment these three—Natura, Mary, Sophia—seem to fade into one another, shadowing forth an always evasive reality. And this, I think, is what we must expect when human thought reaches toward the mystery of the world's existence: an almost visible, almost palpable presence of a reality more accessible to poetry than to experiment, never fully to be revealed by any medium of human knowledge. And yet it is to be, it can be, learned and known, not by peering through a lens or by assemblies of data, but perhaps only by being quietly observant for a long time. Merton's vision does not explain or clarify Alan of Lille's, but between the two there is a sort of recognition and a mutual verification.

I am not entirely confident of my grasp of Alan's *Plaint of Nature*, partly because of my very reasonable doubt of my scholarship and understanding, but also because I am looking back at Alan from my knowledge of later writers who seem to be his successors, and from my own long preoccupation with the issues he addresses. For I do not wish, and I have not tried, to read Alan as a writer of historical or literary interest only. Despite the always considerable differences of times and languages, I have thought of him as a fellow writer with immediately useful intelligence of the world that is both his and mine.

His concept of the integrity of the natural world, and of the dependence of the world's integrity upon the integrity of human nature, leads by the most direct and simple logic to our own more scientific recognition of the integrity of ecosystems, the integrity ultimately of the ecosphere, and to the recognition (by not enough of us) of the necessity of an ecological ethic.

But a large part of the value of the *Plaint* is that, though I suppose it is as full as it could be of the biology and taxonomy of its time, it cannot be reduced to the sort of knowledge that we call scientific. It cannot, for that matter, be reduced to the sort of knowledge that we call poetic. It belongs instead to the great Western family of writings that warn us against what we now call reductionism, but which traditionally we have called the deadly sin of pride or hubris: the wish to be "as gods," or the assumption that our small competence in dealing with small things implies or is equal to a great competence in dealing with great things. In our time we have ceased to feel the traditional fear of that equation, and we have a world of waste, pollution, and violence to show for it.

Plaint of Nature cannot be comprehended within the bounds of any of our specialties, which exclude themselves by definition from dealing with one another. But once we acknowledge, once we permit our language to acknowledge, the immense miracle of the existence of this living world, in place of nothing, then we confront again that world and our existence in it, forever more mysterious than known. And then the air swarms with questions that are scientific, artistic, religious, and all of them insistently economic. Some of the questions are answerable, some are not. The summary questions are: What are our responsibilities? and What must we do? The connection of all questions to the human economy is finally not escapable. For our economy (how we live) cannot leave the world or any of its parts alone, as the ideal of the wilderness preserve seems to hope. We have only one choice: We must either care properly for all of it or continue our lethal damage to all of it.

That this is true we may be unable to know until we have understood how, and how severely, we have been penalized by the academic and professional divorces among the sciences and the arts. Division into specialties as a necessity or convenience of thought and work may be as old as civilization, but industrialism certainly has exaggerated it. We could hardly find a better illustration of this tendency than Shelley's "Defense of Poetry," in which he makes, with characteristic passion, a division between imagination and reason, assigning things eternal and spiritual to imagination, and things temporal and material to reason. *Plaint of Nature*, as if in answer, resolves exactly that duality in the person of Nature herself, who joins Heaven and Earth, and whose discourse is of the vices that break her laws and her world, and of the virtues by which her laws would be obeyed, her rule restored, and her work made whole.

Nearly all of the *Plaint* occurs in Alan's dream vision, which is to say in his mind. It is an intensely mental work, if only because he worked so hard to render the style of it, and it becomes rather stuffy. Going from Alan to Chaucer is like stepping outdoors. Nature, the "noble emperesse" herself, is presented twice in Chaucer's work, once with acknowledgement of "Aleyn" and "the Pleynt of Kynde."[17] But in Chaucer, as never in Alan, the natural world itself is present also.

It has been said that in Chaucer nature is mainly idealized in dreams or paradisal visions. And I suppose it could be said that in his treatment especially of birds, he is a mere fabulist or a protocartoonist. But to me, his attitude toward the outdoor world seems in general to be familiar, affectionate, sympathetic, and, as only he could be, humorous. This we would know if he had written only the first twelve lines of *The Canterbury Tales*. A teacher required me to memorize those lines, and I did, more or less, sixty-some years ago. Since then I have found no other writing that conveys so immediately the *presence* (the freshness of the sight, feel, smell, and sound) of an early spring morning, as well as the writer's excitement and happiness at the thought of it.

Chaucer was a man of the city and the court, but I think he was not a "city person," as we now mean that phrase. London in Chaucer's time was comparatively a small city. Inundated as we are by the commotions of internal combustion, I doubt that we can easily imagine the quietness of fourteenth-century London, from any part of which, above or beyond the street noises, Chaucer probably could have heard the birds singing. Travel on horseback through the countryside was then an ordinary thing. This involved familiar relationships with horses, and on horseback at a comfortable gait anybody at all observant participates in the life of the roadside and the countryside with an intimacy impossible for a traveler in a motor vehicle. City people then would have had country knowledge as a matter of course. If they dreamed or imagined idealized landscapes, that may have been a "natural" result of their close knowledge of real ones.

And so in *The Parliament of Fowls* we have an ideal or visionary garden with real trees. And Chaucer's list of its trees is not just an inventory. He clearly enjoys sounding their names, but he also introduces them, so to speak, by their personalities: "The byldere ok, and ek the hardy asshe, / The piler elm,"[18] and so on. A little later he identifies the birds in the same way. *The Knight's Tale* also has its list of trees, but this one names the membership of a grove that has been cut down, "disinheriting" its further membership of gods, beasts, and birds, and leaving the ground "agast"[19] at the novelty of the sunlight falling upon it. Ronsard too felt this shock, this sympathy and dismay, at the exposure and vulnerability of the ground after the "butchery" of the Forest of Gastine (Elegy XXIV), and some of us are feeling it still at the sight of our own clear-cut forests. There is nothing fabulous or visionary about the Knight's small elegy for the fallen grove. It is informed by observation of such events, and by a real regret.

That the ground under the fallen grove was "agast" (aghast, shocked, terrified) at its new nakedness to the sunlight is not something that the Knight or Chaucer knew by any of the "objective facts" that industrial foresters would use to deny that such a thing is possible. The much older, long-enduring knowledge came from sympathy and compassion.

If Chaucer heard the birds singing in his own English, that was owing to his sympathy for them. Birds and animals use human speech by convention in literary fables, but that usage came into literature, I am sure, from the conversation of country people who lived, as some of them live still, in close daily association with the birds and animals of farmsteads and with those of the natural world. People who are in the habit of speaking to their nonhuman neighbors and collaborators are likely also to have the habit of translating into their own speech the languages and thoughts of those other creatures. There are practical reasons for this, and obviously it can be amusing, but it comes from sympathy, and in turn it increases sympathy.

Some years ago I wrote the introduction for a new printing of Theodora Stanwell-Fletcher's *Driftwood Valley*, a book I had loved since I was in the seventh or eighth grade. When I sent my typescript to the author, her strongest response was to my anticipation of the objection of some readers "to Mrs. Stanwell-Fletcher's anthropomorphizing of animal thoughts and feelings."[20] One of her degrees was in animal ecology; she was "scientific" enough to know that I was right. But her marginal note, as I remember, said: "How else could we understand them?" She spoke with authority, for she and her husband had spent three years in a remote part of British Columbia, where their nearest neighbors were the native plants and animals they had come to study.

From *The Nun's Priest's Tale* we know that Chaucer was a perfect master of the literary fable, but that tale signifies also that he was a close observer of the manners of household poultry, and he no doubt had listened with care to the conversation of country people—several of whom, after all, were in his company of Canterbury pilgrims. That his attention to them and their kind had been deliberate and lively we know from two of his portraits in *The Canterbury Tales*: those of the Plowman in the *General Prologue* and the "poor widow" of *The Nun's Priest's Tale*. The descriptions of those two characters give us a sort of compendium of agrarian values—that are, by no accident, agreeable to Nature's laws.

The Plowman is said to be one of Chaucer's "ideal characters," and I suppose he is, but his idealization does not make him in any way simple. His description, though brief, is ethically complex. The Plowman is an exemplary man and countryman because he is an exemplary Christian. He loves God best, and then he loves his neighbor as himself. He is a hard worker, good and true, and a man of peace. And those virtues enable his charity, for he will work without pay for those who need his help. If I am not mistaken, Chaucer's sense of humor is at work here, pointed at those who think of goodness as a sacrifice paid here for admission to Heaven. The Plowman's virtues are understood as solidly practical and economic. He is a good neighbor, and good neighbors are likely to *have* good neighbors. The payoff, to complete the joke, may be Heavenly, but it is also earthly: A good neighborhood is an economic asset to all of its members.

The portrait of the elderly widow in *The Nun's Priest's Tale* attends to other practical and necessary virtues: patience, frugality, and good husbandry. These are congenial with the virtues of the Plowman and complete them, as his virtues complete hers. That the whole set of virtues is divided between the two characters is a matter only of appropriateness. The widow lives with her two daughters in a small cottage. She owns (God has "sente"[21] her) three large sows, three cows, a sheep named Malle (Mollie?), seven hens, and a rooster. She works "out" as a "dairymaid," but it is clear that her economy is most securely founded upon her own small holding and her few head of livestock, also upon needing little. She needs no "poignant sauce"[22] for her food because the food is good and hunger seasons it well. Her charity is to need no charity, another recognized way of being a good neighbor in a country community. This widow is a first cousin to the old Corycian farmer in Virgil's fourth Georgic. She practices exactly the "cottage economy" later praised and advocated by William Cobbett (and others).

My approach to Chaucer's first representation of Nature has been backward, from late work to early, as a way of knowing how he understood her. If we read *The Parliament of Fowls* simply as an exemplary "dreamvision" by a master poet and courtier, then perhaps we are free to regard the figure of Nature as a pleasing, even a beautiful, "picture" borrowed from Alan's *Plaint* and requiring little more of us than to place the poem historically and to appreciate it critically. But if we would like to take seriously this appearance or apparition of Nature, then we have to ask how seriously Chaucer took it, and that is not so easy. It helps, I think, if we conceive of Chaucer not only as the great poet and sophisticated "man of the world" that he certainly was, but also, and on the evidence of his writing, a man on easy speaking terms with the countryside and all of its inhabitants.

The poem is a dream-vision, a lighthearted fantasy, above all a comedy. It also takes place in a landscape in which the poet is well acquainted with the trees, the flowers, and the birds. The birds speak English, sometimes at length, but they speak also in their own tongues. We hear from the goose, the cuckoo, and the duck all together and all in the same line: "Kek kek! kokkow! quek quek!"[23] When they speak English, they use images that might have been used at court or by a farmer's hearth, but they certainly came from people who had spent time outdoors at night: "There are more stars, God knows, than a pair" and "You fare by love as owls do by light."[24]

Faced with the possibility of copying Alan's vision of Nature in her extremely elaborate finery, Chaucer politely declines by referring us to the *Plaint*, where we can find her in "such array."[25] This is a part of the comedy, but it leaves him free to describe her in his own way, which he does by a single graceful compliment which serves to acknowledge her sanctity and her standing: She is so far fairer "than any creature"[26] as the summer sun's light surpasses that of any star. And then, it seems, he draws aside a curtain:

She is sitting in a forest glade on a flowery hill. She is "set off" by halls and bowers of branches—evergreen branches, as Chaucer's readers must always have assumed—that have been "wrought"[27] according to her design. This is Nature in her English vicarage. She sits before us as a distinctly hieratic figure, yet made familiar by the homely setting that combines art and nature. This is clearly akin to the scene in which, two and a half centuries later, Robert Herrick's Corinna will go a-Maying:

> Come, my Corinna, come; and comming, marke
> How each field turns a street; each street a Parke
> Made green, and trimm'd with trees: see how

Devotion gives each House a Bough,
Or Branch: Each Porch, each doore, ere this, An arke a
   Tabernacle is
Made up of white-thorn neatly enterwove . . .[28]

Chaucer's "noble emperesse, ful of grace"[29] seems perfectly to belong
here, in the center of such a mating ritual as he must have witnessed
many times. She is there, not in May but on Saint Valentine's day, as
in every year, to see to the matchmaking of all the birds, according to
her judgment. To see that they in their great numbers find mates and
reproduce after their kinds is her high office. Following Alan's doctrine,
Chaucer has her presiding as

       the vicaire of the almyghty Lord,
That hot, cold, hevy, light, moyst, and dreye
Hath knyt by evene noumbres of acord . . .[30]

Her work is to reconcile the world's opposites and contentions into a
lasting, self-renewing composure.

From Nature enthroned our attention is drawn to the assembly
of all the birds, to the clamorous low "common sense" of the goose,
the cuckoo, and the duck, and finally to the elegant "roundel" that the
mated birds all sing together at the end. These incongruities take nothing away from Nature's dignity and they don't need to be justified or explained. They notify us of the range of Chaucer's art and his knowledge,
authenticated by the world itself, which often puts high seriousness and
low comedy into the same event or the same instant.

But let us go ahead and ask the modern question: Did Chaucer "believe in" this Nature? Did he "know" her? Did he "actually see" her seated
in her glade "upon an hil of floures"? Well, he seems to have seen her
there, he seems to have invited me to see her, and I too seem to have seen
her. Where are the proofs? There are of course no proofs, no photograph,
no second witness. But we are talking here about the imaginative life of
a country—not a nation, a *country*—which, in its apprehension of the

natural world and its "invisible fecundity," its "hidden wholeness," always must outreach its proofs, its sciences, its mechanic arts, its political economy, its market. If it fails in that, as it has with us, then we get probably what we have got: a country, mainly unknown to its occupying humans, rapidly melting into a toxic slurry and flowing away through its rivers.

That Alan's Nature appears again, years later, in *The Canterbury Tales* suggests that Chaucer thought her important enough to keep her in mind to the end of his life. At the beginning of his tale, the Physician "quotes" what he imagines she would say of the singular beauty of Virginia, his chaste heroine. Though the Physician is a man whose honesty needs watching, we need not doubt his characterization of Nature. Following his professional habit of learned speech, he has Nature describe herself in keeping with Alan's description, and with Chaucer's in *The Parliament of Fowls*. She is God's "vicar general,"[31] in charge of the sublunar creation, whose "forming and painting"[32] of the creatures is work done "to the worship of my lord."[33] What may be unique here is her insistence that her work cannot be "counterfeited."[34] In this, she takes the side of William Carlos Williams* and others in our own time, against Hamlet et al. who have argued that the "end" of art "was and is to hold . . . the mirror up to Nature . . ."[35]

This disagreement is of interest now because it clearly defines the problem confronted by scientists of the last hundred or so years who have, against the industrial declivity, taken an ecological approach to our use of the land, primarily in agriculture. To those scientists, whose work I will discuss later in this essay, two truths have been obvious: first, that we humans cannot live in unaltered natural settings, for we passed up our chance to be "rational apes" too long ago; and, second, though we cannot make mirror images of natural places, even if we could do so, even if we could live in them if we could make them, we nonetheless are obliged to obey Nature's laws, which are imposed absolutely and will never change.

• • •

---

* In especially some of the most lucid prose passages of *Spring and All*.

From Alan's vision of Nature, and then from Chaucer's, came Spenser's (as he testifies) in the fragmentary seventh book of *The Faerie Queene*, and of these three Spenser's is the finest. It is the most fully developed and detailed and the richest in meaning. The story he places Nature in, as he tells it, is the most dramatic. And the problem he sets for her is one that was urgent for him then, and that seems still more urgent for us.

Book VII of *The Faerie Queene* contains only the sixth and seventh cantos and two stanzas of an eighth. These are known as "the Mutability cantos," for they tell how "the Titanesse," Mutability, rebels against the classical deities and attempts to establish her sovereignty over them, and over all creation. She disdains the rule of Jove, and refuses to accept his judgment, appealing instead to "the highest him . . . Father of Gods and men . . . the God of Nature."[36] And so great Nature herself, as God's deputy, comes to preside over a trial to determine the justice of Mutability's claim. For this all the creatures are assembled on Arlo hill, where they are "well disposed" by Order, who is "Natures Sergeant."[37]

And then Nature enters with the great processional dignity that Spenser seems to have learned from the twenty-fourth Psalm,* as maybe of all poets only he could have learned from it:

> Then forth issewed (great goddesse) great dame *Nature*,
>> With goodly port and gracious Maiesty;
>> Being far greater and more tall of stature
>> Then any of the gods or Powers on hie:
>> Yet certes by her face and physnomy,
>> Whether she man or woman inly were,
>> That could not any creature well descry:
>> For, with a veile that wimpled euery where,
> Her head and face was hid, that mote to none appeare.

---

* This assumption is fairly obvious if one is thinking also of the twelfth stanza of his "Epithalamion." Only a poet of the greatest skill, and confidence, would have attempted this.

That some doe say was so by skill deuized,
>   To hide the terror of her vncouth hew,
>   From mortall eyes that should be sore agrized;
>   That eye of wight could not indure to view:
>   But others tell that it so beautious was,
>   And round about such beames of splendor threw,
>   That it the Sunne a thousand times did pass,
Ne could be seene, but like an image in a glass.

That well may seemen true: for, well I weene
>   That this same day, when she on *Arlo* sat,
>   Her garment was so bright and wondrous sheene,
>   That my fraile wit cannot deuize to what
>   It to compare, nor finde like stuffe to that,
>   As those three sacred *Saints*, though else most wise,
>   Yet on mount *Thabor* quite their wits forgat,
>   When they their glorious Lord in strange disguise
Transfigur'd sawe; his garments so did daze their eyes.

. . . .

This great Grandmother of all creatures bred
>   Great *Nature*, euer young yet full of eld,
>   Still moouing, yet vnmoued from her sted;
>   Vnseene of any, yet of all beheld . . .[38]

This representation of Nature clearly derives from those of Alan of Lille and Chaucer, but the resemblance, though unmistakable, is distant. Here there is nothing at all of Alan's relentless accumulation of details. And in our own time, when poets are supposed or expected to disown their forebears, it is a relief to come upon Spenser's filial devotion to Chaucer, but nothing here reminds us of the at-home conviviality of Nature's presidence over the Parliament of Fowls.

Spenser's Nature is altogether hieratic and luminous. In a way that recalls Dante's frustration in the *Paradiso*, Spenser describes this "great goddesse" mostly by describing his inability to describe her. Though she is heavily veiled like perhaps a nun and he refers to her always by feminine pronouns, she may be "inly" either a man or a woman, and her face is either unendurably terrible or so radiantly beautiful that it could not be seen except "through a glass darkly." And in describing her, Spenser, unlike Alan and Chaucer, recalls the Gospels, for her garment was "so bright and wondrous sheene" as to recall the garments of Christ at the Transfiguration. And here Spenser must be remembering also the Gospel of John 1:3: "All things were made by him; and without him was not any thing made that was made."

That she is veiled we may take as Spenser's admonishment to the scientists, from Francis Bacon to the highest-funded prophets and oracles of our time, who have proposed, by their merely human wits and devices, to wring from Nature her ultimate Truth, and thus to mate every problem with its ultimate solution. There is nothing so "progressive" in Spenser's view of Nature—or, hence, of nature. Knowing as he knew, he would have recognized Bacon's arrogance as old under the sun. He could not have expected Science, our own allegorical giant, to quiz Nature face to face.

Furthermore, Mutability, in pleading her case before Nature, addresses her as "greatest goddesse, only great"

> Who Right to all dost deale indifferently,
> Damning all Wrong and tortuous Iniurie,
> Which any of thy creatures doe to other
> (Oppressing them with power, vnequally)
> Sith of them all thou art the equall mother,
> And knittest each to each, as brother vnto brother.[39]

Any twenty-first-century reader familiar with the formal principle of interdependence, as it operates in ecosystems, will recognize this "knitting" for what it is and means, as they will recognize also Nature's "equal" motherhood of "all" the creatures. Her "indifference" is not apathetic; she is merely impartial, preferring no single species over any other, just as the realists of present-day biology know her to be. And this supposedly modern perception is much older than Spenser, for he took it from the *Plaint* in which, four hundred years earlier, Nature had warned Alan that "my bounteous power does not shine forth in you alone individually but also universally in all things."[40] We have our lives by no right of our own, but instead by the privilege of sharing in the life that sustains all creatures. This great convocation is the work of Nature, its "equall mother," which makes her not only, as Alan saw, our teacher, but also, as Spenser was first to see, our judge.

And so, submitting to Nature as the supreme worldly authority, Mutability presents her argument, and summons a procession of witnesses: the earth, the four elements, the seasons, the months, day and night, and finally life and death, all of whom support her argument. Jove then argues that worldly change is ruled by the "heavenly" gods. But Mutability charges and proves the changingness of the planetary deities, of the sun, which is sometimes eclipsed, and of Jove himself, who once was not and then was born. She is an unbluffable, brilliant lawyer, and her case is nearly perfect, as is the poetry that Spenser gives to it.

Finally, after a long considering pause, Nature gives her verdict:

> I well consider all that ye haue sayd,
>> And find that all things stedfastnes doe hate
>> And changed be: yet being rightly wayd
>> They are not changed from their first estate;
>> But by their change their being doe dilate:
>> And turning to themselues at length againe,
>> Doe worke their owne perfection so by fate:
>> Then ouer them Change doth not rule and raigne;
> But they raigne ouer change, and doe their states maintaine.[41]

C. S. Lewis speaks, with justice, of the "deep obscurity"[42] of those lines. But we may clarify them somewhat by placing beside them these earlier lines in which Mutability argues that

> For, all that from [Earth] springs, and is ybredde,
>> How-euer fayre it flourish for a time,
>> Yet see we soone decay; and, being dead,
>> To turne again vnto their earthly slime:
>> Yet, out of their decay and mortall crime,
>> We daily see new creatures to arize;
>> And of their Winter spring another Prime,
>> Vnlike in forme, and chang'd by strange disguise . . .[43]

Mutability here seems to argue, rather craftily, that change is absolute, leading invariably to something "unlike" and entirely new. Nature, if at the end she is remembering those lines, sees them as an imperfect description of a natural cycle capable of endlessly repeating itself—with, we would now say, occasional variations or "mutations," and depending on appropriate human cooperation. In her verdict, Nature readily acknowledges the ceaselessness of change, but she confirms, if not quite clearly, its cyclicality as greater, and as a form, or *the* form, of stability. She would have been confirmed in this by the *Plaint* where, in Alan's vision of her, Nature says (more clearly) that

> it was God's will that by a mutually related circle of birth and death, transitory things should be given stability by instability, endlessness by endings, eternity by temporariness, and that the series of things should ever be knit by successive renewals of birth.[44]

This will be better understood about three and a half centuries later by scientists aware of the biology, and the supreme economic importance, of the fertility cycle.

At the end of Canto VII, Nature, having completed her work for the time being, "did vanish, whither no man wist."[45] *The Faerie Queene*, as we have it, ends two stanzas later with Spenser's prayer for the "Sabaoths sight"

Of that same time when no more *Change* shall be,
But stedfast rest of all things firmely stayd
Vpon the pillours of Eternity . . .[46]

Nature's standing in the order of things, as Spenser understood it, is exalted, well above that of humanity, and she has about her the nimbus of sanctity. Her equitable motherhood of all the creatures and her judgeship over them impose upon humans a responsibility that is both worshipful and relentlessly practical. But the order in which she is placed is firmly Christian, and her jurisdiction is limited to the incarnate world. Reassuring as may be her verdict against Mutability, it offers little comfort to individual humans in their suffering of their own mortality and that of their loved ones. And so *The Faerie Queene* as we have it, though incomplete, ends appropriately by invoking our so far undying hope for a "time," beyond Nature's world and all of its stories, "when no more change shall be."

Within the compass of my reading, Spenser's vision of Nature is the highest and fullest, the most responsibly imagined, the most complete, and the most instructive. And this, I think, is because it is the most thoughtful. In the Mutability cantos, Spenser confronts a question serious enough to have no definitive or final answer: On what terms are we to live with the perpetual changingness of this world? And he answers with an argument meticulously constructed. That his stanzas on Nature's appearance are so complex and beautiful must be partly the result of his thoughtfulness. I do not mean that he used his poetry as a vehicle to express or communicate his finished thought, but rather that his poetry was the vital means by which his thinking was done. Strange as it may seem to say this after the division of the mental functions into departments, it is clear that some poets have recognized that poetry in its way, like prose in its way, can be serviceable to thought, and when they have needed to do so they have used it as a way to think.

• • •

After Spenser, so far as I have read or remember, no other English poet acknowledged the influence of Alan of Lille or thought so carefully about Nature—probably because, after Spenser, no poet needed to think so carefully about her. But there certainly have been other English poets who appear to have been influenced by the earlier visions of Nature, and who have contributed to a line of thought about the proper human use of the natural world.

Passages in the eleventh and twelfth parts of *Piers Plowman* suggest that William Langland, for one, had read *Plaint of Nature.* C. S. Lewis assumed that he had.[47] A remarkable difference is that, to Langland, Nature or "Kynde," rather than the Vicar of God, is God Himself. Langland, anyhow, was a better naturalist than either Chaucer or Spenser. Kynde instructs him in a dream to study the creatures, "the wonders of this world," to gain understanding and to learn to love his creator. And he observes carefully the variety of the creatures and their ways of mating, the skills of the nesting birds, the woodland flowers and their colors. His intimate knowledge of these things authenticates his wonder at them and his sense of the miraculousness of their existence. His wonder involves a tenderness unlike any other that I know: Of the flowers, the stones, and the stars only Kynde "himself " knows the causes; He is the magpie's patron and tells her, "putteth it in hir ere," to build her nest where the thorns are thickest.[48]

Langland and Chaucer both died in 1400. After them, and after Spenser, I have in mind poems by Milton and Pope, in which they seem to have remembered Alan's Nature or Chaucer's or Spenser's and called her, so to speak, by name.

John Milton's *Comus* is a masque, an elegant play in verse, presented at Ludlow Castle in 1634 when the poet was twenty-five years old. It tells the story of a temptation, remembering the story of Satan's temptation of Christ (Matthew 4:1–11), and anticipating *Paradise Regained*, first published in 1671. As Spenser in the Mutability cantos had asked on what terms we are to live with the perpetual changing of this world, a question that had become urgent for him in the latter part of his life, so Milton in *Comus* was asking a question no doubt urgent in his youth but approximately parallel to Spenser's: On what terms are we to live with the material abundance of this world? Human nature, by any honest measure, is limited strictly and narrowly—we don't live very long, and we don't know very much—whereas the nature of the world at large by comparison seems a limitless plenitude. The two poets, then, were asking how to make human sense, a *little* sense, of an immensity.

In *Comus* a young maiden, identified simply as "The Lady," becomes lost in the woods. Alone and vulnerable, she meets Comus, perhaps the Tempter himself, disguised as a shepherd, who offers to guide her to safety. Instead, he takes her to "a stately palace, set out with all manner of deliciousness: soft music, tables spread with all dainties."⁴⁹ He then proves himself the masterful and eloquent seducer he really is. He makes the conventional argument of *carpe diem*, "seize the day," which Jonson, Waller, Herrick, and Marvell also made in famous poems of elegant wit, giving to their dire and perfect logic a characteristic lightness of heart. The poet, as would-be lover, reminds his lady, as Marvell would put it, that "The grave's a fine and private place, / But none, I think, do there embrace."

This is exactly Comus's argument, but he makes it with a philosophic impudence and gravity that greatly enlarges its bearing. Milton's poem is sometimes described as a defense of "the sage / And serious doctrine of Virginity."⁵⁰ It is that, but also far more than that. The poem's great question, as Comus himself raises it, is about the proper use and care of natural gifts:

> Wherefore did Nature pour her bounties forth
> With such a full and unwithdrawing hand,
> Covering the earth with odors, fruits, and flocks,
> Thronging the seas with spawn innumerable,
> But all to please and sate the curious taste?

. . . .

> If all the world
> Should in a pet of temperance feed on pulse,
> Drink the clear stream, and nothing wear but frieze,
> The All-giver would be unthanked, would be unpraised,
> Not half his riches known, and yet despised . . .[51]

He eventually takes up the conventional *carpe diem* theme of the transience of mortal beauty and roses that wither, but he is arguing, as the Lady quickly understands, not for using the world but for using it up. His ideology goes beyond mere personal gluttony and lust to a modern avarice and utilitarianism: the assumption, laid bare in our own time, that all of the natural world that we humans do not consume either is worthless or is wasted.

The Lady, threatened by Comus's passionate intensity and his power of enchantment, is protected only by her inner light—even Comus can see that "something holy lodges in that breast[52]—and her hope of rescue, which eventually comes, but she easily overmatches Comus as a debater, arguing from a better premise and with sufficient courage. Nature, she says,

> Means her provision only to the good,
> That live according to her sober laws
> And holy dictate of spare Temperance.
> If every just man that now pines with want
> Had but a moderate and beseeming share
> Of that which lewdly-pampered luxury
> Now heaps upon some few with vast excess,
> Nature's full blessings would be well dispensed
> In unsuperfluous even proportion . . .[53]

Comus and the Lady are too allegorical in character to allow for much in the way of drama, but I don't think Milton can be accused of rigging their debate. He seems to have taken care to make Comus's argument as attractive as a vital man of twenty-five would have known it to be. The Lady's argument, attractive in a way perfectly opposite, more soundly appreciative of Nature's abundance, and approving temperance as the only safeguard of abundance, is Christian and democratic. (The "Christian conservatives" of our day would call it socialism.) Her argument serves my own by what I take to be its completion of the poets' long-evolving characterization of Nature. The Lady enlarges the import of Nature's demand upon humanity by making it, at last, explicitly economic. It remained for Milton to perceive clearly that Nature requires of us a *practical* reverence. Temperance in the use of natural gifts is certainly a religious obligation, but it is also an economic virtue. *Comus* requires us to think of the right use of gifts. To be in one's right mind is to know the right use of gifts. The Lady reacts so fiercely to Comus's proposition, not just because it assaults her personal virtue, but because it disdains and destroys the idea of economy. The word "economy," taken literally, as I am taking it, does not designate a financial system, but rather the management and care of the given means of life.

Alexander Pope was a poet in many ways unlike John Milton, and yet from the Lady's rebuke to Comus it is only a step to certain poems and passages of Pope. In spite of his physical debilities, Pope had more fun than Milton, but he certainly would have recognized his kinship to the Lady in *Comus*. As the Lady puts it, the human obligation to Nature is defined by obedience "to her sober laws" and the "holy dictate" of temperance. To Pope, that obligation is defined by "Sense" or "Good Sense," which in his use of those terms is pretty much the same. As he understood her, Nature requires of us certain proprieties, not only of manners but also of work. To him, everything depended on a proper sense of scale. We must act and work with the awareness always of the magnitude of Nature's work and of our own comparative smallness as individuals and as a species. And so Pope was another enemy of prodigality, of ostentation and the utter silliness of every kind of extravagance or waste.

In the "Epistle to Burlington," his satire is against the owners of country estates who surround themselves with houses and gardens magnificent to the point of ugliness and discomfort, far exceeding in dimensions and cost any use or pleasure: "huge heaps of littleness" built to display the wealth of the owner, who by comparison is "A puny insect, shiv'ring at a breeze."⁵⁴ This is contrary to "Good Sense, which only is the gift of Heaven"⁵⁵ and is worth as much as all the sciences. Against the Prodigals who waste their wealth on expensive, fashionable things they don't even like, and especially against their grotesque extravagances in what we now call "landscaping," Pope lays down two rules—"In all, let Nature never be forgot" and "Consult the Genius of the Place in all"⁵⁶—that my friend Wes Jackson and I have quoted back and forth for years in confirmation of our efforts for good husbandry of the land.

I need to confess, however, that I have often wondered how seriously I ought to take, not Pope's rules, which I think are sound, but Pope himself as a critic of land use. In the "Epistle to Burlington," after all, he is talking about the country houses and pleasure gardens of wealthy gentlemen, not working farms and forests. He goes so far as to say that even the worst examples, which he curses for "lavish cost, and little skill,"⁵⁷ are pardonable at least for giving employment to the poor—too much as polluting industries now are justified by "job creation." I forgive him for that because of his prophecy, clearly hopeful and immediately following, that these show places of extravagant littleness in "another age" will be wheat fields.⁵⁸ Moreover, his understanding of the relation of art and nature is authentically complex and practical, appropriate to land use of any kind. Good sense leads to a proper mindfulness of Nature, which leads to collaboration between Nature and the gardener. The gardener's intention or design is completed by Nature's gathering of the parts into wholeness. By her gift, moreover, the land is made useful:

'Tis Use alone that sanctifies expense,
And Splendor borrows all her rays from Sense.⁵⁹

The lawns of the estate should not be ashamed to be grazed by live-stock, or the beautiful forests to yield timber. Though with less passion and not so explicitly, Pope thus consents to Milton's argument in *Comus*, that the human economy should be appropriate to the human dependence on Nature.

Pope is the last of the English poets to be mindful of Nature as mother, maker, teacher, giver of patterns and standards, and judge—so far as I know. I have repeatedly acknowledged the limits of my knowledge, first as a duty, but also with the hope that my deficiencies will be supplied by better scholars. What I am sure of is that we have lost the old apprehension of Nature as a being accessible to imagination, linking Heaven and Earth, making and informing the incarnate creation, and requiring of humanity an obedience at once worshipful, ethical, and economic. Her stern instruction, never disproved, that we humans have a rightful but responsible place in the order of things, has disappeared, and has been absent a long time from our working consciousness and our formal schooling.

Nature, as she appeared to Chaucer, Spenser, Milton, and Pope, does not appear in the "nature poetry" of the Romantic poets, and she is absent from the history of their influence upon both poetry and the conservation movement. By the time we come to Wordsworth, who often wrote about the natural world and often was on foot in it, there is already a powerful sense of being alienated from it, with a concomitant longing to escape into it from "the din / Of towns and cities," "the heavy and the weary weight / Of all this unintelligible world," "the fretful stir / Unprofitable, and the fever of the world."[60]

I am quoting now from the poem familiarly called "Tintern Abbey," which displays pretty fully our modern love for nature, our often-lamented distance from it, and the vacationer's sensibility and economy that bring us occasionably "close" to it again, allowing us to feel more or less a religious sense of beauty and peace.

In "Tintern Abbey," addressed to his sister, Dorothy, who accompanied him, the poet has returned after a five-year absence to the Wye valley, "a wild secluded scene" of "beautiful forms," where the weight of the busy world is lightened and

> with an eye made quiet by the power
> Of harmony, and the deep power of joy,
> We see into the life of things.[61]

In the quiet and beauty of that "wild" place he feels or perhaps recalls

> A presence that disturbs me with the joy
> Of elevated thoughts; a sense sublime
> Of something far more deeply interfused,
> Whose dwelling is the light of setting suns . . .[62]

There can be no doubt of the strength of his emotion here, or of the loftiness of his language. Perhaps the presence he feels is that of Nature as the older poets imagined her, but these lines, however intense, are vague by comparison, and his thought is entirely dissipated by his resort to "something." His claim, soon following, that he recognizes

> In nature and the language of the sense
> The anchor of my purest thoughts, the nurse,
> The guide, the guardian of my heart, and soul
> Of all my moral being[63]

is devoid of any particular thought or any implication of a practical responsibility. His version of "nature" thus lacks altogether the intelligence and moral energy of Nature as she appeared to the older poets. Of Wordsworth she seems to have required nothing at all in particular, except perhaps his admiration.

In line 122 the poet personifies Nature by capitalizing her name, but he then also sentimentalizes her:

> Nature never did betray
> The heart that loved her; 'tis her privilege,
> Through all the years of this our life, to lead
> From joy to joy . . .[64]

and thus she becomes the poet's guardian against human evils and "The dreary intercourse of daily life . . ."[65] To perceive in Nature this favoritism is clearly more self-indulgent and less true than Spenser's characterization of her as the "equall mother" of all creatures, which conforms exactly to Jesus's reminder that God "maketh his sun to rise on the evil and on the good, and sendeth rain on the just and on the unjust."[66] Since Nature is so exceptionally kind to Wordsworth and his sister, it is in a manner logical that he declares himself a "worshipper of Nature."[67] Here he departs maybe as far as possible from the Nature of his predecessors, to whom she was God's Vicar and thus forever subordinate to Him. The older poets were, as C. S. Lewis said of Spenser, Christians, not pantheists.

In comparison to the imaginative force and complexity of the earlier poets, this poem looks simpleminded and slack. Nature is understood merely as the purveyor of a sort of consolation or what we now call "mental health." Nobody could take from this version of Nature any sense of our economic dependence upon her, much less of her dependence upon our virtue. The wonder is that this poem contains in lines 11–17 a fine and moving description of an economic landscape— "pastoral farms / Green to the very door," "plots of cottage ground," orchards, and hedge rows—but he makes no approach to the economic life of that place or to its farmers, who certainly could have enlightened him about Nature's special preferences and favors. In this poem, the farms rate only as scenery, as they do for nature lovers of our own time.

A further wonder is that two years later Wordsworth wrote "Michael," a poem that penetrates the scenery. In that poem, the poet imagines in plenitude of detail the lives of a "pastoral" family of the Lake District: Michael, an elderly shepherd, Isabel, his wife, younger by twenty years, and their late-born only son, Luke. They live in difficult country, in weather that can be harsh. Like the many generations of their forebears, they live by endless work, from daylight to dusk and on into the night, the aging parents

> neither gay perhaps,
> Nor cheerful, yet with objects and with hopes,
> Living a life of eager industry.[68]

There is something of the quality of legend in the telling, for their life was old in the poet's memory, and old beyond memory. But I think there is little if any idealization, no "romanticizing." Above all, Wordsworth passed unregarding the temptation to present these people as "clowns" or, as we would say, "hicks." Michael's mind "was keen, intense, and frugal." As a shepherd, he is "prompt / And watchful." He knows "the meaning of all winds."[69]

The poem tells of Luke's upbringing, during which he learned his people's world and their work by accompanying his father almost from infancy, by being "Something between a hindrance and a help" at the age of five in helping his father to manage their sheep flock, and by becoming his father's "companion" in the work by the age of ten.[70]

Theirs is a "world" in itself almost complete and everlasting. But when Luke is eighteen trouble comes from the outside, as trouble is apt to come from the outside in, for instance, the novels of Thomas Hardy. Michael has mortgaged his land "in surety for his brother's son,"[71] to whom misfortune has come, and Michael is called upon to pay the debt, which amounts in value to about half his property. To preserve the land undivided as Luke's inheritance, his old parents decide to send him away, to work for another kinsman, "A prosperous man, / Thriving in trade."[72] Working for this man, Luke would earn enough to lift the debt from the land. As Michael says to Isabel,

> He quickly will repair this loss, and then
> He may return to us. If here he stay,

What can be done? Where everyone is poor,
What can be gained?[73]

For a time, Luke does well, the kinsman is pleased with him, he writes
"loving letters" home.[74] And then doom falls with terrible swiftness
upon the family and their long history:

> Luke began
> To slacken in his duty; and, at length,
> He in the dissolute city gave himself
> To evil courses: ignominy and shame
> Fell on him, so that he was driven at last
> To seek a hiding-place beyond the seas.[75]

Thus an ancient story receives almost abruptly its modern version: The
Prodigal, the far-wandering son, does not now finally make his way
home to continue the family lineage in its home place. Now he is gone
forever. The forsaken parents live on alone, and die, and the land, at
such great cost held to, is sold "into a stranger's hand."[76]

In "Tintern Abbey," without of course intending to do so, Wordsworth laid out pretty fully the model of industrial-age conservation,
which reduces too readily to the effort to preserve "wilderness" and "the
wild," in certain favored places, as if to compensate or forget the ongoing industrial devastation of the other landscapes. This version of conservation, industrial and romantic, orthodox and dominant for at least
a century, simplifies and sentimentalizes nature as friendly, wild, virgin, spectacular or scenic, picturesque or photogenic, distant or remote
from work or workplaces, ever-pleasing, consoling, restorative of a kind
of norm of human sanity. Conservationists of this order have thus established and ratified a division, even a hostility between nature and
our economic life that is both utterly false and limitlessly destructive of
the world that they are intent upon "saving." Such conservationists are
no threat at all to the economy of industry, science, and technology, of
recreational equipment and vacations, which threatens everything those

conservationists think they are defending, including "wilderness" and "the wild." Meanwhile the absolute dependence, even of our present so-called economy, even of our lives, upon the natural world is ignored. In my many years of advocacy for better care of farms and working forests, the silence of conservationists and their organizations has been conspicuous. They oppose sensational abuses such as global warming or fracking or (sometimes) surface mining, but they don't oppose bad farming. Most of them would not recognize bad farming if they saw it, and they see plenty of it even from the highways as they drive toward the virgin forests and the snowcapped mountains. It seems never to have occurred to them that soil erosion and stream pollution in agricultural lands threaten all of this natural world, even "the wild," and that such abuses are caused by an economy that ruins farmers and farms by policy.

"Tintern Abbey" is an archetypal poem, for it gives us the taste, tone, and "spiritual" justification of the escapist nature-love of the many romantic nature poems that descended from it, and of the still-prevailing mentality of conservation. "Michael" also is an archetypal poem, but in a sense nearly opposite. Wordsworth understood it as no more than a family tragedy. Two centuries later, we must see it as uncannily predictive of millions of versions of its story all over the world: the great and consequential tragedy, little acknowledged or understood, of the broken succession of farm families, farm communities, and the cultures of husbandry. Generation after generation the children of farm couples have moved away, leaving the land's human memory, often of great ecological and economic worth, to die with their parents. Whether they have gone away to fail or succeed by the measures of their time, they still have gone away, and their absence is a permanent and enormous loss. And so "Michael" is great both because of its achievement and stature as a work of art and because of its rarity and significance as a cultural landmark. It stands high among the poems that have meant most to me. I first read it more than sixty years ago.

The second tragedy of "Michael" has to do with the history of the poem itself. Unlike "Tintern Abbey," it has had, so far as I am aware, no influence on our thinking about the natural world and our use of it, and little or no influence on the subsequent history of poetry. It stands almost alone. The only poem I know that I think worthy of its company is "Marshall Washer," by my friend Hayden Carruth. Marshall Washer was for many years Hayden's neighbor, a dairy farmer near Johnson, Vermont. Like Michael, Marshall lived a life of hard work on a small farm in a demanding place and climate. As, like Michael, the master and artist of his circumstances, Marshall earned Hayden's love and respect, and from his companionship and example Hayden learned many things that he valued. Hayden, moreover, saw Marshall in perspective of the hard history of such farmers before and after the time of Wordsworth. In the poem, Marshall has lived and worked and aged into a loneliness known to millions of his kind and time. His wife has died, and his sons have

> departed, caring little for the farm because
> he had educated them—he who left school
> in 1931 to work by his father's side
> on an impoverished farm in an impoverished time.[77]

Beyond Marshall's life, the life of the farm had become unknowable and unimaginable, and all such farms were coming under the influence of "development." Land prices and taxes were increasing. It was becoming less possible for a small farmer to own a small farm. And Hayden imagined Marshall's sorrow:

> farming is an obsolete vocation—
> while half the world goes hungry. Marshall walks
> his fields and woods, knowing every useful thing
> about them, and knowing his knowledge useless.[78]

This describes the breaking of what Hayden called "the link of the manure"—"manure" in the senses both of fertilizing and caring for, hand-working, the land—which cannot be ignorantly maintained. The "link of the manure" is the fundamental economic link between humans and the natural world. No matter the plain necessity of this link, it is breaking, or is broken, everywhere.

Ignorance certainly will break it. But so also will forces imposed upon it by what we falsely and too readily think of as the "larger" economy. There obviously can be no economy larger than its own natural sources and supports. Less obvious, farming being "an obsolete vocation" as far as most of us are concerned, is the impossibility that any economy can be larger or more important or more valuable than the economies of land use that connect us practically to the natural sources. Nevertheless, we have this small contrivance we call "the economy," utterly detached from our households and our need for food, clothing, and shelter, in which people "put their money to work for them" and sit down to await the increase, in which money interbreeding with money enlarges itself to monstrosity, glutting on the world's goods. This small economy, centralized and concentrated in the larger cities, imposes in its great equation of ignorance and power a determining and limitlessly destructive influence upon the economies of land use, of farming and forestry, which are large, dispersed, and weak.

Those of us who would like to understand this could do worse than consult with poets, or with the too few of them who have taken an interest and paid attention. Those two widely separated and lonely poems, "Michael" and "Marshall Washer," are tragedies of the modern world. The stories they tell become tragic because the interest of the land, the human investment of interest and affection in the land, becomes subordinated to the interest of a "larger" economy that removes the human interest native to a place and replaces it with its own interest in itself.

After the story of the westward migration, the dominant American story so far is that of the young people who have departed from their rural birthplaces, "humble" or "small" or "backward" or "poor," to find success or failure in the big city. The story of the loneliness of the elders left behind, though surely as common, is rarely told. The implication of its rarity is that it does not matter, but is only a small sorrow incidental to the quest for a greater happiness. But sometimes a backward look will occur, bringing a recognition of loss and suffering that matter more than expected. The example I have in mind is a Carter Family song, "The Homestead on the Farm":

> I wonder how the old folks are at home,
> I wonder if they miss me when I'm gone,
> I wonder if they pray for the boy who went away
> And left his dear old parents all alone.[79]

The song, which I like, carries the story only as far as nostalgia: The departed boy looks back with fondness for his old home, which his memory no doubt has improved, and with some regret, but he clearly has no plans to return. Maybe we can do no better than this, having as yet no common standards or a common language to deal with social disintegration, much less with diminishments of culture and the loss of local memory, all of which will enter into an accounting indivisibly cultural, ecological, and economic.

I don't know if Ezra Pound ever actually knew such people as Michael or Marshall Washer. But his poems on usury, "sin against nature," cast on the stories of these men what has been for me an indispensable light. Maybe nobody ever gave more passionate attention than Pound to the ability of a monetary system by means of usury to drive the cost of land and its products beyond any human measure of their worth, and thus to prey upon and degrade the work and the health that sustain us. And nobody has ever instructed us about this with more economy or grace or beauty:

> With usury has no man a good house
> made of stone, no paradise on his church wall

With usury the stonecutter is kept from his stone
the weaver is kept from his loom by usura
Wool does not come into market
the peasant does not eat his own grain
The girl's needle goes blunt in her hand
The looms are hushed one after another

. . . .

Usury kills the child in the womb
And breaks short the young man's courting
Usury brings age into youth; it lies between the bride
and the bridegroom
Usury is against Nature's increase.[80]

Pound had the misfortune, self-induced, of becoming more notorious for his prejudices and political mistakes than famous for sanity. But he did have in him a broad streak of good sense. He could see all the way to the ground, not invariably a talent among poets, and he had moments of incisive agrarianism. He wrote in these lines a clarifying history of modern land husbandry:

Dress 'em in folderols
                        and feed 'em with dainties,
In the end they will sell out the homestead.[81]

He praised with perfect soundness "Chao-Kong the surveyor," who "Gave each man land for his labour"[82]—wages being always vulnerable, whereas the value of land, like the value of a life, is unreckonable and absolute. And he wrote these lines,

                        Pull down thy vanity, I say pull down.
Learn of the green world what can be thy place
In scaled invention or true artistry . . .[83]

in which he stood before Nature much in the posture of Alan of Lille eight hundred years before.

Whoever would think at the same time of the home ecosystem on the one hand, and on the other of the home community (ecosystem plus humans), is all but forced to think of the local economy—and its tributary local economies elsewhere. Very few poets—very few people—have thought of both at once, because, I suppose, of the intensity of the stretch. It is something like standing with one foot on shore and the other in a loosely floating small boat. It requires a big heart and a strong crotch.

Of the poets I know of my own time, Gary Snyder is the one whose thought and work (in poetry and prose) have most insistently inclined toward the daily and practical issues of our economic life, which is to say our life: the possibility of bringing our getting and spending into concordance with terrestrial reality. This has been, for Gary, a lifelong effort, involving the events and materials of his life, much travel, much reading, much study and thought of his home geography. At a loss as to how to represent this effort in its complexity, I will say only that I think it has begun and renewed itself again and again in realizations of the profound, indissoluble link, the virtual identity, between the world's life and the lives of creatures. How is it with us who live our ever-changing lives as parts or members of the ever-changing world? Or to use language Gary has borrowed from Dogen: How is it with us who are walking on mountains that are walking? This question is not comfortable, and we sometimes would like to ignore or wish against it. But it means at least that the world is always with us, new and fresh:

Clear running stream
            clear running stream

Your water is light
            to my mouth

And a light to my dry body

                            your flowing

Music,

                  in my ears. free,

Flowing free!
With you
              in me.[84]

It is not hard to imagine thoughts of economy and of "the economy" starting from the tenderness, intimacy, and inherent delight of this kindness, this kinship. But the poem also is a thanksgiving, the proper conclusion to such thoughts.

And I ask myself, Can it be that, by way of Buddhism and American Indian anthropology, Gary Snyder is another who has come face to face with the great goddess, great dame Nature, and he makes her this cordial greeting? Maybe.

It must be clear enough by now that I am a reader who reads for instruction. I have always read, even literature, even poetry, for instruction. I am a poet, and so I have read other poets as a poet, to learn about poetry, and, just as important, to learn from poetry. I am also in a small way a farmer devoted to farming, as my father and his father made me, and I have read poetry, and everything else, also as a farmer. As a farmer I have lived daily with the inherent hardships and pleasures, but also with an ever-fascinating and utterly intimidating question: What should I be doing to care properly for this (as it happens) very difficult and demanding place? And a further one: How can I make myself a man capable of seeing what is the right thing to do, and of doing it?

Such questions now are typically addressed to experts, and are answered by a letter or a pamphlet replete with statistics, graphs, diagrams, and instructions, all presumed to be applicable to all persons and to any and every place within a designated region or zone. This may in fact prove helpful, but it is not enough. It is not enough because it includes no knowledge of the particular and unique place where the expertise is to be applied. Moreover, expertise which is credentialed and much dependent on the demeanor and language of authority is typically unable to acknowledge either its inner ignorance or the immense mystery that surrounds equally the asker and the answerer. And so askers are in effect left alone with the expert answer on their singular small places within the mostly uninformative universe.

Supplements and alternatives are available. One can talk with one's neighbors and elders, who never are oracles but are usually worth listening to. One can consult with other experts. I have always liked to consult older or earlier experts, whose knowledge may be seasoned with affection and humility. Or one can read, following one's nose as good hounds and readers do, always on watch for what people in other times and places have known or learned, what penalties they paid for ignorance, what satisfactions they gained by knowledge. These benefits can come from books of every kind.

Such broad and even random conversation is necessary because the present industrial world is not an isolated empire fortified against history or incomparable by its improvements with other times and ways. As I have conversed and read for the last fifty years, I have been reminding myself that many new ways of doing work have been adopted not because they were better for land and people, but simply because the old ways were technologically outmoded. Industrial agriculture, as probably the paramount example, is better than pre-industrial agriculture by the standard mainly of corporate profitability, excluding by a sort of conventional or fashionable blindness the paramount standard of mental, bodily, and ecological health. One can learn this by the study of rural landscapes, but conversation and reading also are necessary. To think responsibly about land use, the whole known spectrum of means and ways must be available to one's thoughts. If, for example, one cannot compare a tractor (and its attendant economy and ecological effects) with a team of horses (and its attendant economy and ecological effects), then one has the use of less than half of one's mind.

Do I, then, think that farmers, or persons of other vocations, can find actual help in reading Chaucer or Milton or Spenser or Pope? Yes, that is what I think. To know Chaucer's plowman is not to know something merely of historical interest. It is to know, to recognize immediately, something that one needs to know. It would be too much to say that *all* farmers, foresters, economists, ecologists, and conservationists should know what Chaucer, Spenser, Milton, and Pope wrote about Nature, but it is a pity and a danger that none or only a few of them do.

Having argued that it is possible to learn valuable, even useful and necessary things from poetry, I now have to answer two further questions. First: Is it necessary for a poem to be instructive in order to be good? I hope not, and I don't think so. There is nothing very instructive, for example, in hearing that "the cow jumped over the moon," but who is not delighted by that poem's exuberant indifference to the possibility of making sense? It is a masterpiece. Even so, I am happy to know that some poems delight *and* instruct, which is a richer possibility.

Second: How does an instructive poem instruct? The answer seems obvious—by containing something worth knowing—but there is one condition: It must teach without intending to do so. In support of this I offer a sentence by Jacques Maritain, who said of the cathedral builders: "Their achievement revealed God's truth, but without *doing it on purpose*, and because it was not done on purpose."[85] The point, I believe, is that what the cathedral builders were doing on purpose was building a cathedral. Any other purpose would have distracted them from the thing they were making and spoiled their work. Teaching as a purpose, as such, is difficult to prescribe or talk about because the thing it is proposing to make is usually something so vague as "understanding." My own best teachers, as I remember, sometimes undertook deliberately to teach me something: "You handed me that board wrong, and made my work harder. Now I'm going to hand it back to you *right*. Now you hand it back to me *right*." But this was rare. When I was most learning from them, I think, they were attempting something besides teaching, if only to make a sentence that made sense. They taught me best by example, unaware that they were teaching or that I was learning. Just so, an honest poet who is making a poem is doing neither more nor less than making a poem, undistracted by the thought even that it will be read. Poets, or some poets, bear witness as faithfully as possible to what they have experienced or observed, suffered or enjoyed, and this inevitably is instructive to anybody able to be instructed. But the instruction is secondary. It must be embodied in the work.

One remarkable thing I have noticed in my reading is that agrarianism, readily identifiable by certain themes (the importance of the small holding, the relationship to Nature, etc.), appears throughout the written record from as far back as Homer and the Bible. A second remarkable thing is that these appearances are intermittent, sometime widely separated. When this vital strand of human thought and concern has disappeared from writing—as it does, in poetry, from Wordsworth's "Michael" to Hayden Carruth's "Marshall Washer"—it has continued in the conversation of farmers. I was (I am still) Hayden Carruth's friend. I knew him from much conversation and many letters. In Hayden's company I met and talked at some length with Marshall Washer. Though Hayden was far better read than I am, I am confident that the agrarianism of Hayden's poem did not come from his reading. It came straight from Marshall himself, who had it from his father, who had it from a lineage of living voices going back and back, more or less parallel to, but rarely, maybe never, intersecting with the lineage of writings. I know this also from my own long participation in such conversation. The appearances of agrarian thought in the written record are like stepping stones, separate and irregularly spaced, but resting on a firm and (so far) a continuous bottom.

Who were, and to a much-reduced extent still are, the people who have passed this tradition by living word from generation to generation for so long? The answer, obviously, is the country people who have done the work of field and forest, generation after generation. They are the people once known as peasants, serfs, or churls, and now, still doing the same work, as farmers or country people, when "farmer" and "country" are still as readily used as terms of abuse as "peasant" and "churl" ever were. My friend Gene Logsdon says that when he was a schoolboy in Wyandot County, Ohio, "*Dumb farmer* was one word." Here I need to remember two sentences from G. G. Coulton's *Medieval Panorama*. The first is this: "Four-fifths, at least, of the medieval population had grown their own food in their own fields; had spun and woven wool from their own sheep or linen from their own toft; and very often it was they themselves who made it into clothes."[86] I should add that they also kept themselves housed, and they fed and sheltered their animals. Anybody who has done any part of such work knows that it involves knowledge of the highest order and value, for the human species has survived by it, and it is neither simple nor easy to learn.

But how were these people with their elaborate and indispensable knowledge valued in the Middle Ages? Here is the second sentence from *Medieval Panorama*: "Froissart shows us plainly enough how, after the bloody capture of a town or castle, the gentles [knights and nobles] were spared, but the common soldiers [churls] were massacred without protest from their more exalted comrades in arms."[87] They were thought to be, in a word, dispensable.

I don't believe that this thought has changed very substantially from then until now. We, whose humane instincts have so famously evolved and improved, are firmly opposed to outmoded forms of massacre, but we still regard farmers as dispensable, and by various economic constraints and social fashions we have dispensed with many millions of them over the last sixty or so years. If the twenty-first-century American farmer is farming several thousand acres and employing a million dollars' worth of equipment, he still is a member of a disparaged, and therefore a vanishing, population. He does not control any part of his economy. He has no more influence over the markets on which he buys

and sells than he has over the weather. No prominent politician, economist, or intellectual is thoughtful either of him or of the condition of
the land he works, or of the health of the ecosystem that includes his
land. In the entire food industry he will be dependably the most at risk,
the least valued, and the lowest paid, except, of course, for the migrant
laborers he may at times be constrained to hire. If he miscalculates or
has a bad year and is ruined, that will register among the professional
onlookers as a minor instance of "creative destruction."

In the course of this progress of industrialization and depopula-
tion, farming itself has become so radically simplified as to be unworth
the name. Most damaging has been the division between the field crop
industry and the meat-animal industry. To remove the farm animals
from farming is to remove more than half of the need for knowledge,
skill, and intelligence, and nearly all of the need for sympathy. To
crowd the animals into the tightest possible confinement to live and
function exclusively as meat-makers is to do away with sympathy as a
precondition, to reduce mindfulness to routine, and to replace all the
free helps of Nature and natural health with purchased machinery and
medicines.

But when plants and animals, croplands and pastures, are gathered
into the care of a single farmer, this calls for a mind versatile and accomplished, competent to deal with the fairly stable natures of the kinds
of plants and animals, as well as the variable and sometimes surprising
circumstances of mortality, the weather, and the economy. Among the
good farmers I have known, I have found also a formal intelligence by
which they ordered the spatial arrangement of fences, fields, and buildings to be most conserving of the land and most usable, and by which
they formed also the temporal structures of their crop rotations and the
days, seasons, and years of their work.

Good farmers, whose minds are comparable to the minds of artists
of the "fine arts," have been instructed so often for so long that they
are "dumbfarmers," that they only half believe how smart and capable
they actually are. I have heard too many of them describe themselves
as "just a farmer." It is, at any rate, impossible for highly credentialed

professionals and academics to appraise justly the intelligence of a good farmer. They are too ignorant for that. You might as well send a bird dog to judge the competence of a neurologist.

About such things there are no "objective" measures. I can offer only my testimony. In my by-now long life, I have known well and observed closely the work of a good many farmers whom I have respected. I have thought carefully about them for a long time, and some of them I have written about. In general: I have found them alert, observant, interested, interesting, thoughtful of their experience, conversant with the experience of others. By midlife or sooner they have come to know many things so completely as to be unconscious of knowing them. They have had, in general, the humorous intelligence that recognizes natural limits and their own limits. They have had also a commonplace sense of tragedy that permitted them to accept their helplessness in the face of loss and suffering—as Marshall Washer faced his burning barn with thirteen heifers trapped inside, and kept on, still working, by the testimony of his friend Hayden Carruth, within weeks of his death at eighty-eight. That is not indicative either of "dullness" or "stoicism," nor does it mean that farmers in general are better or more virtuous than other persons. It means simply that farmers live and work in circumstances unremittingly practical, and for this certain strengths of mind are necessary.

In general, the good farmers I have known have had no taste for self-display, did not parade their knowledge, and would say little where their knowledge might not be respected. But if you had a mind and ear for their conversation, and some ground of friendship or common knowledge, you were likely to hear sound sense that came from their experience of the natural world, and of farming and its local history. As late as my own generation, because the young then were still working with and listening to their elders, the talk of farmers was still carrying the traditional themes and attitudes. Many of the things I heard from them I have kept always in my mind, their words and their voices.

· · ·

Probably in the summer of 1965, after my family and I had moved here
to the "twelve acres more or less" where we still live, I was not equipped
for some mowing that needed to be done. I hired a neighbor of my
parents' generation, a man I had known from my childhood, liked, and
respected. When he had finished the work, he turned off the tractor
engine and we talked a while, he much in the spirit of welcoming me
to my new place. He had been renewing his own acquaintance with the
place as he worked. We spoke of the ways it had been used (not always
kindly), and of the uses I might make of it.

When he was ready to go, he started the tractor and, to end the
conversation, said cheerfully, "Well, try a little of everything, you'll hit
on something."

He knew, and he knew I knew, how little of "everything" the old
place was actually capable of producing on its steep slopes and its one
pretty good "garden spot" by the river. But he had said a good thing,
and we both knew that. He had stated one of Nature's laws: the Law of
Diversity, vital both to ecological and to economic health. One of my
father's father's rules was "Sell something every week," a different version of the Law of Diversity.

Another of my older friends, a fine farmer whose friendship I inherited from my father, once told me a crucial part of the story of his
beginning on his own farm. This, I think, would have been in 1940 or a
little earlier. He and his wife had gone into debt to buy their place, and
they had no money. My friend went early in the year to a grocery store
in town and asked the owner if he would "carry" him until he sold his
crop. The owner knew him, trusted him, and agreed. When my friend
sold his crop at the year's end and went to settle up at the store, his bill
came to eleven dollars and some cents. He and his wife had been thrifty
and careful, living so far as possible from their place, thus obeying another of Nature's laws, the Law of Frugality: Don't be prodigal.

A man of about the same age, a dear friend who was conscientiously
my teacher for thirty years, once told me with an emphasis amounting
to passion: "If you've got grass and room to keep a milk cow [for family
use] and you don't do it, you've *lost* one milk cow." The absent cow he

saw, not as a neutral matter of mere preference, but as a negative economic force, a subtraction from thrift and thriving. This was in respect for the Law of Diversity and the Law of Frugality.

A steadying influence on my mind for most of my life has been the metaphor by which my father referred to a patch of abused land that had been healed and grassed as "haired over." He thus perceived a wound to the earth as a wound to a living creature, perhaps a collar gall on the shoulder of a workhorse. We could say that this phrase observes another of Nature's laws—Keep the ground covered—but much else of value is concentrated in it. By it my father wakened my mind to the thought of the system of kinships by which the world survives, and to the thought of the whole significance of the smallest healing. I don't know whether or not this language originated with my father, but I knew *his* father and so I know that it was not the thought of one mind. Such a thought is as far as possible unlike the thought of the earth as an inert material mass to be shoved about, poisoned, and blasted at human discretion.

None of those sayings comes from a note I made at the time or from any record I kept, but only from memory, and to me this signifies their importance and value. I have remembered them and many others, I believe, because I recognized them not quite consciously as parts of a whole, a kind of mind which, like my mentors, I inherited, which probably is as old as farming and necessary to it. This mind, which I think has never been fully conscious or coherent in any one person, never perfect, always in some manner failing, almost never having the incentive of public appreciation or adequate economic support, has nonetheless cohered, coming to consciousness as needed, and expressing itself in an articulate local speech that takes its heft and inflection from the reconciliations between people and their circumstances, their work and their feelings about it. This mind, much to the credit of its inherent good sense, has survived all its adversities until now, living on, talking to itself, so to say, in the conversation of its local memberships. It still speaks, where it survives, of the importance of the well-doing of small tasks that the dominant culture has always considered degrading but which are nonetheless essential and worthy of care: "Don't think of the dollar," my friend and teacher said to me. "Think of the *job*." And it still speaks of our dependence on the particular natures of creatures and on the natural world, and, more practically, of a necessary respect and deference toward Nature. In this speech, Nature customarily is personified: the great dame herself, who knows best and will have her way. Always there is the implication that Nature helps when you work *with* her, with knowledge of her ways, their value, and their ultimate dominance, and that she does not help but works against you when you work against her.

Recently my son brought me an issue of a conventional industrial farming magazine, containing an article, by a "semi-retired" rancher, Walt Davis, about the need to manage a cow herd so as "to be in sync with nature."[88] Though some of the vocabulary ("in sync") is new, this advice is old. I know nothing that suggests it is wrong. The point, as often, is economic: To be in sync with Nature is to make full use of her helps that are free or cheap, as opposed to the use of industrial substitutes that are expensive. By observance of Nature's laws, the land survives and even thrives in human use. By the *same* laws, farmers can hope at least to survive in the almost conventional adversity of the farm economy.

Almost typical of young farmers is the impulse to intervene in natural processes with some "latest" expertise, requiring typically some "latest" merchandise in order to increase production or fend off some perceived threat. Older farmers are more likely to be suspicious of anything that costs money, and to rely instead on the gifts of their own intelligence and the nature of creatures. Young shepherds, in their eager and self-regarding sympathy, may try to help a newborn lamb to stand and suck—may even succeed, or seem to. Older shepherds will know that such "help" is most likely a waste of time. They know when to walk away and "leave it to Nature." They are likely to know also that Nature bids them to get rid of a ewe whose lamb can survive its birth only with human help.

Going on forty years ago, because I knew his grand reputation as a breeder of Southdown sheep, I had the honor of becoming a little acquainted with Henry Besuden of Vinewood Farm in Clark County, Kentucky. Mr. Besuden was seventy-six years old then and not in good health; it had been several years since he had owned a sheep. But when I visited him, which I did at least twice, and he showed me his place and we talked at length, I found that his accomplishments as a farmer excelled in fact and in interest his accomplishments as a sheepman.[89]

In 1927, at the age of twenty-three, he inherited a farm of 632 acres, a large holding for that country, but it came to him as something less than a privilege. The land had been ruined by the constant row-cropping of renters: "Corned to death." Gullies were everywhere, some of them deep enough to hide a standing man. Between Mr. Besuden then and an inheritance of nothing was the stark need virtually to remake his farm. To do this he had to return the land from its history of human carelessness to the care of Nature: Every gully, through which the land was flowing away, had to be transformed into a grassed swale that would check and retain the runoff. This required a lot of work and a long time, but by 1950 all of the scars at last were grassed over.

To this effort the sheep were not optional but necessary. They would thrive on the then-inferior, weedy and briary pastures, and, rightly managed, they were "land builders." He became a sheepman in order to become the farmer Nature required for his land. The constant theme of his work was "a way of farming compatible with nature" or, as Pope would have put it, with "the Genius of the place." I have not known a farmer in whose mind the traditional agrarianism was more complete or more articulate.

He wrote in one of his several articles entitled "Sheep Sense": "It is good to have Nature working for you. She works for a minimum wage." Soil conservation, he wrote, "also involves the heart of the man managing the land. If he loves his soil he will save it." He wrote again, obedient to Nature's guidance, of the need "to study the possibilities of grass fattening." He wrote of the importance of "little things done on time." He told me about a farmer who would wait until he came to a spot bare of grass to scrape the manure off his shoes: "That's what I mean. You have to keep it in your mind."

In any economy that becomes exploitive of land or people or (as usual) both, it appears that some of the people working within it will recognize that its special standards of judgment are inadequate. They will see the need for a more comprehending standard by which the constrictive system can be judged, so to speak, from the outside. At present, for example, some doctors and others who work in the medical profession have the uneasy awareness that their industrial standards are failing, and their thoughts are going, as always in such instances, toward Nature's laws, which is to say, toward the health that is at once bodily, familial, communal, economic, and ecological. The outside standard invariably will turn out to be health, and perceptive people, looking beyond industrial medicine, see that health is not the painlessness of a body part, or the comfort of parts of a society. They see that the idea of a healthy individual in an unhealthy community in an unhealthy place is an absurdity that, by the standards of industry, can only become more absurd.

In agricultural science the same realization was occurring at the beginning of the twentieth century. The first prominent sign of this, so far as I know, was a book, *Farmers of Forty Centuries*, in which F. H. King, who had been professor of agricultural physics at the University of Wisconsin, recounted his travels among the small farms of China, Korea, and Japan. As a student of soil physics and soil fertility, King must be counted an expert witness, but he was also a sympathetic one. He was farm-raised, and his interest in agriculture seems to have come from a lifelong affection for farming, farmers, and the details of their work.

The impetus for his Asian journey seems to have been his recognition of the critical deficiencies of American agriculture, the chief one being the relentless exploitation of soil and soil fertility by practices that were supportable only by the importation to the farms of "cargoes of feeding stuffs and mineral fertilizers."[90] This, he knew, could not last. It was, we would say now, unsustainable, as it still is. It was possible in the United States because the United States was still a thinly populated country.

Such extravagance had never been possible in China, Korea, and Japan, where "the people . . . are toiling in fields tilled more than three thousand years and who have scarcely more than two acres per capita, more than one-half of which is uncultivable mountain land."[91] This long-enduring agriculture was made possible by keeping the fertility cycle intact and in place. The "plant food materials" that we were wasting, "through our modern systems of sewage disposal and other faulty practices," the Asian farmers "held . . . sacred to agriculture, applying them to their fields."[92]

As a sample of the economic achievement of the peasant farms he visited, King says in his introduction that "in the Shantung province [of China] we talked with a farmer having 12 in his family and who kept one donkey, one cow, both exclusively laboring animals, and two pigs on 2.5 acres of cultivated land where he grew wheat, millet, sweet potatoes and beans."[93] The introduction ends with this summary:

> Almost every foot of land is made to contribute material for food, fuel or fabric. Everything which can be made edible serves as food for man or domestic animals. Whatever cannot be eaten or worn is used for fuel. The wastes of the body, of fuel and of fabric worn beyond other use are taken back to the field . . .[94]

The chapters that follow contain finely detailed descriptions of one tiny farm after another, every one of them exemplifying what I have called Nature's Law of Frugality, or what Sir Albert Howard would later call her "law of return." Fertility, we might say, was understood as borrowed from Nature on condition of repayment in full. "Nothing," King wrote, "jars on the nerves of these people more than incurring of needless expense, extravagance in any form, or poor judgment in making purchases."[95] No debt was to be charged to the land and left unpaid, as we were doing in King's time and are doing still.

Farmers of Forty Centuries was published in 1911. In 1929, J. Russell Smith, then professor of economic geography at Columbia University, published *Tree Crops*, another necessary book, another of my stepping stones. I don't know whether or not Smith had read King's book, but that does not matter, for Smith's book was motivated by the same trouble: our senseless waste of fertility and the prospect of land exhaustion.

What Smith saw was not only our fracture of the fertility cycle, but also another, an opposite, cycle: "Forest—field—plow—desert—that is the cycle of the hills under most plow agricultures . . ."[96] Smith was worried about soil erosion. He had seen a part of China that King had not visited:

> The slope below the Great Wall was cut with gullies, some of which were fifty feet deep. As far as the eye could see were gullies, gullies, gullies—a gashed and gutted countryside.[97]

And Smith knew that there were places similarly ruined in the "new" country of the United States. The mistake, everywhere, was obvious: "Man has carried to the hills the agriculture of the flat plain." The problem, more specifically, was the agriculture of annual plants. "As plants," he wrote, "the cereals are weaklings."[98] They cannot protect the ground that their cultivation exposes to the weather.

As Henry Besuden had realized on his own farm two years before the publication of Smith's book, the reaction against the damage of annual cropping could only go in the direction of perennials: Slopes that were not wooded needed to be permanently grassed. So Mr. Besuden rightly thought. J. Russell Smith took the same idea one step further: to what he called "two-story agriculture,"[99] which would work anywhere, but which he saw as a necessity, both natural and human, for hillsides. The lower story would be grass; the upper story would consist of "tree crops" producing nuts and fruits either as forage for livestock or as food for humans.

The greater part of Smith's book is devoted to species and varieties of trees suitable for such use, and to examples (with photographic plates and explanatory captions) of two-story agriculture in various parts of the world. He was, he acknowledged, a visionary: "I see a million hills green with crop-yielding trees and a million neat farm homes snuggled in the hills."[100] But he was careful to show, by his many examples, that two-story agriculture *could* work because in some places it was working, and in some places it had been working for hundreds of years. He was promoting a proven possibility, not a theory.

Like Alan of Lille, Smith understood Nature's condemnation of prodigality, and he accepted her requirement that we should save what we have been given. The passion that informs his book comes from his realization that Nature's most precious gift was given only once. The Prodigal Son could squander his inheritance of money, repent, and be forgiven and restored to his father's favor. But Nature, "the equall mother" of all the creatures, has no bias in favor of humans. She gave us, along with all her other children, the great gift of life in a rich world, the wealth of which reduces finally to its thin layer of fertile soil. When we have squandered that, no matter how we may repent, it is simply and finally gone.

Smith was above all a practical man, and he stated one of Nature's laws in terms exquisitely practical: *"farming should fit the land."* The italics are his. He said that this amounted to *"a new point of view,"*[101] and again his italics indicate his sense of the urgency of what he was saying. He was undoubtedly right in assuming that this point of view was new to his countrymen, or to most of them, but of course it was also very old. It was implicit in Nature's complaint to Alan of Lille, it was explicit in Virgil's first Georgic, more than a thousand years before Alan, and it certainly informed Pope's instructions to consult "the Genius of the Place." The point is that, in using land, you cannot know what you are doing unless you know well the place where you are doing it.

. . .

In the long lineage that I am discussing, the fundamental assumption appears to be that Nature is the perfect—and, for our purposes, the exemplary—proprietor and user of any of her places. In our agricultural uses of her land, we are not required to imitate her work, because, as Chaucer's physician says, she is inimitable, and in order to live we are obliged to interpose our own interest between her and her property. We are required instead to do, not *as* she does, but *what* she does to protect the land and preserve its health. For our farming in our own interest, she sets the pattern and provides the measure. We learn to farm properly only under the instruction of Nature: "What are the main principles underlying Nature's agriculture? These can most easily be seen in operation in our woods and forests."[102]

Those are the key sentences of *An Agricultural Testament*, by Sir Albert Howard, published in 1940. Howard had read *Farmers of Forty Centuries*, and his testimony begins with the worry that had sent King to Asia:

> Since the Industrial Revolution the processes of growth have been speeded up to produce the food and raw materials needed by the population and the factory. Nothing effective has been done to replace the loss of fertility involved in this vast increase in crop and animal production. The consequences have been disastrous. Agriculture has become unbalanced: the land is in revolt: diseases of all kinds are on the increase: in many parts of the world Nature is removing the worn-out soil by means of erosion.[103]

From this perception of human error and failure he made the turn to Nature, that we can now recognize, across a span of many centuries, as characteristic and continuing in a lineage of some poets, some intelligent farmers and farm cultures, and some scientists. Howard's study of agriculture rests solidly upon his study of the nature of the places where farming was done. If the land in use was originally forested, as much of it was and is, then to learn to farm well, the farmer should study the forest.

Industrial agriculture, far from consulting the Genius of the Place or fitting the farming to the land or remembering at all the ecological mandate for local adaptation, has instead and from the beginning forced the land to submit to the capabilities and the limitations of the available technology. From the ruinous and ugly consequences, now visible and obvious everywhere the land can be farmed, one turns with relief to the great good sense, the mere sanity, the cheerful confidence of Howard's advice to farmers: Go to the woods and see what Nature would be doing on your land if you were not farming it, for you are asking her, not just for her "resources," but to accept you as her student and collaborator. And Howard summarizes the inevitable findings in the following remarkable paragraph:

> The main characteristic of Nature's farming can therefore be summed up in a few words. Mother earth never attempts to farm without livestock; she always raises mixed crops; great pains are taken to preserve the soil and to prevent erosion; the mixed vegetable and animal wastes are converted into humus; there is no waste; the processes of growth and the processes of decay balance one another; ample provision is made to maintain large reserves of fertility; the greatest care is taken to store the rainfall; both plants and animals are left to protect themselves against disease.[104]

Howard was familiar with the work of F. H. King and other scientific predecessors. *An Agricultural Testament*, he says, was founded upon his own "work and experience of forty years, mainly devoted to agricultural research in the West Indies, India, and Great Britain."[105] He had the humility and the good sense to learn from the peasant farmers his work was meant to serve. He came from a Shropshire farm family "of high reputation locally,"[106] and so I assume he had grown up hearing the talk of farmers. I don't know what, if anything, he had learned from the poets I have learned from, but of course I am delighted that he called Nature personally by name as Chaucer, Spenser, Milton, and Pope had done.

As Milton in *Comus* had enlarged the earlier characterizations of Nature by recognizing the economic significance of her religious and moral demands, making it explicit and practical, so the work of Sir Albert Howard completed their ecological significance. The agricultural economy, and the economies of farms, as determined by the economies and technologies of industrialism, would by logical necessity run to exhaustion. Agriculture in general, and any farm in particular, could survive only by recognizing, respecting, and incorporating the integrity of ecosystems. And this, as Howard showed by his work, could be understood practically and put into practice.

Spenser's problem of stability within change, moreover, we may think of as waiting upon Howard for its proper solution, which he gives in *The Soil and Health*, published in 1947:

> It needs a more refined perception to recognize throughout this stupendous wealth of varying shapes and forms the principle of stability. Yet this principle dominates. It dominates by means of an ever-recurring cycle, a cycle which, repeating itself silently and ceaselessly, ensures the continuation of living matter. This cycle is constituted of the successive and repeated processes of birth, growth, maturity, death, and decay. An eastern religion calls this cycle the Wheel of Life and no better name could be given to it. The revolutions of this Wheel never falter and are perfect. Death supersedes life and life rises again from what is dead and decayed.[107]

As Howard of course knew, religion would construe that last sentence analogically or symbolically, but he does not diminish it or make it less miraculous by treating it as fact. The Wheel of Life, or the fertility cycle, is not an instance of stability as opposed to change, as Spenser may have hoped, but rather an instance, much more interesting and wonderful, of stability dependent upon change. The Wheel of Life is a religious principle of which Howard saw the scientific validity, or it is a principle of Nature, eventually of science, which has long been "natural" to religion. This suggests that beyond the experimental or empirical proofs of science, there may be other ways of determining the truth of a solution, a very prominent one being versatility. Is the solution valid economically as well as ecologically? Does it serve the interest both of the land and of the land's people? The Wheel of Life certainly has that double validity. But we can go on: Does it fit both the farm and the local ecosystem? Does it satisfy the needs of both biology and religion? Is it imaginatively as well as factually true? Can it reconcile utility and beauty? Is it compatible with the practice of the virtues? As a solution to the problem of change and stability, the Wheel of Life answers affirmatively every one of those questions. It is complexly, and joyously, true.

Such a solution could not have originated, and cannot be accommodated, under the rule of industrial or technological progress, which does not cycle, which recycles only under compulsion, and makes no returns. Waste is one of its definitive products, and waste is profitable so long as you are not liable for the cost or replacement of what you have wasted.

Waste of the gifts of Nature from the beginning of industrialism has subsidized our system of corporate profits and "economic growth." Howard, judging by the unforgiving standard of natural health, described this "economy" unconditionally: "The using up of fertility is a transfer of past capital and of future possibilities to enrich a dishonest present: it is banditry pure and simple."[108]

The falsehood of the industrial economy has been disguised for generations by the departmentalization and over-specialization of the essential academic and intellectual disciplines. In the absence of any common or unifying standard of judgment, the professionals of the schools have been free to measure their work by professional standards exclusively, submitting only to the "peer review" of fellow professionals. As in part a professional himself, Howard understood the ethical blindness of this system. Against it he raised the standard of the integrity of the Wheel of Life, which is comprehensive and universal, granting no exemptions.

Whether because of his "instinctive awareness of the importance of natural principle"[109] or because of respect for his own intelligence or because of an evident affection for Nature's living world and the life of farming, Howard kept the way always open between his necessarily specialized work as a scientist and his responsibility to the Wheel of Life. His personal integrity was to honor the integrity of what he called the "one great subject": "the whole problem of health in soil, plant, animal, and man."[110] The practical effect of this upon his work was his insistence upon thinking of everything in relation to its context. In his "revolt against 'fragmentation' of knowledge," his investigation of a crop would include its "whole existence": "the plant itself in relation to the soil in which it grows, to the conditions of village agriculture under which it is cultivated, and with reference to the economic uses of the product."[111] As a researcher and teacher, he would not offer an innovation to his farmer clients that they could not afford, or that they lacked the traction power to use.

There clearly is no break or barrier between Howard's principles and his practice and the "land ethic" of his contemporary, Aldo Leopold, who wrote:

Health is the capacity of the land for self-renewal. Conservation is our effort to understand and preserve this capacity.[112]

And:

A thing is right when it tends to preserve the integrity, stability, and beauty of the biotic community. It is wrong when it tends otherwise.[113]

Moreover, there is no discontinuity between the ethics of Howard and Leopold and Nature's principle, given to Alan of Lille, that her good, the good of the natural world, depends upon human goodness, which is to say the human practice of the human virtues. And here I will say again that the needs of the land and the needs of the people tend always to be the same. There is always the convergence of what Nature requires for the survival of the land with what economic demand or economic adversity requires for the survival of the farmer.

From Alan's *Plaint of Nature*, and surely from the conversation of farmers and other country people before and after, it is possible to trace a living tradition of deference, respect and responsibility to Nature and her laws, carried forward by many voices speaking in agreement and in mutual help and amplification. They speak in fact with more agreement and continuity than I expected when I began this essay. And they speak, as also I now see, without so much as a glance toward moral relativism.

For many years I have known that the books by King, Smith, Howard, and Leopold, supported by other intellectually respectable books that I have not mentioned, constitute a coherent, sound, and proven argument against industrial agriculture and for an agricultural ecology and economy that, had it prevailed, would have preserved both the economic landscapes and their human communities. It is significant that all of those books, and others allied with them, were in print by the middle of the last century. Together, they might have provided a basis for the reformation of agriculture according to principles congenial to it. If that had happened, an immeasurable, and so far an illimitable, damage to the land and the people could have been prevented.

The opposite happened. All specifically agricultural and ecological standards were replaced by the specifically industrial standards of productivity, mechanical efficiency, and profitability (to agri-industrial and other corporations). Meanwhile, the criticisms and the recommendations of King, Smith, Howard, Leopold, et al., have never been addressed or answered, let alone disproved.

That they happen to have been right, by any appropriate standard, simply has not mattered to the academic and official forces of agriculture. The writings of the agrarian scientists, the validity of their science notwithstanding, have been easily ignored and overridden by wealth and power. The perfection of the industrial orthodoxy becomes clear when we remember that King, Smith, and Howard traveled the world to search out and study examples of sustainable agriculture, whereas agri-industrial scientists have traveled the world as evangelists for an agriculture unsustainable by every measure.

The truth of agrarian scientists, and their long cultural tradition, casts nevertheless a bright and exposing light upon the silliness and superficiality of the industrial economy, the industrial politicians and economists, and the industrial conservationists. Industrial politicians and economists ignore everything that can be ignored, mainly the whole outdoors. Industrial conservationists ignore everything but wilderness preservation ("Give us the 'wild' land; do as you please with the rest") and the most sensational and fashionable "environmental disasters."

In opposition to industrial and all other sorts and ways of subhuman consumption of the living world, the tradition of cooperation with Nature has persisted for many centuries, through many changes, sustained by right principles, the proofs of experience and eventually of science, and good sense. Its diminishment in our age has been tragic. If ever it should be lost entirely, that would be a greater "environmental disaster" than global warming. It is reassuring therefore to know that it has lasted until now, in the practice of some farmers, and in the work of some scientists. I now have in mind particularly the scientists of The Land Institute, which to me has been a source of instruction and hope for nearly half my life, and which certainly belongs in, and is in good part explained by, the cultural lineage I have been tracking.

The Land Institute was started forty years ago. It is amusing, amazing, and most surely confirmative of my argument, that when Wes Jackson laid out in his mind the order of thought that formed The Land Institute, he had never heard of Sir Albert Howard. The confirming gist of this is that Wes's ignorance of the writings of Sir Albert Howard at that time did not matter. What matters, and matters incalculably, is that Wes's formative thought developed exactly according to the pattern followed by the thinking of King, Smith, and Howard: perception of the waste of fertility and of soil, recognition of the failure of the current standards, and the turn to Nature for a better standard.

Wes had read *Tree Crops*, which had given him the fundamental principle and pattern, which he must more and more consciously have needed. He had in himself the alertness and the sense to look about and see where he was. And like King and Howard he had grown up farming—in, as I know, an agrarian family of extraordinary intelligence and attentiveness. He grew up loving to farm. He knew, and probably long before he knew he knew, the essential truth spoken by Henry Besuden: that soil conservation "involves the heart of the man managing the land. If he loves his soil he will save it." The entire culture of husbandry is implicit in that last sentence. The practical result was, again exactly, Albert Howard's comparison of human farming to Nature's farming—or, as Wes has phrased it in many a talk, a comparison of "human cleverness" to "Nature's wisdom." Whereas Howard had looked to the woods for this, Wes, a Kansan, looked to the native prairie, a possibility that Howard himself had foreseen and approved. If you want to know what is wrong with a Kansas wheat field, study the prairie. And then, taking his own advice, Wes conceived the long-term and ongoing project of The Land Institute: to replace the monocultures of annual grains with polycultures of grain-bearing perennials, which would have to be developed by a long endeavor of plant-breeding.

Among those who are interested, this project is well known. I want to say only two things about it: First, it is radical, for it goes to the roots of the problem and to the roots of the plants. Second, there is nothing sensational about it. To Wes, having thought so far, it was obviously the next thing to be done. To any agricultural scientist whose mind had been formed as Wes's had been formed—and Wes, unique as he is, could not have been *that* unique—it ought to have been obvious. If one of only two possibilities has failed, the alternative is not far to seek. That the need for an agriculture of perennials was obvious to nobody but Wes, and that it is still by principle unobvious to many agricultural scientists, suggests that the purpose of higher education has been to ignore or obscure the obvious.

The work of The Land Institute is as dedicated to the best interests of the land and the people as if it, rather than the present universities, had sprung from the land-grant legislation. And so the science of The Land Institute is significantly different from the industrial sciences of product development and product addiction—also from the "pure" science that seeks, with the aid of extremely costly and violent technology, the ultimate truth of the universe.

I am talking now of a science subordinate and limited, dedicated to the service of things greater than itself, as every science and art ought to be. There are some things it won't do, some dangers it won't risk. It will not, I think, commit "creative destructions," for the sake of some future good or higher truth. It is a science founded upon the traditional respect for Nature, the natural world, the farmland, and those farmers whose use of the land enacts this respect.

This old respect, really one of the highest forms of human self-respect, provides an indispensable basis, unifying and congenial, for work of all kinds. It might unify a university. In evidence, I offer the friendship that for nearly forty years has kept Wes Jackson and me talking with each other. According to the departmentalism of thought and the other fragmentations that beset us, a useful friendship or a conversation inexhaustibly interesting ought to be impossible between a scientist and a poet. That such a conversation is possible is in fact one of its most interesting subjects. Different as we necessarily are, we have much in common: an interest in the natural world, an interest in farming, an inherited agrarianism, an unresting concern about the problems of farming, of land use in general, and of rural life. Making a common interest of these subjects depends of course on speaking common English, which we can do. But that is not all.

I have heard Wes say many times that "the boundaries of causation always exceed the boundaries of consideration." The more I have thought about that statement, the more interesting it has become. The key word is "always." Mystery, the unknown, our ignorance, always will be with us, to be dealt with. The farther we extend the radius of knowledge, the larger becomes the circumference of mystery. There is, in other words, a boundary that may move somewhat, but can never be removed, between what we know and what we don't, between our human minds and the mind of Nature or the mind of God. To ignore or defy that division, wishing to be as gods, believing that the human mind is so capacious as to contain the whole universe and its whole truth, is characteristic of a kind of science that is at once romantic and industrial, ever in search of new worlds to conquer. From its work, I fear, we can expect only a continuing spillover of violence, to the world and to ourselves.

But a scientist who knows that the boundary exists and accepts, even welcomes, its existence, who knows that the boundary has a human side and elects to stay on it, is a scientist of a kind opposed to the would-be masters of the universe. A poet, too, can choose the human side of that boundary. Any artist, any scientist can so choose. Having so chosen, they can speak to one another congenially, in good faith and friendship. When we know securely the smallness of our minds relative to the immensity of our ignorance, then a certain poise and grace may become possible for us, and we can think responsibly of the circumstances in which we work, of the issues of limits and of the proprieties of scale. If we can talk of limits and of scale, we can slack off our obsession with quantities and immensities and take up the study of form: of the forms of Nature's work, of the forms by which our work might be adapted to hers. We may then become capable of the hope, that Wes and I caught years ago from our friend John Todd, for "Elegant solutions predicated upon the uniqueness of place."[114]

And now the long journey of my essay is ended. I have written it in order to encounter once again, and more coherently than before, the writings and the thoughts among which my own writings have formed themselves. The newest to me of the predecessors I have discussed is the oldest: Alan of Lille's *Plaint of Nature*. My reading and re-reading of that book over the last four or five years helped me to see the thread that connects the others: the books and the voices—to borrow Alan's happiest metaphor—that through many years have been in conversation in "the little town of my mind."[115]

Notes

1. C. S. Lewis, *Studies in Words*, second edition, Cambridge University Press, 1975, p. 42.
2. Alan of Lille, *Plaint of Nature*, translation and commentary by James J. Sheridan, Pontifical Institute of Medieval Studies, 1980, p. 33.
3. Ibid., p. 67.
4. Ibid., pp. 124–25.
5. Ibid., p. 75.
6. Ibid., p. 86.
7. Ibid., p. 94.
8. Ibid., p. 99.
9. Ibid., p. 104.
10. Ibid., p. 108.
11. C. S. Lewis, *The Allegory of Love*, Oxford University Press, 1973, p. 108.
12. Alan of Lille, *Plaint of Nature*, p. 128.
13. Ibid., p. 59.
14. Ibid., p. 46.
15. Thomas Carlyle, *Past and Present*, Everyman's Library, 1947, p. 46.
16. Thomas Merton, *The Collected Poems*, New Directions, 1977, pp. 363 and 370.

17. Geoffrey Chaucer, *The Poetical Works of Chaucer*, Cambridge Edition, F. N. Robinson, editor, Houghton Mifflin, 1933, p. 367, line 316. All further Chaucer citations are to this edition.
18. Chaucer, *The Parliament of Fowls*, p. 365, lines 176, 177.
19. Chaucer, *The Knight's Tale*, p. 54, line 2931.
20. Theodora Stanwell-Fletcher, *Driftwood Valley*, introduction by Wendell Berry, Penguin Books, 1989, p. x.
21. Chaucer, *The Nun's Priest's Tale*, p. 238, line 2828.
22. Ibid., line 2834.
23. Chaucer, *The Parliament of Fowls*, p. 369, line 499.
24. Ibid., p. 370, lines 595, 599.
25. Ibid., p. 367, line 318.
26. Ibid., p. 366, line 301.
27. Ibid., line 305.
28. Robert Herrick, "Corinna's Going A-Maying," lines 29–35.
29. Chaucer, *The Parliament of Fowls*, p. 367, line 319.
30. Ibid., lines 379–81.
31. Chaucer, *The Physician's Tale*, p. 175, line 20.
32. Ibid., line 12.
33. Ibid., line 26.
34. Ibid., lines 13, 18.
35. *Hamlet*, III, ii, 24.
36. Edmund Spenser, *Spenser's Faerie Queene*, J. C. Smith, editor, Clarendon Press, 1909, Book II, Canto VI, stanza xxxv, lines 4–6.
37. Ibid., Canto VII, stanza iv, lines 6–7.
38. Ibid., Book VII, Canto VII, stanzas v, vi, vii, and lines 1–4 of stanza xiii.
39. Ibid., stanza xiv, lines 1, 4–9.
40. Alan of Lille, *Plaint of Nature*, p. 118.
41. Spenser, *The Faerie Queene*, Book VII, Canto VII, stanza iii.
42. Lewis, *The Allegory of Love*, p. 356.
43. Spenser, *The Faerie Queene*, Book VII, Canto VII, stanza xviii, lines 1–8.
44. Alan of Lille, *Plaint of Nature*, p. 145.
45. Spenser, *The Faerie Queene*, Book VII, Canto VII, stanza lix, line 9.
46. Ibid., Canto VIII, stanza ii, lines 2–4.
47. Lewis, *The Allegory of Love*, p. 160, footnote.
48. William Langland, *The Vision of Piers Plowman, A Critical Edition of the B-Text*, edited by A. V. C. Schmidt, J. M. Dent and Sons, 1978, passus XI, lines 320–66, and passus XII, lines 218–28.
49. John Milton, *Comus*, stage direction, after line 658.
50. Ibid., lines 786–87.
51. Ibid., lines 710–14, 720–24.
52. Ibid., line 246.
53. Ibid., lines 765–73.

54. Pope, "Epistle to Burlington," lines 109, 108.

55. Ibid., line 43.

56. Ibid., lines 50, 57.

57. Ibid., line 167.

58. Ibid., lines 173–76.

59. Ibid., lines 179–80.

60. William Wordsworth, "Lines Composed a Few Miles Above Tintern Abbey," lines 25–26, 39–40, 52–53.

61. Ibid., lines 47–49.

62. Ibid., lines 94–97.

63. Ibid., lines 108–11.

64. Ibid., lines 122–25.

65. Ibid., line 131.

66. Matthew 5:45.

67. Wordsworth, "Tintern Abbey," line 152.

68. Ibid., "Tintern Abbey," lines 120–22.

69. Ibid., lines 46–48.

70. Ibid., lines 189, 194–98.

71. Ibid., line 211.

72. Ibid., lines 249–50.

73. Ibid., lines 252–55.

74. Ibid., line 433.

75. Ibid., lines 442–47.

76. Ibid., line 475.

77. Hayden Carruth, "Marshall Washer," in *Collected Shorter Poems, 1946–1991*, Copper Canyon Press, 1992, p. 171.

78. Ibid., p. 175.

79. Lester Flatt and Earl Scruggs, "The Homestead on the Farm," in *Songs of the Famous Carter Family, Featuring Mother Maybelle Carter and the Foggy Mountain Boys*, CD, Columbia Records, n.d.

80. Ezra Pound, *The Cantos of Ezra Pound*, Faber & Faber, 1964, Canto LI, p. 261.

81. Ibid., Canto XCIX, p. 734.

82. Ibid., Canto LIII, p. 278.

83. Ibid., Canto LXXXI, p. 556.

84. Gary Snyder, "Water Music II," *No Nature*, Pantheon, 1992, p. 196.

85. Jacques Maritain, *Art and Scholasticism with Other Essays*, translated by J. F. Scanlan, Charles Scribner's Sons, 1947, p. 52.

86. G. C. Coulton, *Medieval Panorama*, Meridian Books, 1955, pp. 103–4.

87. Ibid., p. 240.

88. *Beef Producer*, Oct. 2015, p. 7.

89. Mr. Besuden's story and his several remarks come from my essay "A Talent for Necessity," *The Gift of Good Land*, North Point Press, 1981, pp. 227–37.

90. F. H. King, *Farmers of Forty Centuries*, Rodale Press, 1911 (reprinted, n.d.) p. 1.
91. Ibid.
92. Ibid.
93. Ibid., p. 3.
94. Ibid., p. 13.
95. Ibid., p. 234.
96. J. Russell Smith, *Tree Crops*, Harcourt, Brace and Company, 1929, p. 4.
97. Ibid., p. 3.
98. Ibid., p. 11.
99. Ibid., p. 16.
100. Ibid., p. 259.
101. Ibid., p. 260.
102. Sir Albert Howard, *An Agricultural Testament*, Oxford University Press, 1940, p. 1.
103. Ibid., p. ix.
104. Ibid., p. 4.
105. Ibid., p. ix.
106. Louise E. Howard, *Sir Albert Howard in India*, The Rodale Press, 1954, p. 221.
107. Sir Albert Howard, *The Soil and Health*, Schocken Books, [1947] 1972, p. 18.
108. Ibid., p. 63.
109. L. E. Howard, *Sir Albert Howard in India*, p. 20.
110. Howard, *The Soil and Health*, p. 11.
111. L. E. Howard, *Sir Albert Howard in India*, p. 42.
112. Aldo Leopold, *A Sand County Almanac*, Oxford University Press, 1966, p. 236.
113. Ibid., p. 240.
114. John Todd, "Tomorrow Is Our Permanent Address," in *The Book of the New Alchemists*, edited by Nancy Jack Todd, E. P. Dutton, 1977, p. 116.
115. Alan of Lille, *Plaint*, p. 193.

～

The Order of Loving Care

By now many of Andy Catlett's mentors and old schoolmates among the writers, in Kentucky and elsewhere, have left the visible world to take their places only in the convocation of his mind. With that company of friends, while it lasted, he carried on a many-branched conversation that he had grown into and so had grown up in his trade.

But his growth had been slow, and it had taken a long time. He was not fully grown up as a writer until he was fully grown as a man. For that he had to accept and own the influence of his grandfather Catlett and of his father, of his father's deliberate teaching, of the example of Elton Penn, of his conversations with Elton that had helped him to understand his grandfather and his father. These were the articulate ones, who spoke, as Andy would realize, not only for themselves, but also for those among their neighbors who put their agrarianism mostly into practice rather than words.

That influence, complex and profound as it was, lay in his mind only half awake and nearly speechless until he had come home, settled with his family on the Harford place, and knew that he would stay. And then at last he began consciously to inherit from that familial and local lineage the tradition, the agrarianism, ancient as he eventually would know it to be, that was theirs and now was his—his own, not because he had chosen it, but because it apparently had chosen him.

Once he was at home and committed, married to his marriage to Flora, their marriage then married to what had become its place, then a sort of providence, or so it seemed, began to work in his behalf.

In the years following his homecoming, Andy and Henry, his brother, began an alliance and collaboration founded of course upon liking and pleasure but also, more and more consciously, upon their father's passion for land conservation, for grass and grazing, and his agrarian politics. Their conversation on these subjects lasted until Henry's death in 2016. But for some years still after the middle 1960s these subjects, so far as Andy knew, were only local. They had not entered at all into any of his schooling. Agrarianism had no standing or presence at his alma mater, the state's land-grant university. Nor was it to be found, so far as Andy could discover, in the agricultural bureaucracy. It had been there once, as he knew from his reading, but it was there no more. In his own experience, the ways, values, subjects, passions, and politics of agrarian culture belonged only to his conversations with his father, his brother, and Elton Penn.

And then in 1970, Andy met Gene Logsdon, who was living in Philadelphia, working improbably for *Farm Journal*, but who belonged to his family's land in Wyandot County, Ohio, where from his childhood he had learned farming and the love of farming, most speakingly from his mother, and where in a few years he and Carol, his wife, would buy a small acreage and farm it almost perfectly as long as he lived. It was as if Gene and Andy had met before. The two of them sat down and talked. Their talk immediately had the feel and tone of a conversation far older than themselves, a language of matters long ago settled. They knew much in common, much they never had to explain. They talked on for forty-six years, until Gene died, also in 2016, at the end of May, about five months before Henry's death in late October. They talked and they laughed, both of them out of key with their time and glad to be, enjoying their own contrariness and each other's. When one of them said about exactly what the other thought he would say, they laughed.

It was a good while then before Andy met Maury Telleen. Andy had been at home ten years by then. He had begun an argument against industrial agriculture. He had known for some time that he needed to learn about Amish farming. A friend sent him a note: "Maurice Telleen, editor of the *Draft Horse Journal*, maybe could help." And he gave Andy the address. Maury, as Andy would learn, had been raised in a family devoted to farming in central Iowa. His father had been a dairyman who bred and showed Brown Swiss cattle. At the time Andy met him, Maury and Jeannine, his wife, were living and publishing the *Journal* in the town of Waverly, north of Waterloo. In response to a letter from Andy, Maury wrote him to come to Waverly. He could stay at Maury's house. Maury would help. That was in 1974. Elton Penn died that year in late March. In April, mourning the loss of his friend and teacher of thirty years, Andy met Maury Telleen, who would be his friend, sometimes his publisher, always his ally, for thirty-seven years.

The old conversation, again, seemed merely to resume from no beginning that either of them knew, and they were in it together until Maury died in 2011. Maury had an interesting mind, intelligent, principled, practical, aware and alert, quick-witted, often funny. He was a great companion. By way of Maury, as he only could have done by way of Maury, Andy met a sizeable number of good farmers in good Amish communities and a number of non-Amish holdouts in the Midwest. He met, for one, Arnold Hockett in northwest Iowa who, when tractors were coming to replace the draft horses, had sometimes driven after a truck hauling a good team to slaughter, bought them at something above the going price per pound, brought them home, and put them back to work and into his kind care.

For his meeting in 1980 with Wes Jackson, Andy had been prepared directly, as if purposefully, by his father's argument in favor of grass. "The only crop our people can grow to advantage year after year

forever," Wheeler would say to his boys and to anybody who would listen. What he had in mind was the long-established symbiosis of blue-
grass and white clover that he had loved from his childhood. *Grass!* He
could not speak the word without an emphasis denoting the actuality
that it named and all that it had meant to him. The advantage of grass
to the farmers of his home country was that it was perennial. It did not
have to be planted every year. It thatched over the ground and protected
it from erosion. It preserved and increased fertility. It conserved the
rain and resisted drouth. It fed grazing animals who for eight or nine
months of the year harvested it for themselves. It admitted Nature and
her gifts freely into the service of the farmer. Moreover, it looked right.
A well-kept pasture was a consolation to look at. It was beautiful.

And so when Wes Jackson started talking about the importance to
agriculture of perennial plants, Andy was ready to listen and to know
what he meant. The work of The Land Institute, which Wes had helped
to start in Kansas, was the development of perennial grain crops as
probably the only answer to soil erosion and other problems that had
always belonged to the agriculture of annual crops. Wes was a scientist,
a geneticist, and plant breeder who read the Bible and Dante. Andy,
by his own training and reading, was at best a non-scientist ready to
listen. In some ways perhaps he was Wes's opposite. But never opposed.
Whereas Andy had been concerned about problems *in* agriculture,
Wes said that he and his Land Institute colleagues were addressing the
problem *of* agriculture. The problem of agriculture from the beginning
had been the association of annual planting with soil erosion, the waste
of soil and fertility. But Wes himself was addressing that problem from
the vantage point of his family's land-sense that had shaped their highly
diversified truck farm in a state under the rule of industrial wheat fields.
If it was Wes's science that at first attracted Andy's attention, it was
their mutual agrarianism that made them friends. And though he could
approach it only by way of agrarianism, his encounter with Wes's science and his proofs was a big step in Andy's education. He knew from
his own observation that Nature regarded the annual plants as an emergency measure, as wound dressing. Over time, in both woodland and

grassland, she clearly preferred perennials, perennial roots and perennial leaves, to take hold of the soil and cover it, granting to the land itself a perennial life. This clearly underwrote the needs for pastures and for crop rotation that Andy already understood, but his new acquaintance with the science of The Land Institute carried his understanding to a more exacting clarity and to a standard, Nature's standard, more requiring than he had thought.

Though their schooling had made them different, both Andy and Wes had grown up in farming, which both of them respected and loved. They could talk to each other because they knew many of the same things, valued many of the same things, and spoke the same language. When they met it was, again, not as though they started talking, but as though they continued. The same conversation that had included Andy, his teachers, and his brother at home, and then Gene Logsdon in Ohio, and then Maury Telleen in Iowa, now included Wes Jackson in Kansas. Of all his friends, Andy has talked most with Wes, by now for hundreds of hours, face to face or on the telephone. Their conversations have been purposeful, serious, helpful to their work, but reverting almost always to something funny, a new joke or a remembered story. And they have happily let duty wait, or happily run up their phone bills, while they laughed.

And then in 1983, when Andy spoke in a large, nearly empty auditorium at Oberlin College in Ohio, and his speech included the Amish and what he had so far learned from them, a young Amish couple were sitting neatly side by side in the front row. After Andy had finished talking, the Amish couple started to leave with the driver they had hired to bring them, and then they changed their minds and came back. They were David and Elsie Kline, who lived in Holmes County, near Wooster, about fifty miles south. David wanted to talk with Andy, and they did talk for a long time, standing in a hallway while students passed around them. And as it had been in Andy's meetings with Gene and Maury and Wes, so it was with David. The two of them seemed merely to recognize each other as members of a conversation long-established, and they continued it that day until David *had* to get back to the work that was waiting for him at home.

David was a farmer. By heredity, upbringing, and passionate choice, he was a farmer. He would become a minister and then a bishop of his church, but after the way of his people he would remain a farmer. Much more than he had known before they met, Andy needed David's friendship and conversation. Both of them were hereditary farmers, both the products of farm communities, but the communities they belonged to were in some ways fundamentally, even radically, different. Port William—or Old Port William, Port William past and gone, as Andy is now obliged to think of it—was a happenstance, an accidental community, gathered on the hill above its river by the individual choices or fates of its members, but it was nonetheless a conscious community, bound together by common knowledge of its place and membership, and by a shared awareness of its life and continuance in time, until it was distracted and disintegrated by its acceptance of the allure of industrial progress and the impositions of domestic colonization. David's community, co-extensive more or less with his church, but within a much larger community of similar and associated churches, was a community both conscious and conscientious, made coherent by its members' willing assent to the Christian Gospel, most significantly the Gospel's principles of neighborly love and of nonviolence.

Port William, virtually from the beginning, had been sectioned by its churches, the Methodist with its steeple prominently in the center of town and the Baptist on the southern outskirt. A third section was composed, in a manner of speaking, of those who did not attend either church. Most of the farmers, particularly the smaller ones, lived by a principled, neighborly sharing of work and fate that was truly Christian in practice and in practical results but was never called "Christian," and Andy never heard it noticed in a sermon. Such Christianity as Port William had never was able to see the practical difference between the teachings of Jesus and the aggressively secularizing economy that opposed them and deprived them of earthly standing and practical effect.

David's community, conscientiously self-aware as it was and had often needed to be, had responded to the blandishments of the industrial economy and industrial progress with a single question: "What will this do to our community?" This question came from the resolve, in all the souls consenting to their membership, never to allow their children or their neighbors to be replaced by machines. As David's friend, Andy was able to observe fairly closely the working and the effect of this resolve in the large Amish population of Holmes County. He saw the surpassing elegance of the Amish people's one simple question to the modern world. And he saw an equally admirable sophistication in the complexity of their answer—for of course the answer and the answers had necessarily to come from themselves.

And so, gradually, Andy came to know that the language most intimately his own could be spoken, understood, and answered in Ohio, Iowa, and Kansas. And from 1983, when he met David Kline, until sometime late in the 1990s, these friends, Gene and Maury and Wes and David, were the four allies he knew he had away from home. That these friendships came to Andy at the time they did seems to him to bespeak the presence in this world of a generosity that all the sciences together cannot reach and had better be quiet about. Andy knows that he is not the only person who had had this thought. He has talked to a good many people, friends and others, who have confirmed his experience of the arrival in one's life of friends and books that were most needed *when* they were most needed.

Equally remarkable to Andy were the ways that these particular friends answered to his particular needs. He needed Gene Logsdon's understanding and experience of the mentality of industrial agriculture, as opposed to, and by, his inborn and inherited agrarianism. He needed Maury Telleen's own heritage of agrarianism, his livestockman's point of view, and his conviction that teams of draft horses and mules still had and would continue to have a viable place in farming, and moreover in farming of the best kind. And somewhat desperately in fact, Andy needed Wes Jackson's science with its orientation both to agrarianism and to ecology, just as he needed Wes's willingness to teach and correct him. He needed, as Gene and Maury and Wes did also, the friendship of David Kline and David's articulate sense of the achievement of his people in Holmes County within the ecological, agricultural, economic, and social catastrophe of industrial agriculture.

By their recognition of the excellence of the farms of David and his people, the four non-Amish members of this friendship were forever set apart from the hermetic orthodoxy of "agribusiness" in the schools and the government. They knew that every axiom and principle of that orthodoxy was overturned in Holmes County and in the best Amish farming everywhere. They knew upon proof that a farmer working a team of horses on a small farm, in a community of other such farmers, could not only survive but prosper, even in the adversity of the national "farm economy" as it had nearly always been. This clarified and confirmed their knowledge, steadied their commitment, and gave them hope. It amused them to think that any solid-minded scientist of a land-grant college of agriculture who gave Holmes County a straight look would go stone blind and fall to the earth like St. Paul on the road to Damascus.

Of all he has seen of the United States, and he has seen a good bit, Andy knows of two counties that seem to him to offer visions of Heaven. One of those is Woodford County, Kentucky, where the backroads, sometimes for miles on end, pass through large pastures with board fences and ancient oaks and ashes standing about, darkening the green grass with their shade. The pastures, grazed by beautiful horses, are perfectly maintained, so that the turf lies like a caress upon every swell and swale. The landscape is in fact a great work of art, and it has the same improbable and fragile life as the great works of art in the great museums, for its sustenance is the fabulous wealth of the horse racing industry, wealth unimaginably disproportionate to the world's actual economy of food, clothing, and shelter. As much as Andy loves looking at those pastures with their bands of grazing horses, and he never has got his fill of looking at them, he knows that they are anomalous, both in the poor state of Kentucky, where the land and the people suffer together, and in the long, hard history of human survival.

The other vision, virtually opposite to that one, is of Holmes County, Ohio, where David Kline's people have lived and farmed for generations. The topography there is much like that of Andy's home countryside in Kentucky. It is a landscape rolling to sloping, much divided by streams, with some level bottomland. The economy is still predominantly both agricultural and agrarian, and it is directed at every point to the practical needs of human life. The landscape is ruled by the wish that the community members together might prosper—as opposed to the wish long on the loose, and forever frustrated, among non-Amish farmers that they, individually and separately, might become rich.

The farms of Holmes County are small, from perhaps eighty to perhaps a hundred and twenty acres. The fields proportionately are small, given mainly, in rotation, to pasture, hay crops, small grains, and corn. Wes Jackson speaks of "the eyes-to-acres ration," or the balance between Nature's landscape and the attention paid to it by its human inhabitants and users. In Holmes County the eyes-to-acres ratio is manifestly correct. The attention paid would justly be described as "loving." The fields are kept and cherished by people obviously given to the noticing of details, the "minute particulars," to use William Blake's term, both of places and of work. The field work is done on foot and by hand or with teams of horses, and this imposes, you might say, a natural speed limit. The right scale of the work and the doing of it without hurry *free* the resident minds and eyes to pay attention. And the attention paid need not be limited to the economic details. The lives and the workdays of David and his family are continually lightened and enlivened by the notice they give to the natural creatures who complete the life of the country: the stages of the vegetation in brushy fencerows, along the roadsides, and in the woods; the comings and goings of the birds and animals and insects; the events of the sky and the weather.

This attentiveness, this decent domestic pride, becomes more concentrated and more discriminating when it comes to the heart and center of every farm: the house, the barn, the outbuildings, the farmyard, the house yard. Here the economic life of the place becomes more diverse, more cunningly structured, and more beautiful. Here to the larger life of the place are added poultry flocks, maybe some hogs, vegetable gardens, flower beds, bird houses and bird feeders. Often there are bee hives. At David and Elsie's place, there is a large picnic table and a number of chairs for sitting and resting, especially in the cool of the evenings after work. Tellingly, the well of good water just outside the back door is equipped with a hand pump and a drinking cup. David's father made it a rule never to harness a team after supper, which Andy has always thought highly civilized. Why have a beautiful farm if you have no time and place to sit down to look at it and enjoy it?

Now that his own home country has been invaded by factory-fields of corn and soy beans, Andy has become too well acquainted with fields and farms that are painful to look at, for they have only the one purpose of one crop grown only for money. The only thing above the ground is the crop. All else—every tree, every building, every fence—has been wiped away by a bulldozer. This way of farming imposes upon the land a rigid geometry dictated by the needs of machines, ignoring the country's natural forms and features, ignoring its wounds.

And so, in a kind of self-defense, Andy recovers and cherishes his memories of a hillside field on the farm of Monroe Miller, another of his Holmes County Amish friends. Monroe, who has now joined the convocation of ghosts in Andy's mind, was a farmer, a minister, and a respected breeder of Percheron horses. His farm included some very good bottomland along a creek, but a sizeable part of it was fairly steep hillside. Because he needed corn for his horses and his dairy cows, Monroe was constrained to use every acre to greatest advantage. This meant that he had to crop the hillside.

Andy first visited Monroe's farm with Maury Telleen early one fall maybe forty years ago. They arrived after dark, having stopped for supper on the way. When the family gathered before bedtime, Monroe rather pointedly handed Andy the open Bible, laid his finger at the head of a chapter, and asked Andy to read it. Andy would wonder why Monroe had selected him, and he would never know for sure. Perhaps Monroe had wondered if he would read with proper reverence and understanding. If that was the reason, Andy must have read well enough, for he and Monroe became friends. Andy still owns, and is still using, a pair of Percheron geldings that he bought from Monroe as weanlings twenty-one years ago.

The next morning, after Monroe had milked by lantern light and they had eaten breakfast in the big kitchen with his family, he led Maury and Andy up onto the hillside beyond the barn. He wanted them to see it, as they understood, because he was proud of it. He had reason to be. The hillside had been plowed and planted in corn in contoured strips sixteen rows wide. Between the plowed strips were grassed strips, equally wide, that were mowed for hay. Not long before, the corn had been cut and bundled with a binder. And then, to clear the ground for a cover crop and the rotation back to grass, the bundles had been carried off the plowlands and shocked on the grass, eight rows up the hill and eight rows down. Monroe, who had given careful thought to the raising of children, said that shocking the corn, carrying the bundles up and down the slope, greatly improved the behavior of teenage boys.

The morning was somewhat overcast, giving precision to the light, in which they could see the winter crop of wheat sprigging up in the drillmarks. That hillside, as Andy knew well, was a difficult and demanding place for such farming. Like any slope, it increased the burden of gravity for the humans and the horses who worked there. By the same unalterable fact, it was extraordinarily vulnerable to erosion. But in the discriminating light of that morning, they saw no marks of erosion. The field, as Monroe was using and caring for it, was a kind of masterpiece. It was very beautiful. Neither Andy nor Maury would forget it as it looked that morning.

In response to their obvious appreciation of it and their questions, Monroe told them its story. In the history of his family's use of it there had been times, he said, when heavy rains had washed soil from the slope down onto the road. When Monroe came into ownership, he felt required to do something to correct this problem. He asked the Soil Conservation Service for help.

The local office of that agency sent out surveyors with transit, marking pole, and stakes, and they laid out the first of the contour strips. After only one day, Monroe no longer needed their help, for he perfectly understood the principles of their work. He attached a rear-view mirror to an ordinary carpenter's level. This allowed him to see the bead in the window of the level while he sighted along the top of it. Using this, he and one of his brothers completed the work. Making the corn rows approximately horizontal, as Thomas Jefferson had realized in the Virginia mountains long before, was a check against erosion. So was the alternation of the plowed strips with the strips of equal width that were grass-covered. Using a "two-way plow" that turned every furrow in the same direction, Monroe made a practice of turning all the furrows uphill. Reversing the principle of the shingled roof, this made every furrow a water-catcher. This too was a check against erosion. A further check against erosion was the use of horses for traction power. Hooves do not compact the soil as much as wheels. Under the footsteps of his horses, the soil structure remained porous and thus capable of absorbing water. The surface of the ground was more a sponge than a roof.

Andy remembers walking up that hillside alone on another fall day in a later year. What he was noticing that day, and making sure of, was that the dead-furrows on the lower sides of the strips were still as open, as free of silt, as they had been when the plowing was finished in the spring. And he remembers his happiness at what he felt then that he securely knew. He thought he had as good a proof as he was likely to get of the significance of Wes Jackson's eyes-to-acres ratio. When that ratio was right, it implied the preceding rightness of scale, and it enabled the formal completeness in which the parts interdepended and reinforced one another, and every part received enough attention. The result, there on Monroe's vulnerable, even somewhat improbable, hillside plowlands was a demonstration of the effective order of loving care. Certain possibilities, as Andy then saw and rejoiced, came within the reach of close attention and loving care that are forever inaccessible to mere technology, money, and the "big brain."

And now in the Age of Billionaires, who want everything that they don't already have, from everybody's government to anybody's farm, Andy's thoughts are often recalled to another enlightening visit to Monroe Miller's farm. He is unsure now of the company that day, for it was a long time ago. Maybe he had come with Maury Telleen. He is certain that Leroy Stutzman, another good Amish horseman, was there. David Kline, he thinks, was there, perhaps one or two of Monroe's boys, and it seems to Andy that he had his own son, Marcie, with him. Monroe had led the company of them down the road to his new horse barn, which was remarkable, among other things, for its all-weather drinking trough. Monroe had captured the outflow of a good spring and piped it into the barn, where it filled the trough, keeping it constantly full. The surplus water entered a standpipe and drain, which carried it to the streambed below the barn.

Their pleasure in the new barn, its ever-filling water trough, and the horses that were stabled there had made it already a memorable day. When they had looked their fill, they started back along the road toward Monroe's house, Monroe in front, the others in a loose bunch behind him. Their conversation led presently to a story somewhat famous in Holmes County, for it concerns the conflict of values that the Amish continually live with. Andy cannot remember who told it that day, but this is the story.

Too far to the east for its own good, Holmes County shares the Appalachian curse of coal, the curse compounded by the closeness of the coal to the surface of the ground, making it possible to be strip-mined. The Amish are somewhat of two minds about this. On the one hand it is a desecration, some of the ministers including Monroe have preached against it, and Andy knew that David forever hated it. On the other hand it offers money to landowners, who sometimes need it. Sometimes the sale of its underlying coal can be used to pay for a farm.

And it provides employment to some young Amish men who can use the work.

There was, back a while, an ex-Amish coal operator by the name of Mullet. Mr. Mullet had hired a young Amish man, perhaps just a big boy, to run a bulldozer, clearing away the trees, buildings, fences, everything above the surface, ahead of the first cut into the ground. The young man was working his way through an old farmstead, shoving the collapsed timbers and siding into a pile to be burned. He came to a small outbuilding, pushed the roof and walls clear of the floor, and took them to the pile. On his return he saw something shining between the joists of the broken floor. He climbed off the great machine to go and look. He had to look a while to persuade his eyes that they were looking at money. It was actual money, coins of silver and gold still mostly contained in the rotting box in which they had been hidden—by whom and how long ago?

Nobody was there but the young bulldozer operator. Nothing was there but the big rumbling machine, the burn pile of broken and splintered lumber, and the in fact very large stash of old coins that, as the young man knew, for a long time nobody had seen and now nobody had seen but him. He got his lunch box and filled it with only some of the coins. When he shut the lunch box and started to lift it, the handle came off in his hand.

He got the stout cloth sack in which he had wrapped his water jug. The sack was big enough and strong enough to hold all the coins. He tied it, put it in a secure place, and finished his day's work.

When he went home he carried the sack of coins with him and said nothing about it. He had explained nothing even to himself, his mind still unsettled by his astonishment. But in the night his upbringing returned to him, and his conscience performed its work. By morning he knew that he must not waste a minute in taking the treasure he had found to Mr. Mullet.

He did so. And Mr. Mullet, having examined his new property, did not waste a minute calling his lawyer, who did not waste a minute getting there to see to matters so urgent. And then, without waiting too many more minutes, there they were, the lawyer and the young Amish bulldozer operator and Mr. Mullet and the sack of money, in the lawyer's car, at the curb in front of the bank.

The sack of money being heavy, the young man politely offered to carry it into the bank, or to help Mr. Mullet to carry it in. But Mr. Mullet said no. Trusting nobody but himself, he would be the one to carry the money. And so, stooping and hurrying as he had to do with so heavy a burden clasped in his arms, Mr. Mullet carried his money into the bank alone.

It was a good story, well told. Nobody knew a story to match it, and for a while nobody said anything. Monroe also was silent. He was walking still a little ahead and apart from the others, bent a little forward, his arms drawn back, his right wrist held in his left hand, looking apparently only at the road.

At last he said, "To be satisfied with little is difficult. To be satisfied with much is impossible."

But still Andy's sense even of his home countryside and what to do with it was incomplete. He needed to know far more than he knew about forestry, and he was getting on past fifty years old.

He had loved the woodlands around Port William from the earliest wanderings of his boyhood, through his years as a squirrel hunter, and then his first efforts, after his homecoming, to teach himself the names of the flowers, the trees, and the birds. By then he was needing the woodlands, his own and his neighbors', as places of refuge and consolation, where he could sit down, grow quiet, and watch for whatever might be revealed. Or if he was weary, he could lie down on the dry leaves and sleep a clearer, simpler sleep than was possible anywhere else. For perhaps fifteen years following his return, the wooded valley sides of his familiar country were mostly undisturbed. Trees were reclaiming the hillside croplands and pastures abandoned after World War II. But in some places also the woods had grown old, and there were tall oaks and poplars whose trunks two men could not encircle with their arms.

He had learned, moreover, to regard the woods as a place of instruction. For this his principal teacher had been the English agricul-
turist Sir Albert Howard, who taught that in their use of the natural
world farmers should follow Nature's laws in order to avoid the already
manifest high cost of failing to do so. To learn to farm in the right
way, Howard said, you must study the woods. For in the woods, where
Nature unmolested does her farming, she employs the greatest possible diversity of plants and animals; she keeps the ground covered to
preserve the soil and prevent erosion; by the slow burning of decay she
converts death to life; she wastes nothing; nothing that dies stays dead;
she presides at the balances of life and death, growth and decay; her soil
in endless passages gathers and keeps the rain. On the farm as in the
woods what Howard called "the Wheel of Life"—birth, growth, matu-
rity, death, and decay—must be kept turning in place. This is Nature's
answer to humanity's unnatural and inhuman concept of "waste."

Howard's two most significant books, *An Agricultural Testament*
and *The Soil and Health*, were in print before the middle of the twentieth
century. Sound, scientifically reputable, and persuasive as they are, they
have been mainly ignored by agricultural scientists and by conservationists. Even so, they have continued to inform the work of a lineage,
a sort of cadre, of agrarian farmers and scientists. But Howard's advice
to study the woods had no comparable influence on forestry. This is
somewhat astonishing, if only because the farm woodlot is valuable, not
merely as an example or pattern to the farm, but also as an economic
asset to be used well and so conserved. But even as the giver of a sustainable pattern to the farm, let alone as a sustainable asset, the woodlot
must be ecologically intact, both in itself so far as possible and as one
in a neighborhood of communicating woodlots. In the woods Nature is
self-sustaining only insofar as the woods is whole. In a place naturally
whole, everything is living. As long as the Wheel of Life turns in place,
undiminished and uninterrupted, death is alien; nothing is "dead" that
is not already transforming into new life. Insofar as the nature of a place
is fragmented, the balance is thrown over in favor of death, of what we
call "waste." The need for the farm to emulate the wholeness of the local

forest implies the need to keep the local forest whole. A local economy would be self-sustaining, and thus locally adapted, if it preserved the wholeness of the local forest and the local farms. This of course would require a local culture competently aware of, and capable of meeting, the needs of the local ecosystem and the local economy. Attention to the history of any local countryside—as certainly the countryside around Port William—reveals the necessity of such a local culture, but Andy Catlett does not know of any local school that has noticed, or that has been notified of, any such necessity. So far as he knows, the subject of health, as an endless, endlessly beautiful, order of interdepending wholes, is held by all the schools to be not a subject.

But Aldo Leopold, whose land ethic and whose work as a whole accords with Howard's—and who, like Howard, was reputably schooled and fully credentialed—has also been ignored by scientists and conservationists insofar as his work had to do with farming. And his interest in forestry, about equally practical and urgent, has been about equally ignored. In 1942 he published an essay, "The Last Stand," in which he described the Spessart forest, which he had seen in Germany in 1935. Half of this forest, he said, had been selectively logged, keeping it ecologically intact, since 1605, and it was still producing "the finest cabinet oak in the world." The other half was "slashed," meaning clear-cut, during the same century and had never recovered, but was producing "only mediocre pine." Leopold thus distinguished emphatically between forestry oriented to the forest ecosystem and forestry oriented only to production—essentially the same distinction he made between kinds of farming. So far as Andy Catlett has discovered, Leopold's essay has not had the least influence on commercial logging or the recommended "best management practices"—not, anyhow, in Kentucky.

Industrial forestry appears to be as impenetrable an orthodoxy as industrial farming, but it has been much slower to produce, in reaction, a publicly accessible alternative, which, as with agriculture, could only be a way of forestry oriented to forest ecology, or forest health, or to the long-term productivity of the forest, or (remembering Howard) to Nature's forestry. There were, as Andy would discover, good examples of such forestry, but they were widely scattered and little noticed. They were the work mainly of foresters sensible enough to recognize the economic value of sustained productivity, who merely went about their work in what they considered the best way. To the extent that they succeeded, they recognized their success and improved on it, but they were in no hurry to invite attention to their work. There was no "movement." In acquiring a public presence or reputation, sustainable forestry lagged behind sustainable agriculture by fifty or sixty years.

As so in the 1980s when commercial logging began to establish itself in the woodlands around Port William, on the steep valley sides along the creeks and up and down the river, Andy was both troubled and in the dark. He could see only locally. He could see that a logging company bought a tract of standing timber with the sole object of "harvesting" every marketable stick. He could see that the purchaser, having bought the trees, then owned also the privilege of extracting them from the woods as cheaply, which is to say as quickly, as possible, using all available power. And he could see that the woods, as it remained, was too much reduced, too much altered in its nature and character, and too much damaged by carelessness and haste. But he knew no example of better forestry by which he might have measured and understood what he was seeing.

For perspective he had only the examples of the best farming he had known, and these he knew pretty well. He knew that the attentiveness, the care, the skill, and the enacted affection of the best farming would necessarily carry over into forestry. And he knew that the virtues and practices of good husbandry had been permitted and even encouraged in his own country by the tobacco program, combining price supports and production control, which during most of his life had given the farmers an asking price for at least one of their products. For want of an asking price, through the long history of farming, farmers had lived and worked in a colonial economy, carrying their products to market and accepting, without recourse, whatever price they were offered.

As self-defense they had only the knowledge of how to live poor. This certainly had been true of the lives of Andy's own people well into the early years of his parents' generation. From this he knew, as logging grew more prominent all around him, that he was seeing the colonization of the woods. The trees were bringing to the landowners what the buyer would pay. Sawlogs were being trucked away with minimal benefit and much damage to the land owners, and with no benefit to the community.

For most of his life by then, Andy had been watching the deterioration of the human fabric of Port William and its countryside. Farmers died without heirs, almost by rule. No place of business that closed ever opened again. Old houses in the town, on farms, on places that once were farmed, were neglected, abandoned, demolished, or burned. Young people went away and returned only for funerals. Or they commuted to work and returned only to watch television and sleep. The sitting places in front of the stores that were almost never deserted in the old days, when the wild big boys would be replaced by the bed-weary old men in the stillest hour before daylight, came finally to be empty all night long, even on Saturday night, even in the best weather. The old sounds of the early morning, roosters crowing, men calling their milk cows, had been replaced by the starting of tractors and commuters' cars and pickup trucks, and by the passing of school buses carrying the children away from early morning to late evening. A new kind of time had come, a new kind of history. Now when one of the old ones died, there would be something the survivors would want to know that could no longer be known. Or there would be something they did not have that they would need to go farther to get, or would never find again anywhere.

When Mr. Milo Settle died and his garage that had earned so fine a reputation far and wide was closed forever and his gas pumps were removed, people had to drive their cars and trucks ten or fifteen miles to get them fixed, or pay to have them towed. They had to burn gas to get gas. When the town's one remaining grocery store went out of business, people had to drive ten or fifteen miles to shop, and everybody was depending more and more on store-bought food. The cost of living in Port William was going up. And so the industrialization of the woods, when that came, was a new sorrow to Andy, but it came as a part of an established pattern and was no surprise.

Maybe the mind is most alert when it is most troubled. Maybe the fox is most alert, most inhabiting and at home in his native country, when he is hardest run by the hounds. Anyhow, Andy now had the woods on his mind, he was troubled, and he was listening. Because he was listening he began to hear things that he knew he needed to hear.

From his conversations with his friend William Martin, forest ecology became a term and an idea that he could use with some understanding. He learned to transfer the idea of culling livestock from farm animals to forest trees. A competent livestockman would not sell his best animals and keep the worst. Just so, a competent forester or woods owner would not commit or tolerate the malpractice known as "highgrading," by which the best trees are sold and the worst left standing. And so, yes, the principles of good management and good care did pass freely back and forth between plants and animals, farming and forestry—though a farm and a forest were different, and the difference imposed limits.

At a farming conference in New Hampshire, Andy caught a few words from a man who evidently was making a living from his own woods. The man was about Andy's age. He was talking, clearly, about something he *did*, not something he had thought of doing or was planning to do. He was an intelligent man, friendly, glad to talk about the enterprise in which his life and interest were fully invested, glad to answer Andy's questions. He owned, he said, a good many hundreds of acres, enough so that he worked only in his own woodland. His logging equipment consisted of a tractor and a portable sawmill. Because of the small scale of his work and his low operating costs, he was able to do a sort of custom logging. Unlike the big, industrial outfits, he could fill special orders. One of his customers, for example, had asked him to supply thirty hornbeam logs, and he had been able to do so. Hornbeams are small trees of limited use, beneath or beyond the notice of most loggers, but this forester was pleased and somewhat amused by his own ready ability to fill the order. Because of his dependence on the yield from a limited acreage, this man, as Andy would realize only later, had to be restrained and selective in choosing which trees to cut in any year. But at that time Andy was too ignorant to ask him what his principle of selection was. He was too ignorant or too distracted to ask the man, whose name he soon forgot, for his address or telephone number.

But Andy's new interest in forestry had got around among his friends. He was talking to anybody he met who might enlarge his knowledge. Somebody sent him a magazine article about the forest and the forestry of the Menominee Indians in Wisconsin: "Menominee Sustained-Yield Management," by Marshall Pecore. And *that*, Andy realized, was what he had been looking for, that phrase, "sustained-yield management." It sounded like what he needed because it sounded like what his home woodlands needed.

In his conversations with his friend Bill Martin he was learning, if not forest ecology, at least something of the principles of forest ecology. Standing on a height overlooking the Kentucky River near Port William, they could see thousands of acres of forest along the steep sides of the valley in three counties. They knew that the forest they were looking at was more or less continuous along the river and its tributaries for 255 miles between its entrance into the Ohio and the three forks at Beattyville, and from there, along the forks, through the interruptions and damages of the strip mines, almost to the Virginia line.

"It's a great resource," Andy said. "A lot of people could take a living from it."

"*If* they would use it well," Bill Martin said. "*If* they knew how to use it well. *If* they wanted to use it well."

There came a time—not normal in Kentucky politics—when Bill Martin, an ecologist, a conservationist, was employed in state government. He was, he said, "a man in a white hat," unexpected in the circumstances, and he was working in the Department of Natural

Resources for Philip Shepherd, another man in a white hat. Because of those two men whose heads were willing to be so conspicuously adorned, Andy was invited to speak at the Kentucky Forest Summit to be held in Louisville in the fall of 1994. Bill Martin came to Andy's place on Harford Run to ask him if he would make the speech. Sitting on the porch, looking into the woods, they talked at length of what needed to be done, and so of what needed to be said. As always in their conversations, there was some laughter, for they mutually were amused at a number of things. For one thing, they both were aware of the likelihood that Bill was inviting Andy to waste his breath. But they knew also that the circumstances called for seriousness, and they were as serious as they needed to be.

To be invited to waste his breath at a conference sponsored by state government was at least an honor, and Andy took it seriously. His problem, too familiar to him by then, was that he did not know enough. He knew the outline, and some of the contents, of his dissatisfaction, but he still was without an example of something better. To prepare himself to write his speech, he went to Wisconsin to look at the Menominee Forest.

The Menominee originally inhabited a homeland of fifteen thousand or so square miles in Wisconsin and northern Michigan. By the middle of the nineteenth century, in accordance with the conventional charity of their white Christian neighbors, they had been pushed into what is now Menominee County in east central Wisconsin. Their holding had thus been reduced to 235,000 acres, of which 220,000 were forested. That was it. That was all.

Like the New Hampshire forester whose livelihood was limited to his own forest, like the Amish who accept the limits of neighborliness and the working gait of a draft horse, like in fact the human race on the earth, the Menominee in 1854 faced the classic predicament of so much and no more. If they were to live, they would have to live from their forest. If they were to live long from their forest, they could not simply cut it all to the ground, as was then the way of forestry in the dominant society. And so, before they started logging, they determined on a way of doing the work so as not to destroy either the natural character of the forest or its ability to reproduce itself. This they were able to do, obviously, because they already possessed intimate knowledge of the forest. They knew both where they were and what they had to do to remain there. The result was, as Andy said in his speech, that "after 140 years* of continuous logging, the forest still is believed to contain a billion and a half board feet of standing timber"—or about the same number of board feet that it had contained in 1854. Thus, like the New Hampshire forester and like the Amish, the Menominee succeeded, not by increasing their acreage to achieve the "economy of scale," which is the recommended way, and typically the disaster, of industrial forestry and farming, but instead by accepting the given or imposed limit and then making the best possible use of what they had. As Andy would know more assuredly later, from more examples and further thought, nothing good can happen in the human use of the land except within known and accepted limits. Without limits there can be no propriety of scale, no coherence of form, no saving ratio of eyes to acres, no close attention and loving care. That the Menominee, having once freely inhabited an immense territory and then become contained by their much smaller "reservation," were able to devise an art of sustainable forestry is more than admirable. It was and is, like the Amish achievement, a work of communal genius, far higher and finer than the works of individual genius that so enrapture us today.

By the kindness and courtesy of the forest office staff, including Marshall Pecore himself, Andy was given as thorough a look at the forest and as complete a grasp of its working principles as was possible in two days. In his Forest Summit speech he described the management of the forest this way:

> About 20 percent of the forest is managed in even-aged stands
> of aspen and jack pine, which are harvested by clear-cutting

---

* As of 1994.

and which regenerate naturally. The rest of the forest is divided into 109 compartments, to each of which the foresters return every fifteen years to select trees for cutting. Their rule is to cut the worst and leave the best. That is, the loggers remove only those trees that are unlikely to survive for another fifteen years, those that are stunted or otherwise defective, and those that need to be removed in order to improve the stand. Old trees that are healthy and still growing are left uncut. As a result, this is an old forest, containing, for example, 350-year-old hemlocks, as well as cedars that are probably older. The average age of harvested maples is 140 to 180 years.

And there was one further, most important point he had to make: "[T]he Menominee forest economy is as successful as it is," Andy said, "because it is not understood primarily as an economy. Everybody I talked to . . . urged me to understand that the forest is the basis of a culture, and that the unrelenting cultural imperative has been to keep the forest intact."

And so to balance his dissatisfaction with what he was seeing at home, Andy now had seen with his own eyes the most reassuring available example of a way of forestry that had actually worked sustainably and continuously for 140 years. He had also the key to the failure of his own people, who had inhabited Kentucky in 1994 for only 219 years. Their failure, as he knew, had certainly been economic, for they had wasted or destroyed much of the natural wealth they had possessed at the beginning. Even the agrarians, the land husbanders, who had come wishing to stay, nevertheless squandered the forest. But before their failure was economic, it had been cultural. They had destroyed so much, partly no doubt in ignorance, but mostly for want of a cultural imperative to save it. In this way also, as Andy knew, the economic success of the Holmes County Amish demanded to be understood: Their economic success had depended upon a practical culture that was always securely preceded by love for God and for their neighbors.

• • •

By then Andy could see that he had begun to gather the substantial parts of an understanding of forestry that was parallel to, and at critical points belonged to, his and his friends' understanding of farming.

And then, in 1996, Maury Telleen asked him to go to the farthest northeast corner of Ohio to write for the *Draft Horse Journal* an article about Charlie Fisher, who logged with horses. Andy and Flora then made the long drive north, Andy to write the article, Flora to take photographs. They had worked together in this way before, to write and illustrate articles about farming. They were a good team, and their collaboration was useful, for Andy's writing would be improved by their understanding of what could and could not be adequately described in words, and by their discussions about how to picture what had to be pictured.

It was late in the fall. The hard frosts had come and the leaves were down, making it easy to see into the woods. Flora and Andy spent two days with Charlie Fisher, learning about his way of logging, how it was done, and its effect. Charlie was then half-owner and working partner in a company consisting of a logging operation and a sawmill. His partner managed the sawmill, and Charlie purchased the standing timber, selected and marked the trees to be cut, and supervised the crews at work in the woods. The work in the woods was what Andy had come to see and what he was most capable of seeing, but it mattered to him that the woods work, employing local people, supplied a local mill also employing local people and serving a local need for sawed lumber. And so the two-man partnership enlarged itself into a partnership with the local economy and the local community, and finally, logically enough, with the only locally owned bank in their neighborhood.

Andy had been prepared for his meeting with Charlie by the years, from his earliest boyhood to the coming of the tractors, that he had spent in the old way of farming in his own country, using some draft horses but mostly mules. And by the time of his conversation with Charlie he had been working teams of horses on his own farm for more than twenty years. And so, as in the most significant of his previous encounters, he and Charlie began with some common understanding that included a good many things that did not need to be explained.

Charlie's advance work of purchasing boundaries of timber and selecting and marking the trees kept three logging crews busy in the woods. Each crew was made up of one sawyer who felled the marked trees and two teamsters who skidded the logs usually five or six hundred feet to where they were yarded up to await a trucker. Each teamster worked a pair of horses to a two-wheeled cart or "logging arch." And so Charlie's woods operation routinely employed nine men and twelve horses. Mostly their work was done in small privately owned woodlots within a radius of forty or fifty miles.

It was a pleasure to listen to Charlie's description of the way the horses worked, for his language was finely detailed and clear, and Andy enjoyed writing it down:

> We watched a team drag out a twelve-foot log containing about 330 board feet. They were well-loaded but were not straining. Charlie says that a team can handle up to five or six hundred board feet. For bigger logs, they use an additional team or a bulldozer. A good teamster can skid 3,000 to 3,500 board feet a day in small logs. The trick, Charlie says, is to know what your horses can do, and then see that they do that much on every pull. Overload, and you're resting too much. Underload, and you're wasting energy and time. The important thing is to keep loaded and keep moving.

Charlie had no settled prejudice against mechanical equipment, which he used according to need, but he had obviously a settled preference for the use of horses in the woods. For this he gave four reasons:

1. As his first reason, he said, "I've always liked horses." And Andy fully agreed to the primacy he gave to this. Without the liking, the other good reasons don't count.

2. He also liked the woods, and horses are kinder to the woods than a mechanical skidder. They use a much narrower roadway; if well used, they are not so likely to bark the trees; they don't leave deep ruts. Charlie said, "The horse will always be the answer to good logging in the woods."

3. Whereas the purchase and use of a mechanical skidder siphons money out of the local community, the horse logger both earns and spends his money at home.

4. Horses cost much less and work much cheaper than a mechanical skidder. The lower operating costs are compatible with lower per acre yields, thus freeing the horse logger to be as selective and conservative as the woods requires. Andy knows now far better than he knew then that this is a benefit of an accepted limit on power and speed.

When Charlie selected and marked the trees to be cut, Andy wrote: "His purpose is to select a number of trees, often those that . . . are diseased or damaged or otherwise inferior, which will provide a reasonable income to landowner and logger alike, without destroying the wood-making capacity of the forest." This Charlie opposed to the sort of cutting that removes every marketable tree, after which another cutting cannot be made for sixty to a hundred years. He was necessarily conscious always of both the economic issues and the good health of the woods, but he stated his aim in a way that was admirably personal and immediate: "I always hope maybe there'll be trees here for my son to cut in ten or twenty years." Thus he involved his affection, which Andy was sure would work to better results than any mere knowledge or methodology.

Charlie took Flora and Andy to woodlands that he had marked for logging, woodlands that were being logged, and finally to a woodland that had been logged three years before, of which Andy wrote:

Very few of the remaining trees had been damaged by trees felled during the logging. I saw not a single tree that had been barked by a skidded log. The skid trails had completely healed over; there was no sign of erosion. And, most striking, the woodland was still ecologically intact. It was still a diverse, uneven-aged stand of trees, many of which were over sixteen inches in diameter . . . After logging, the forest is still a forest, and it will go on making wood virtually without interruption or diminishment. It seems perfectly reasonable to think that, if several generations of owners were so inclined, this sort of forestry could eventually result in an "old growth" forest that would have produced a steady income for two hundred years.

Charlie's stock in trade was his good work, which appealed to the wish, fairly general among landowners, to have their woods well treated. It had been a long time since he had needed to hunt for work. He was sixty-six years old, he said, and busier than ever.

Andy said, "Well, you seem to be enjoying it."

Charlie said, "Oh, I *love* it."

When Maury Telleen had read Andy's article, he called him up. "You *liked* him, didn't you."

To complete Andy's education in forestry, as it stands so far, he needed two further teachers and friends. By the grace or generosity that often has been the providence of his life, he found them when he most needed them and was best prepared to meet them. He needed their examples and their language.

He met Jason Rutledge, a breeder of Suffolk horses and a horse logger in the Virginia mountains, whose way of forestry accords closely with that of the Menominee and that of Charlie Fisher who, not surprisingly, had been Jason's mentor. But it was from Jason that Andy first heard the phrase "worst-first single tree selection," which is how Jason named and described his way of logging. By "worst-first" he meant, as Andy had learned to expect, not only the trees that were inferior in conformation or as species, but also the trees that were diseased or damaged and thus unlikely to survive the ten- or twenty-year interval between loggings. By "single tree selection" he indicated the requirement, at once ecological and economic, to look at and think carefully about every tree in the woods. Jason has the good habit of worrying about language. Andy likes his uneasiness about the word "sustainable," so fashionable now among his fellow Americans who have never sustained much of anything. He prefers "restorative," for as he rightly asks, "How do you sustain a decline?" And his organization is the Healing Harvest Forest Foundation, a name clearly that came from thinking. For logging with horses Jason would give the same reasons as Charlie Fisher: His own liking for the horses and the woods; also, between the creatures and the machine, the forest prefers the creatures.

There is a story about Jason that Andy loves to tell. In the story a man of the modern age, the proud owner of the sophistications of efficiency and speed, is watching Jason as he goes deliberately about the many choices involved in the best work of any kind, and never exceeding the speed at which a team of horses can comfortably work.

"Don't you know," says the sophisticate, "that you'll never get done that way?"

"Yes!" Jason says. "That's the point!"

And so he goes, with a certain exultation, against the grain of "the American way of life," which has the deathly purpose of getting done with everything as quickly as possible. Jason's answer, probably by no accident, is Amish in character and implication. And in being so nearly Amish, it is perhaps also natural: One works, as one lives, not to be done but to keep on.

Another time, at a forestry conference Jason was on a panel with a couple of industrial foresters. He described his own way of selecting trees and of logging with horses. The moderator, to keep the audience from becoming confused, explained, "Mr. Rutledge is from the mountains of Virginia, and he knows you can't log those steep mountainsides with horses."

Jason, whose knowledge of history extends beyond yesterday, said, "Oh. You mean they can't be logged with horses *again*?"

Jason, moreover, is a teacher, who teaches his way of logging in the only way it can be taught: by taking apprentices with him when he goes to work in the woods. The adequate textbook on horse logging will always remain in the minds and bodies of experienced loggers and experienced horses. The paramount reason, as generally, is that the work can be made reasonably safe only by experience, but the next reason, closely following, is that this particular work requires the laying of hands upon everything involved. The use of horses is in every way more physical than the use of a machine.

By Jason's choice and contriving, Andy met Troy Firth, a forest owner in the northwestern corner of Pennsylvania, whose products are sawlogs, milled lumber, and maple syrup. Jason and Troy are friends and allies for the good reason that their lives and livelihoods come to rest upon the same kind of forestry—worst-first single tree selection and logging with horses—and for the same reasons.

Andy once heard Jason say to a crowd at a forest field day: "I am not a man of few words." And that was right enough. He is not. Like Andy Catlett and no doubt only a few others, Jason does not mind hearing what he has to say. Maybe that is because he knows what he is talking about, he knows a lot, and he is always trying to say it better. But on that day he was recommending Troy who, he said, *is* a man of few words. He was right again. Troy perhaps is not eager to listen to himself.

But his words, if few, are rigorously chosen, and Andy has needed them all. At the same meeting, it may have been, where Jason called him a man of few words, Troy offered his hearers as clean and clarifying a distinction as they probably had ever heard: "A bad logger goes to the woods thinking of what he can take out. A good logger goes to the woods thinking of what he can leave." This statement, as Andy understands it, takes the side of Nature, the nature of the land and the land's community, against the dominant current of American history since 1492. The good logger thinks of what he can leave, and whether for the sake of the woods or for the sake of the next logger the result is the same: What is left remains whole.

One learns what to leave and what to take, moreover, by observation. "Forestry," Troy says, "is mainly observational, rather than theoretical." In Troy's vocabulary "observation" means walking and looking, paying attention to details, not once or twice but again and again over a long time. "It takes decades. That's all there is to it." We are a homeless nation, but as Gary Snyder says in his luminous book *The Great Clod*, "Humanistic concerns can be cultivated anywhere, but certain kinds of understanding and information about the natural world are only available to those who stay put and keep looking." There is, of course, a limit to what one forester can observe often and in detail. This implies a necessary humility, and it brings us again to the spatial limit implied by the eyes-to-acres ratio.

To observe in so committed a way one must be rightly motivated. And about this Troy again is characteristically plainspoken. The right motive is love. Andy took part in a conference sponsored by Troy's Foundation for Sustainable Forests; it was called "Loving the Land Through Working Forests," and "loving" as used here does not designate an idle sentiment but rather a way of work. One cannot, because one will not, take good care of anything that one does not love, and this is merely obvious. But from what he has seen and done himself, Andy believes that one cannot authentically or accountably even know anything that one does not love.

Troy's two terms, "observational" and "loving," imply a completeness of character, an ethical completeness, in the forester, who thus will never approach the type of the all-knowing expert, whose knowledge is supposedly universal and usable in every place. The observant and loving forester's knowledge accumulates as a mosaic of parochial details, hoping to preserve, in using it, the ecological integrity of *a* place.

Thus, slowly and over a lot of years, Andy Catlett has gathered from his own place and experience, and the places and experiences of his friends, the principles and the language to describe what might be the good use of the land and a good land-using economy in his home country around Port William.

This understanding, and this kind of understanding as it applies to different places, has been the basis of a public advocacy that Andy and his friends, in their various ways, have carried on for nearly half a century. They have made, the survivors are still making, an argument essentially agrarian that would have been recognized, that in fact was being made, by the best farmers of their parents' generation, for it was more or less the common sense of the countryside. But now, amid the clamors of the parties of industrialism, the agrarian argument has become rare, almost unhearable, almost unheard.

And yet, among a surviving remnant, the little company of Andy's friends among them, the old argument still lives and continues. It is grounded in the obvious truth, the axiom, that the human economy is dependent upon, and limited by, the natural world, which is dependent in turn upon human cherishing, forbearance, and skill.

The argument, as they have made and elaborated it over so many years, begins with the understanding that the human use of the natural world, if it is not to destroy the natural world, must obey the laws of Nature. And Nature's laws, numerous as they clearly are as they are manifested in the variety of native creatures and ecosystems, perhaps can be comprehended as versions of only three: the Law of Fullness, the Law of Diversity, and the Law of Frugality.

Nature appears to wish and to require that the life of any of her places should be as abundant as possible and as diverse as possible in its kinds. Every creature desires and attempts to live fully, and for this it is dependent on the lives of other creatures. And this fullness depends in turn upon a formal interdependence somewhat but not entirely comprehensible by humans. The Law of Diversity, mysterious as it ultimately is, is justified by the Law of Fullness.

For life in its necessary diversity to exist and to continue, there must be no waste. The substances that embody the life of one creature must survive its death to embody the lives of other creatures in a succession with no foreseeable end. One of our names for Nature is Mother Nature, and this surely is not because of her partiality for individuals among her children, but rather because, like a thrifty housewife, she wastes nothing, not a bite of food or a drop of water. She keeps serving a menu of delectable and nourishing leftovers.

Agrarianism, as Andy and his teachers living and dead have understood it, comes to rest upon recognition of Nature's unalterable laws. Agrarian farmers have always understood that disobedience to her laws is uneconomic and a kind of blasphemy, and that obedience to her laws makes her an ally, a provider of free helps. They love her Law of Fullness, and so rejoice when their farms are filled with life. They respect her Law of Diversity, which they understand as opposed to specialization. Rather than put everything at risk on one "specialty," they are drawn as by their own nature toward a diversity of enterprises, of plants and animals, for if one fails, another may succeed. And they regard with love and fear her Law of Frugality. They hate wastefulness. They tell their children, "Waste not, want not."

Agrarian farmers have always understood also that Nature's laws imply certain specifically human laws that also must be obeyed. The Law of Humility requires respect, a kind of reverence, and deference before Nature's ultimately mysterious forms and processes. There will always come times when humans meet their limit, must back off and "leave it to Nature." The Law of Neighborliness forbids prospering alone, requires generosity to human neighbors but also, as our understanding of ecology grows and informs our work, to the neighbors that are not human. The Law of Neighborliness has its proof in the agrarian economy of the Amish, who hold "Love they neighbor as thy self" to be the paramount law of this world, and so they have neighbors, and so they give help, and so they have help, and so they prosper.

Nature's Laws of Fullness and Diversity imply a supreme principle of formal coherence or integration, but this does not become in a direct or simple way a law for humans. They must respect it but they cannot comprehend or imitate it in its complexity and detail. She alone is master of her own work. But insofar as they can understand and obey her Laws of Fullness and Diversity, she hands on to agrarian farmers the problem of form. The best farmers have been ceaselessly occupied with the question, never fully or finally answered, of how the various creatures and things of their living are to be fitted together to their mutual advantage.

This conglomerate of obligations and considerations—which carries over, with obvious differences and changes, to forestry—sets the economy of agrarianism almost completely at odds with the economy of industrialism, just as it leaves Andy Catlett and his friends outside the bounds and the conversation (such as it is) of the liberal and conservative parties of industrialism. Agrarianism proposes an economy of local resources, exchanges, and services that are cheap or free, depending on the virtues of good work and thrift, tending toward the maximum of local self-sufficiency and independence. Such an economy is not like, and can never be made like, the industrial economy that proposes dependence upon expensive products, extravagant wants, excessive consumption, limitless spending, and waste.

Andy knew well, and he has remembered again and again, the household of his Catlett grandparents, who shared pretty fully in the imperfections of their time and place, who no doubt lived in poverty by modern standards as they struggled to hold on to their farm, and did hold on to it, though almost losing it, and never quite "got ahead." They lived from their garden, their flock of chickens, their milk cows, their meat hogs. His grandmother made her own soap. And so they survived, and at least ate well, through the predations and depressions of an economy that glutted upon the primary producers of its wealth, as dominant economies had always done. They spent little, wasted nothing, and saved everything that could be saved. Andy remembers, after his grandmother's death, finding her collections of bits of string, ribbon, and dress trimmings all wound neatly on pieces of cardboard and put away, those and other things too nice, too costly, too potentially useful to be thrown out or burned. It was as though she—and how many thousands like her, fearful of want?—had read and believed, "Gather up the fragments that remain, that nothing be lost." He found her collection of pretty greeting cards that she could not part with because they had so gladdened her heart. And he wonders how in the time only of his own life his nation can have progressed from that old effort and hardship and saving to the normality of spending, consuming, and throwing away.

As he thought over and over again of these things, Andy began to understand the extreme wrong of putting the human economy first, as industrialism invariably does, but as the Menominee feared to do because their culture forbids it, and as Troy Firth for the sake of love refuses to do. Reality itself, the human condition itself, demands that humans should understand themselves as living souls, inhabiting a living world alive by God's spirit that is life itself. If, as William Blake said, following closely certain passages of Scripture, "everything that lives is holy" and "every particle of dust breathes forth its joy," then it is exceedingly dangerous to force our will upon the earth by means of explosives, poisons, enormous machines, and a great numbness that allows our selves and our economy to come first.

But Andy knows, he cannot for very long forget, that while he has been watching, learning, and, with his friends and allies, advocating kinder ways of living in this world, his home community of Port William and its countryside, like every such community from coast to coast—which is to say "rural America"—is wasting and dying. Sometimes it seems to him that his people have scattered like a flushed covey of bobwhites that, by calling to one another, may come together again. At other times it seems to him that people and land together have been shattered and the fragments irretrievably dispersed, like the clods and rock shards blown out of a dynamited post hole, to remain apart and lost forever, or to prepare some hard new beginning from almost nothing, far off and unimaginable.

And then from what he hopes and fears he must back up to what he actually knows. He must withdraw his thoughts from the future, which, in the weakness and fear he knows too well in himself, people are cramming with pipedreams and nightmares. Denying himself the temptations of the emptiness of time-to-come, he must turn back to his place and community as it now is and to what is now there. He knows that in the absence of the old who have died and the young who have gone away, among the abandoned old farmsteads and the fallen and the falling houses, among the misfarmed too-large fields and the plagues of addiction, some have stayed, even some young ones, native to the place, in effect its old belongings, who seem determined to stay. And there are a few newcomers, some with young families, who have come for the old reason, to have, even if small and poor, a piece of ground of their own under their feet to live on and from, who have found their places, and as of old are not easily hanging on. And among the native born and the newcomers he sees friendships forming and acquiring histories, exchanges of work, gatherings at evening for supper and music, the emerging outlines of renewed community. And these things are happening without official notice or help.

Andy and Flora too are still at the headwaters of Harford Run, where their long marriage found and made its place, still at their work, and with their children as helpers and allies. Andy, who twenty years ago knew for sure that he had only four allies outside his family, knows now that he has a good many. He knows that there is now widespread in the cities a "food movement," giving status to somewhat malleable terms such as "organic," "fresh," and "local," and interest in food is only a step from an interest in agriculture. He knows that a perhaps increasing number of doctors are worrying about the economy of health, and worrying about the economy of health is only a step from worrying about agriculture.

But he knows also that the number of people he might count as allies is so small as to be almost unnoticeable, almost invisible, among the millions of consumers and spenders. He knows that food, which is too costly for poor people, is far too cheap as its price affects farmers and farming and the possibility of better farming. He knows that the best land, for bad reasons, has become too costly to be purchased by young farmers for the purpose of farming. He knows that, excepting the few small farms still well-farmed on principle or to supply the food movement, most of the farmland is overworked, bruised by the wheels of heavy machines, eroding, poisoned, and economically marginal.

And so Andy is forced to question the worth of the advocacy that has so occupied him and his friends for so long. He knows that their advocacy has virtually no standing with professors, intellectuals, journalists, and economists, let alone the corporations and the politicians of the capitols. He and his friends have not contributed to a reasonably expectable public conversation about the use and care of the land, as once in their innocence they may have intended to do or supposed they could do, because there is no such conversation.

What then can justify their effort? What compensates? Here Andy must speak only for himself. He refuses, to start with, the sometimes-offered consolation that in his advocacy he has written well, or that what he has written, regardless of its effect, is "literature." Sometimes even he has thought his writing may be literature. It is sufficiently an art, he grants, for there are learnable ways of doing it, and he has learned some of them. But what is the significance of "literature" and the implied "literary value" in a toxic and wasting country? Would even the plays of Shakespeare compensate the loss or ruin of the topsoil of England? Andy knows better than that. As dear as the plays of Shakespeare are to him, as much as he has depended on them, as much as they have instructed and inspired him, he knows that the art that kept the soil fertile and in place, in Shakespeare's time and after, is an art more necessary than Shakespeare's.

He takes some consolation in knowing that he and his friends have kept alive at least their part of a necessary public conversation about land use that may eventually take place. Remnants themselves, they may have helped an agrarian remnant and a remnant agrarianism to survive—a saving remnant it may even be, but that is for the future to know.

But the compensation that he is sure of, that apart from any result has mattered most, has been his love for his advocacy and the companionship among the living and the dead that it has given him. He has loved his friendship with his friends, their long collaboration, and the laughter that has been always at least immanent among them, breaking out often when most needed like the water of a spring. That this collaboration now includes his children more than ever confirms and endears it to him.

And Andy has loved his work, the daily care for his place and his animals, the daily waiting for words and the writing them down. As it was human work it could not be free of trouble that from time to time would come to it, but it has had in it also a constant inherence of pleasure, even of joy. His work, he thinks, the love that was in it, the love that it was for, has given him a happy life.

He has begun to think of happiness as a power of the mind, to be cultivated like thought and imagination. Because he has come to the age when he must think of such things, he recalls the times when he has been happy against reason, and for no reason. He recalls the times when he has been happy for reasons so small and ephemeral that nobody has learned to charge for them: a bright-colored tiny bird feeding in the top of the tallest sycamore, a bird's song, a wild flower, a butterfly, a briar heavy with ripe berries, the sound of a beloved voice, the touches of loved ones. To miss or refuse the happiness of such free, small, beautiful, and passing things would be dangerous, he thinks. It would dishonor life itself, Heaven itself. It would be ingratitude.

A Long Ancestry

A founding theme of Andy Catlett's thinking and his writing has been one of his father's guiding principles, which he put this way:

> If you want people to love their country, let them own a piece
> of it.

Wheeler meant a modest piece, for as always he had the small farmers in mind—most immediately the small farmers of the neighborhood around Port William, Kentucky—and he was talking about the important difference between a citizen of a nation and an inhabitant of a home country: the worth, in short, of having underfoot a piece of ground that one can live from. He was taking for granted the knowing how to live from it.

His father's saying is explained, Andy thinks, by a sort of ritual boast that he heard early in his life from multiple sources, and always in reference to the farmer's subsistence economy:

> They may run me out [or: sell me out], but they'll never starve me out.

As he has enlarged his reading and pondering over many years, Andy has come to see that boast as the statement of a powerful theme of his culture, coming from an ancient longing and a long history of hardship. The longing is expressed in the promise of three verses of Psalm 128:

> 2 For thou shalt eat the labor of thine hands: happy shalt thou be, and it shall be well with thee.

> 3 Thy wife shall be as a fruitful vine by the sides of thine house: thy children like olive plants round about thy table.

> 6 Yea, thou shalt see thy children's children, and peace upon Israel.

As for the hardship, here are a few telling lines from the twenty-fourth book of *The Odyssey*, as translated by Robert Fitzgerald. Odysseus, son of King Laërtês of Ithaka, has been gone from home for twenty years. In his absence his father has grown old. The royal household and the kingdom are now utterly reduced to lawlessness and disorder. The last of the great recognition scenes following Odysseus's return to Ithaka occurs between him and old Laërtês:

> Odysseus found his father in solitude
> spading the earth around a young fruit tree.
> He wore a tunic, patched and soiled, and leggings—
> oxhide patches, bound below his knees
> against the brambles; gauntlets on his hands
> and on his head a goatskin cowl of sorrow.

The king is wearing the clothes and doing the work of a peasant. Thus he has survived so far the disorder of his kingdom. He is cultivating a young fruit tree, and so enacting a covenant with the possibility of renewal and continuity.

This has a parallel in Jeremiah 32. Jerusalem is under siege by the Babylonian army. Jeremiah, whom the king has put in prison for speaking what will prove to be true, is visited by his uncle, Hanameel, who says to him,

> Buy my field . . . that is in Anathoth . . . for the right of inheritance is thine, and the redemption is thine; buy it for thyself.

And though he is in the most desperate of circumstances, Jeremiah buys the field. Surely no banker would have advised this, which again is the enactment of a covenant with the possibility (here the prophecy) of renewal:

> Houses and fields and vineyards shall be possessed again in this land.

This plot is recalled by Shakespeare in *As You Like It*, in which Duke Senior and his friends, exiled in the Forest of Arden, recover and renew the forms of a just, compassionate, and therefore legitimate social order. The greatest wisdom of our lineage seems to have concluded again and again that the renewal of communal order must begin with a bringing down to the land, the ground underfoot.

As You Like It reveals to some of the exiles in the forest the exemplary figure of the good shepherd, Corin, whose identification with his work, his subsistence, and his flock is absolute. Corin is another who eats the labor of his hands:

> Sir, I am a true laborer; I earn that I eat, get that I wear, owe no man hate, envy no man's happiness, glad of other men's good, content with my harm; and the greatest of my pride is to see my ewes graze and my lambs suck.

The emblematic healing in *As You Like It* is the restoration of Corin to a secure place in the economic order. The achievement of a life so admirable and so respected clearly counted with Shakespeare as a success, whereas the success story of the industrial age celebrates people who go *up* from the farm or "the sticks" to a "good job" in a factory or a profession.

A more modern version of the bringing down by disaster to the land is a story, or a part of a story, about a much beloved farmer, breeder of Belgian horses, and Andy Catlett's friend, the late Howard Johnstone of Maple Hill, Kansas. Howard was a draftee in World War II. He was in combat apparently just long enough to be captured by the Germans. As a prisoner of war, he was permitted to send one brief telegram to his parents. Howard's no doubt reassuring message was this:

Breed my two gray mares to a jack.

A theme or plot closely related to the bringing down by disaster to the land and so to renewal is that of exemplary persons who have been brought *up*, as they conceive, to possession of a small piece of land and thus to a secure subsistence, a measure of economic independence, and pleasure in such uneconomic gifts as the beauty of flowers. Andy has kept in mind this passage, from the fourth of Virgil's *Georgics* in David Ferry's translation:

For I remember, down by Tarentum,
Where dark Galaesus waters the yellowing grain,
I saw an old Corýcian man, who lived there,
Under the arches and towers of the fort,
On a little patch of land that nobody wanted,
Too poor for oxen to plow, unfit for pasture,
Not right for planting vines. But this old man
Carefully planted white lilies, vervain, and poppies,
And different sorts of vegetables for his table,
And thus he made for himself a happiness

That was equal to the happiness of kings,
And when he came home at night his feast was free.

Sixteen hundred years later the French poet, Pierre de Ronsard, remembered and praised that old subsistence farmer of Corycia, whose value and significance were still recognized. Ronsard's tribute is in his poem "La Salade," and the translation was made by one of Andy's neighbors:

Ah, but Virgil pleases when he sings
The old father of Corycia who each spring,
Busy with his hoe through daylight's length,
Worked his meagre fields with all his strength,
And coming home at evening bought no wine
Or any costly bread or meat in town,
But spread his frugal table with things to eat
That to his healthy hunger seemed more sweet,
Better and tastier than any Lord's . . .

. . . .

Which do you think was happiest of these two:
That great Crassus, to his "position" true,
Who, envious of Pompey's Triumph, of that *word*,
Went out to die by the Parthian sword,
Or this old husbandman who stayed at home,
Lived in his garden, and never set foot in Rome?

What is dearest to Andy in those lines is Ronsard's emphasis on the old husbandman's independence, which in our time we can understand as first economic and then political. And we can see now that this is a democratic independence. We are as free as we can afford to be. If, having the use of the land and its life-supports, we cannot be starved out, we have freely also the use of our own minds. This was exactly the understanding of Thomas Jefferson, who wrote in *Notes on the State of Virginia*:

> Dependence begets subservience and venality, suffocates the germ of virtue, and prepares fit tools for the designs of ambition.

And that was why he wrote to James Madison:

> The small landholders are the most precious part of a state.

Jefferson wrote his *Notes on the State of Virginia* in 1781. His letter to Madison was written in 1785. According to his own testimony, the soil of the hillsides of Virginia had already suffered from ill use, and so caution requires us to suppose that the small farmers Jefferson knew were not necessarily good farmers. The descendants of some of them, who moved into Kentucky, also were not necessarily good farmers. What we can confidently suppose is that a farmer's attention can be more intimately and kindly concentrated on a small farm than on a large one. If the small farmers, who cherish their few acres always as better than none, do not care well for the land, who will? Will the government, which by nature can cherish nothing? Will the large land owners, who of their many acres can easily ignore or abuse a few?

The interval between Jefferson's lifetime and Andy Catlett's is about two hundred years. The most tragic thing Andy knows in his old age is that those two centuries of American use of American land have drastically reduced the quantity and health of the topsoil along with the number of small farmers. The correlation between those two reductions would be difficult, perhaps impossible, to establish firmly and exactly. But there can be no doubt that the absent farmers have been replaced by mechanical and chemical technologies, of which the ecological costs have been too high.

Andy has lived more than a third of the interval between his time and Jefferson's. As those years of his lifetime and their changes have affected the land and people of the Port William neighborhood, it has been in many ways a history of diminishment and ruin. And now in his latter days, when Port William has become a third-rate "bedroom community" and the land around it is farmed by ever fewer economically threatened and struggling farmers, he looks back studiously at the place as he knew it early in his life, and especially as it was before the industrialization of its farmlands began almost on the day after V-J Day.

In those now far-off days, all of Port William lived by farming. Its bank and its shops, its merchants and mechanics, its doctor, all lived by their services to farmers. The land was then divided mainly into family-size farms that were worked by the people who lived on and from them. But almost everybody in the town and the neighborhood had at least the use of a small parcel of land. The farmers, the tenant farmers, the farmhands, the townspeople, all really who so desired, owned or had the use of a plot for a garden, a pen for chickens, a lot or stall for fattening a hog, pasture for a milk cow. And almost everybody knew, perfectly or imperfectly as might be, how to take the subsistence of their households from the land.

Subsistence and the family hog had the force of law in old Port William, a law that was accorded a sometimes passionate respect. When Uncle Cletus Rowanberry was a young man, courting the girl who would become in time Aunt Mill, the two of them were romancing one night about the house they would live in and how nice their life in it was going to be.

Milly said, "And, Cletus, we'll have a dog!"

"*Naw!*" Cletus promptly told her. "No *mam!*" And he backed his refusal by a sort of poem that has lived long in the memory of Port William:

What'll keep a dog'll keep a *hog*.
We'll have a *hog*. *I'll* be the dog.

Characters such as Virgil's old Corycian or Shakespeare's Corin, as they have cropped up into literature from the substrate of common experience and memory, are presented as separate individuals. But to see them in full figure, as Andy knows, it is necessary to imagine them or remember them in their neighborhoods at work with their neighbors. The word "neighbor" carries the whole radicalism of the Christian Gospels, but Andy did not learn about the radical economy of neighborliness in church. He learned it from the friends he worked with and listened to, who were sure always that

Many hands make light work,

and who went together into the harvest under the rule of a doctrine most human and holy:

Nobody's done until everybody's done.

Andy thinks of those old ones, long asleep in the graveyard plots that all their holdings finally diminished to, most of them now forgotten, a few still remembered by Andy and a dwindling few others. Andy does not remember them sentimentally, as to wish them back again, for he knows their imperfections as he knows his own. His thoughts dwell on them with regret, sorrow, affection, amusement, or great love, as his heart requires, but also with a careful understanding of the possibility that they lived out and proved, however imperfectly. He thinks of the ancient consciousness that dwelt in them of their need for a piece of land under their feet, that they could live from and thrive a little in the face of whatever greedy or powerful "they" may have threatened them. Their consciousness of that need, Andy knows, had not come to them from any parts of the written record such as he happens to know, but from the common talk and common passion of their kind, generation after generation, on back beyond recoverable knowing.

And now he thinks the time is coming when this faltering civilization, like many others, will have to decide: Are the few surviving of Jefferson's "small land holders," in their ancient lineage of need and knowledge, a romantic fiction, as most of us now think, or a "saving remnant" necessary to renew the human life of the earth?

The Branch Way of Doing

Danny Branch is older than Andy Catlett by about two years, which matters to them far less now than when they were young. They are growing old together with many of the same things in mind, many of the same memories. They often are at work together, just the two of them, taking a kind of solace and an ordinary happiness from their profound knowledge by now of each other's ways and of how to do whatever they are doing. They don't talk much. There is little to explain, they both are likely to know the same news, and Danny anyhow, unlike his father, rarely has anything extra to say.

Andy has always known Danny, but he knows that, to somebody who has not known him long, Danny might be something of a surprise. As if by nature, starting with the circumstances of his birth, as if by his birth he had been singled out and set aside, he has never been a conventional man. To Andy he has been not only a much-needed friend, but also, along with Lyda and their children, a subject of enduring interest and of study.

Danny is the son of Kate Helen Branch and Burley Coulter. His family situation was never formalized by a wedding between his parents, who for various and changing reasons lived apart, but were otherwise as loving and faithful until death as if bound by vows. And Danny was as freely owned and acknowledged, and about as attentively cared for and instructed, by Burley as by Kate Helen. "He's my boy," Burley would say to anybody who may have wondered. "He was caught in my trap."

And so Danny grew up learning by absorption the frugal, elaborate housekeeping of his mother through the Depression and afterward, and grew up also, from the time he could walk, in the tracks of his father, which led to work, to the woods, to the river, sometimes to town. Danny learned as they went along what came from work, what came, more freely, from the river and the woods, what came even from the easy, humorous talk of his father and his friends.

The whole story of Burley Coulter will never be known, let alone told. Maybe more than his son, he would have been a surprise to somebody expecting the modern version of Homo sapiens. He loved the talk and laughter of work crews and the loafing places of Port William, but he was known also to disappear from such gatherings to go hunting or fishing alone, sometimes not to be seen by anybody for two or three days. Everybody knew, from testimony here and there, from gossip, that he had been by nature and almost from boyhood a ladies' man. Little girls had dreamed they would grow up and marry him, and evidently a good many bigger girls had had the same idea. But he remained a free man until, as he put it, Kate Helen put a bit in his mouth and reined him up. But nobody had heard much more than that from Burley himself. He was full of stories, mostly funny, mostly at his own expense, but they never satisfied anybody's curiosity about his love life. He never spoke disrespectfully of a woman. He never spoke of intimacy with a woman. And so Port William speculated and imagined and labored over what it believed to be his story, receiving the testimony of many of its own authorities: "Why, he did! I know damn well he did!" And Burley quietly amused himself by offering no help at all. It is possible, Andy thinks, that Burley was the hero of a work of fiction, of which he was hardly innocent, but a work of fiction nevertheless, composed entirely in the conversation of Port William.

Burley knew the way questions followed him, and he enjoyed the chase, preserving himself unto himself sometimes, like a well-running red fox, by arts of evasion, sometimes by artful semi-truths. Those who thought to catch him were most apt to catch a glimpse as he fled or perhaps flew, a mere shadow on the horizon. When he stood and faced you, therefore, as he did stand and face the people he loved, his candor would be felt as a gift given. But in ordinary conversation with the loafers and bystanders of Port William, he could be elusive.

"Where was you at last night, Burley? I come over to see you, and you wasn't home."

"I stepped out a while."

"Well, I reckon your dogs must've stepped out too. I didn't see no dogs."

"My dogs do step out."

"Reckon you all was stepping out off up Katy's Branch somewhere?"

"A piece farther, I reckon."

"Well, now, where?"

"Well, till full day I didn't altogether exactly know."

"If I couldn't hunt and know where I was, damned if I wouldn't stay home."

"Oh, I knew where I was, but I didn't know where where I was was."

Danny, his father's son and heir in many ways, always has been a more domestic man, and a quieter one, than his father. In 1950, two years after the law allowed him to quit school and he started farming "full time" for himself, he married Lyda, and the two of them moved in with Burley, who had been living in the old house on the Coulter home place alone ever since his mother died.

For seven years Danny and Lyda had no children, and then in the following ten years they had seven: Will, Royal, Coulter, Fount, Reuben, and finally ("*Finally!*" Lyda said) the two girls, Rachel and Rosie. Lyda, who had been Lyda Royal, had grown up in a family of ten children, and she said that the Lord had put her in this world to have some more. Like Danny, she had grown up poor and frugal. "If my daddy shot a hawk that was killing our hens, we ate the hawk."

She was about as tall as Danny, stoutly framed but not fat, a woman of forthright strength and presence whose unwavering countenance made it easy to remember that she was blue-eyed. She and Danny are the best-matched couple, Andy thinks, that he has ever known. That they had picked each other out and become a couple when they were hardly more than children and married before they could vote seems to Andy nothing less than a wonder. He supposes that they must have had, both of them, the gift of precocious self-knowledge, which could only have seemed wondrous to Andy, whose own mind has come clear to him slowly and at the cost of much labor.

For a further wonder, Danny and Lyda seem to have understood from the start that they would have to make a life together that would be determinedly marginal to the modern world and its economy—a realization that only began to come to Andy with the purchase of the Harford place when he was thirty. It was already present in Danny's mind at the age of sixteen, when nearly everybody around Port William was buying a tractor, and he stuck with his team of mules.

Marginality, conscious and deliberate, *principled* marginality, as Andy eventually realized, was an economic practice, informed by something like a moral code, and ultimately something like religion. No Branch of Danny's line ever spoke directly of morality or religion, but their practice, surely for complex reasons, was coherent enough that their ways were known in the Port William neighborhood and beyond by the name of Branch. "That's a Branch way of doing," people would say. Or by way of accusation: "You trying to be some kind of Branch?"

To such judgments—never entirely condemnatory, but leaning rather to caution or doubt or bewilderment, for there was a lot of conventional advice that the Branches did not take—it became almost conventional to add, "They're a good-*looking* family of people." The good looks of Danny and Lyda when they were a young couple became legendary among those who remembered them as they were then. Their children were good-looking—"Of course," people said—and moreover they looked pretty much alike. Danny and Lyda were a good cross.

Their economic life, anyhow, has been coherent enough to have kept the Branch family coherent. By 2004, Branch children and grandchildren are scattered through the Port William neighborhood, as Lyda says, like the sage in sausage. They stick together—whether for fear of Lyda, or because they like each other, or just because they are alike, is a question often asked but never settled. Wherever you find a Branch household you are going to find a lot of food being raised, first to eat and then to sell or give away, also a lot of free provender from the waters and the woods. You are going to find a team, at least, of horses or mules. But there are Branches catering to the demand for heavy pulling horses. Some keep brood mares and sell anything from weanlings to broke farm teams. If a team will work cheaper or better than a tractor, a Branch will use a team. But with a few exceptions in the third generation, they also can fix anything mechanical, and so no Branch has ever owned a new car or truck or farm implement. Their habit is to find something that nobody else wants, or that everybody else has given up on, and then tow or haul it home, fix it, and use it.

As they live at the margin of the industrial economy, they live also at the margin of the land economy. They can't afford even moderately good land, can't even think of it. And so such farms as they have managed to own are small, no better than the steep-sided old Coulter place where Danny and Lyda have lived their married life, no better even than the much abused and neglected Riley Harford place that Andy and Flora Catlett bought in 1964.

The Branch family collectively is an asset to each of its households, and often to their neighbors as well. This may be the surest and the best of the reasons for their success, which is to say their persistence and their modest thriving. When the tobacco program failed, and with it the tobacco economy of the small farmers, and the long tradition of work-swapping among neighbors and even acquaintance with neighbors was petering out, the Branches continued to swap work. They helped each other. When they knew their neighbors needed help, they went and helped their neighbors. If you bought something the Branches had for sale, and they were always likely to have something to sell, or if you hired them, they expected of course to be paid. If, on the contrary, they went to help a neighbor in need, they considered their help a gift, and so they would accept no pay. These transactions would end with a bit of conversation almost invariable, almost a ritual:

"Well, what I owe you?"

"Aw, I'm liable to need help myself sometime."

The old neighborly ways of Port William, dying out rapidly at the start of the third millennium, have survived in Danny and Lyda Branch, and have been passed on to their children. The one boast that Andy ever heard from Danny was that he had worked on all his neighbor's farms and had never taken a cent of money in payment. After his boys grew big enough to work, and he knew of a neighbor in need of help, instead of going himself he would sometimes send a couple of the boys. He would tell them: "If they offer you dinner, you can eat, but don't you come back here with any money."

This uneasiness about money Andy recognizes from much else that he has known of the people of Port William and similar places. Free exchanges of work and other goods they managed easily, but transactions of money among friends and neighbors nearly always involved an embarrassment that they had to alleviate by much delay, much conversation, as if to make the actual handing of cash or a check incidental to a social occasion. It was not, Andy thought, that they agreed with the scripture that "the love of money is the root of all evil," but that from a time even older they held a certain distrust against money itself, or the idea of it, as if a *token* of value were obviously inferior to, obviously worse than, a *thing* of value. And so a man, understanding himself as a neighbor, could not accept money as in any way representative of work or goods given in response to a need.

The Branches, then, would have things to sell. They would work now and then for wages. At convenience or if they had to, they would spend. But their aim, as often as possible, was to have a choice: something they could do or make or find instead of spending money, even of earning it.

Of the source and the reasons for this Branch fastidiousness, Andy is still unsure. For himself, he has finally understood that, however it may be loved for itself, money is only symbolic, only the means of purchasing something that is not money. To live almost entirely by purchase, as many modern people do, is to equate the worth of every actual thing with its price. The symbol thus comes to limit and control the thing it symbolizes, and like a rust or canker finally consumes it. And so buying and selling for money is not simply a matter of numbers and accounting, but is a dark and fearful mystery.

Do the Branches know this? Because he so imperfectly knows it himself, Andy has not known how to ask Danny or Lyda if they know it. He knows only that they, and their children too, seem to be living from some profound motive of good will, even of good cheer, that shows itself mainly in their practice of their kind of economy. The Branches are not much given to explaining.

And so in addition to being included in their friendship, benefitting from it, knowing them well, and loving them in just return, Andy has studied them with endless liking and fascination, feeling always that there is yet more that he needs to know. He believes that the way they live, and the way they are, can be summed up, not explained, by a set of economic principles, things Danny could have told his children but probably never did, or needed to. Andy, anyhow, after many years of observing and pondering, has made a list of instructions that he hears in Danny's voice, whether or not Danny can be supposed ever to have said them:

1. Be happy with what you've got. Don't be always looking for something better.
2. Don't buy anything you don't need.
3. Don't buy what you ought to save. Don't buy what you ought to make.

4. Unless you absolutely have got to do it, don't buy anything new.

5. If somebody tries to sell you something to "save labor," look out. If you can work, then work.

6. If other people want to buy a lot of new stuff and fill up the country with junk, *use* the junk.

7. Some good things are cheap, even free. Use them first.

8. Keep watch for what nobody wants. Sort through the leavings.

9. You might know, or find out, what it is to need help. So help people.

Andy heard Danny say only one thing of this kind, but what he said summed up all the rest.

When he was just old enough to have a driver's license, Reuben, Danny and Lyda's youngest boy, raised a tobacco crop and spent almost all he earned from it on a car. It was a used car—Reuben, after all, was a Branch—but it was a fancy car. Lyda thought the car was intended to appeal to a certain girl. The girl, it turned out, was more impressed with another boy's car, so Reuben got only his car for his money, plus, as his mother told him soon enough, his good luck in losing the girl. Though all in vain, the car was bright red, and had orange and black flames painted on its sides, and had a muffler whose mellow tone announced that Reuben was more rank and ready than he actually was.

Andy and Danny were at work together in Andy's barn when Reuben arrived in his new-to-him car. He had promised his help, and he was late. He drove right up to the barn door, where his red and flaming vehicle could hardly have looked more unexpected. He gunned the engine, let it gargle to a stop, and got out. Maybe he had already had a second thought or two, for a touch of sheepishness was showing through his pride. Danny favored his son with a smile that Reuben was not able to look away from. Reuben had to stand there, smiling back, while, still smiling, his father looked him over. When Danny spoke he spoke in a tone of merriment—the epithet he used seemed almost indulgent—but his tone was nonetheless an emphasis upon a difference that he clearly regarded as fundamental: Some people work hard for what they have, and other people are glad to take it from them easily. What he said Andy has remembered ever since as a cry of freedom: "Sweetheart, I told you. And you'll learn. Don't let the sons of bitches get ahold of your money."

The Art of Loading Brush

I

At last full of the knowledge of the wonder it is to be a man walking upon the earth, Andy Catlett is past eighty now, still at work in the fashion of a one-handed old man. He has done without his right hand, given away to a cornpicker, for more than forty years, and he does not miss it much. But he has been old, it seems to him, for only three or four years, and he misses pretty freshly what was once his strength. His farming now is reduced to caring for his livestock and small tasks of upkeep on what he is apt still to think of as the Riley Harford place, its name long before he attached his own to it. As a farm perhaps never better than marginal, the place in its time has known abuse, neglect, and then, in Andy's own tenure and care, as he is proud to think, it has known also healing and health and ever-increasing beauty.

He has supposed, he has pretty well known, that some of his neighbors in Port William and the country around had thought, when he and Flora bought the place and settled in it, that they would not last there very long, for it was too inconvenient, too far from the midst of things, too *poor*. And so Andy has delighted a little in numbering, as disproof and as proof, the decades of their inhabitance: the 1960s, the '70s, the '80s, the '90s. And now they have lived there more than half a century, long past the doubts and the doubters that they would last. Now it has become beyond doubt or question their place, and they have become its people. They have given their lives into it, and it has lived in their lives.

Of all his kindred Andy has become the oldest. He is one of the last who remembers Old Port William, as he now calls it, as it was when it and the country around it were still intact, at one with its own memory and knowledge of itself, in the years before V-J Day and the industrializing of land and people that followed. He is one of the last of the still-living who was born directly into the influence of the best men of his grandfather Catlett's generation, who confidently, despite their struggles, assigned paramount value to the good-tending of their fields, to a good day's work with the fundamental handtools, to the stance and character of a good mule—the inheritance that has made Andy so far out of place in the present world.

Surprised to find that he has grown as old as his grandfathers, who once seemed to him to have been old forever, he sometimes mistakes his shadow on the ground for that of Marce Catlett, his grandfather, whom he was born barely in time to know, or that of Wheeler Catlett, his father, whom he knew first as a man still young in middle age and finally as a man incoherent and old. Their grandson and son, he has come at last into brotherhood with them.

Of all the old crew of friends and neighbors with whom he traded work and shared life, who accompanied him and eased his way, Andy is the last of the older ones still living. Of that about-gone association, the only younger ones still at hand are his and Flora's children and Lyda and Danny Branch's.

Danny was the last, so far, to go. In the absence of the others, and not so often needed by the younger ones, he and Andy had been often at work together in their old age. "Piddling" they called it, for they never hurried and when they got tired they quit, but also it was work and they did it well. They had worked together since they were young. They knew what to expect from each other. They knew, as Danny said, where to *get*, and that was where they *got*. Danny knew, for instance, and maybe before Andy knew, when Andy was going to need a second hand. They worked sometimes, Andy thought, as a single creature with one mind, three hands, and four legs.

Danny was sick a while. And then at breakfast time one morning, answering a somewhat deferential knocking on the front door, Andy was surprised to see Fount and Coulter Branch standing somewhat back from the door in the middle of the porch, formal and uncomfortable. They had never before in their lives come to his front door. Always all of them had followed the old usage: The familiars of a household went to the back door. But now the world had changed. It would have to be begun again. Fount and Coulter had come for that.

As Andy stood in the open door, the brothers looked at him and did not say anything—because, as Andy saw, they were not able to say anything.

And so he spoke for them. "Well, boys. Has he made it safe away?"

And then Fount cleared his throat, and swallowed, and cleared his throat again. "Andy, we was wondering, if maybe you wouldn't mind, if you wouldn't mind saying a few words for him."

They reached for his hand and shook it and went away.

And so Andy stood behind the lectern at the funeral home and spoke of Danny, of the history and company that they both had belonged to, of the work that they had done together, of the love that made them neighbors and friends, and of the rules of that love that they knew and obeyed so freely, that were so nearly inborn in them, as never to need to be spoken. Andy spoke the rules: "When your neighbor needs help, go help. When neighbors work together, nobody's done until everybody's done." Looking at the younger ones, his and Danny's, who now were looking back at him, he spoke the names of the old membership, dead and living, into whose company the younger ones had been born. He spoke of their enduring, their sweat, and their laughter. "This is your history," he said. "This is who you are, as long as you are here and willing. If you are willing, this is yours to inherit and carry on."

Having outlived so many and so much that will not be known again in this world, Andy has come to feel in body and mind sudden afflictions of sorrow for the loss of people, places, and times. He has passed the watershed in his life when he began losing old friends faster than he made new ones. Now he is far better acquainted in the graveyard on the hill at Port William than in the living town. And so he is diminished and so he lives on, his mind more and more enriched by the company of immortals who inhabit it. He is often given to the thought of subtraction, of what has been given, what taken, what remains. He is no longer surprised, when he is alone, to hear himself speak aloud some prayer of gratitude or blessing.

And yet by their absence his old companions have in a way come closer to him than they were when they were alive. They seem to involve themselves intimately in his life as he goes on living it. His thoughts now often seem to come to him in their words and voices.

On a certain kind of warm summer evening with a steady breeze from the west, Elton Penn will say to him again, as Elton said to him when he was a boy, "Do you feel how soft the air is? It's going to rain."

Or sometimes, when he is looking with satisfaction at his steep pastures now healed and "haired over" with grass, he will hear his father say, "This land responds to good treatment."

Or when in the apparently unbreakable habit of the years of his strength Andy catches himself working too fast, Mart Rowanberry will say, as he said to him once with a certain condescension in the overeagerness of his youth: "You aiming to keep that up all day?"

Or he will remember sometimes in the evening, when the weariness of the day and of his years has come upon him, his grandpa Catlett speaking in one sentence the tragedy and triumph of his knowledge: "Ay God, I know what a man can do in a day."

Or he will hear again his granddaddy Feltner on occasions more than enough: "What can't be helped must be endured."

Or when, as sometimes happens, he is listening to somebody who has started talking and can't stop, he recalls the judgment of Art Rowanberry: "I reckon he must be a right smart fellow, but whatever he knows he learnt it from hisself."

As he thinks back over his kinships and friendships, of those he has loved and who have loved him, and of the once worn-out and broken farm that he has cared for, that has responded to his care with health and beauty, he is able to think well enough of himself. But he still has his wits too, and his memory, and he is often enough reminded of his acts of carelessness and selfishness, more in his youth than now, but also now, and he will hear his grandmother Feltner: "Listen to me. Your granny expects better of you." And so she taught him, as he flinched from her gaze, to expect better of himself. And so he is grateful to think of forgiveness and of the persons in high places who recommended it.

From Elton Penn's early death until the deaths as they came of all the older ones, Andy and his children, the Rowanberrys, the Sowerses, the Coulters, and the Branches would often be at work or at rest together. They knew one another well. They talked for hundreds of hours. And now it seems remarkable how little they spoke of public issues. They talked of course of the weather and their work, of things they remembered. They told jokes and stories. They told of other seasons in other years when they were doing what they were doing again. They told stories that all of them were in, that all of them already knew, that they had told and heard and laughed at and revised and told again any number of times. They told and wondered at bits of local gossip. They spoke of the life histories, commented upon the characters, and filled out the pedigrees of remarkable people they knew or had known. Rarely they would lapse into journalism and tell of something they had read in the paper or heard on the news. Almost never did they speak of politics.

Andy can remember now only one political utterance from a member of their old crew in all of those years. This was at one of the annual Rowanberry family reunions. They had gathered that year in a hickory grove in a corner of a bottomland field belonging to Pascal and Sudie Rowanberry Sowers. There was a sizeable crowd of them: at-home

Rowanberrys, Rowanberrys come home for the occasion, Rowanberrys-by-marriage, honorary Rowanberrys, and some self-appointed Rowanberrys who came bearing in pots, kettles, and baskets, as dutifully as the others, their contributions to the feast.

Andy was sitting on a bench among several of the men who had come from away, all of whom had originated within the familiar reach and compass of Port William, but who bore now something of the estrangement of distance and of other places. A little to Andy's surprise, they began to speak of the recent disgrace of an eminent politician. Pascal, who was standing with one shoulder propped against a tree more or less in front of the bench, seemed to be withdrawn under the brim of his hat as he could sometimes seem to be, but Andy knew that he was listening. The talk of the great politician's downfall gradually brought one of the talkers under pressure to confess that he had voted for him, and another to say modestly that he had not.

Pascal then lifted his head so that his countenance emerged from the shadow of his hat. He said, "I'm not going to tell you who I voted for. But I'll tell you this much. I'll never vote for that son of a bitch again."

Ill-fitted as he has always been to the present age of the world, much more ill-fitted to it as he has come to be, Andy is yet in part and inextricably its creature, captured and held to it even by his contrariness against it, drawn too much left or right by the toxic simplifications of its politics, too much subject to the seductions of its economy. Often enough he knows he has spent money he knew he should have kept. Often enough he has been tempted to buy something he knew he did not need, only by a second thought separating himself from the dog-trained "consumers" who obediently pay too much for whatever is new. He knows that among that multitude he would disappear from the ghosts he most needs to remain known by. He rescues himself by vigilance and fear. And then invariably he will hear Danny Branch's admonition to Reuben, his temporarily youthful and extravagant son: "Sweetheart, you'll finally learn. *Don't* let the sons of bitches get ahold of your money."

Often enough in his remembering he will be delighted. He will laugh. And his laughter will be complicated by respect for the completeness and the stature that come only to the dead, and by the knowledge of loss, and by grief.

II

Outliving your friends, hardly a pleasure, is in its way a matter not overly complicated. Time brings the losses and, if you stay in time, it removes the shock or surprise, gathers the new absences into the structures of ordinary days, and carries you past. But Andy also has begun to outlive his fences, and in the present age of the world that is verily a complication.

He had missed by a lifetime or more the age of the rock fences. When he was born some of them were still in use, but they were frost-heaved and crumbling. Nobody any more had the skill or the time to mend them. They were being replaced by wire, the tumbled rocks left lying or cast into piles out of the way or knapped into road gravel. And so as he grew up he learned to fence with wire.

After he and Flora settled on the Harford place he renewed all the old fences and added more, sometimes with help but often alone. As the years passed he repaired and then rebuilt those fences. But then he had been still in his strength, and for a long time when he needed help, he had his friends or his children.

Now in his old age he still knows how to build a fence, but he is without the all-day strength and stamina to do it. And the generation of Port William men who knew either how to build a fence or how to help is by now as decrepit as he is or dead and gone. Of all the ones Andy knows, the only one he could freely call on who could build a fence is Marce, his son. But Marce has his own farm and his own shortage of help. Though he is nearby and watchful and capable and always ready to help when needed, and often does help, Andy doesn't want to ask him to take on a big job. He feels a greater reluctance to call on any of the Branches. He knows that if he asked they would feel obligated and would come whether it suited them or not.

And so when he had spliced and re-tightened and stobbed up a lengthy stretch of old barbed wire to about its and his own limit, he started asking around for somebody else he could hire to rebuild it. A friend of his gave him the name of a friend of *his* who gave him the name of Shad, short for Shadrock, Harbison.

Shad Harbison was an entrepreneur from down about Ellville who farmed some, carpentered some, did about anything anybody wanted done, including fence-building, and had a crew and the equipment to do the job. Andy called Mr. Harbison on the phone and told him what he needed. Would he be interested?

"Sure would," Mr. Harbison said. "I'll be there at eleven o'clock tomorrow morning. Now where you live?"

Andy told him, and told him how to find the place.

At eleven o'clock the next morning Mr. Harbison's pickup truck was in the driveway in front of Andy's house. Andy would not have been surprised if he had been late or had never showed up, but he was on time to the minute. Andy thanked him for his punctuality, and from then to the end of their association he would have no further reason to thank him. Mr. Harbison politely tooted his horn. They introduced themselves and shook hands.

Mr. Harbison, without unduly noticing the absence of Andy's right hand, had given him his own left hand. "Call me Shad."

"All right. And I'm Andy."

They walked the fence together, Andy showing Shad where it started and where it ended. Andy pointed to the old wood posts that were still sound, and to the ones that would have to be replaced. They took note of the considerable amount of brush and the several trees that would have to be removed before the old fence could be taken out and the new one built. They looked and Shad nodded at the half a dozen young oak and walnut trees that were not to be cut. Andy told Shad he wanted the bushes and the tree limbs laid in neat piles, butt ends together, handy to pick up. The old wire should be rolled up and the rolls put into piles. Andy described the fence he wanted: five strands of barbed wire, spaced so as to turn sheep. There was to be one new corner post, and Andy said how he wanted it braced.

Shad took it all in comprehendingly and with approval:

"Aw yeah. I see."

"Yessir, I see what you mean."

"Why sure. It won't be no problem."

They came to an understanding on the price. Too much, Andy thought, but he had expected that. He had made up his mind not to mind.

"Get the wire and everything else you need at Mel Hundley's in Port William. He'll know to look for you, and he'll charge me for what you get."

Shad then figured up and, taking a notebook and pencil from a shirt pocket, made a list of the materials he thought he would need. He read the list to Andy and looked at him.

"All right," Andy said.

And then, prompted by a committee of his ghosts, he said, looking Shad in the eye, "I'm asking you to do this because I think you'll do it right. I hate a damned mess, and I believe you do."

"Aw, I'm with you there. It ain't a *bit* more trouble to do it right than it is to do it wrong."

They shook hands.

"Tuesday week," said Shad. "Early."

"I'll be looking for you."

On Tuesday, not early, a large powerful red pickup truck with a large metal toolbox behind the cab came rumbling up the lane and into the driveway. The truck was pulling a large trailer of the kind known as a "lowboy" upon which was riding a large red tractor.

A large, soft-looking, somewhat sleepy young man got out of the cab and turned to look at Andy.

Andy was grinning to cover his displeasure at the looks of the young man. "If you're looking for Andy Catlett, I'm him." He stuck out his only hand.

Deciding what to do with it occupied the young man for an awkward moment, and then another, and then, turning his right hand approximately upside down, he allowed Andy to shake it.

"I'm Nub," the young man said.

"Are you Shad Harbison's son?"

"Well I *reckon!*" Nub said, implying that this should have been obvious.

By then an assortment of three other men had emerged from the cab. Had the surplus flesh of Nub been distributed evenly among them, they would have been much improved. They were lean with the leanness of wear and tear, of four or five Saturday nights a week for too many weeks. There was not a full set of teeth or a matched pair of eyes among them.

Andy put his hand in his pocket. "Fellows, I'm Andy Catlett."

"I'm Junior," said the first.

"I'm Junior," said the second, who clearly had looked forward to Andy's surprise at the coincidence.

"Twins!" Andy said, and the Juniors got a laugh out of that.

The third neither laughed nor smiled. He said, "Clay."

Andy turned back to Nub. "Where's your dad?"

"Bringing the wire and stuff."

They unloaded the tractor and Andy showed Nub where to leave the trailer. Then with Andy opening the gates and pointing the way, Nub driving the truck and Clay the tractor, they went up the hill to start work.

Andy had a prejudice against heavy machinery. When a big truck or tractor came onto his place, his prejudice was a sort of loose ache somewhere inside him or in the air around him. He had anticipated the truck and the tractor and was reconciled, but he had allowed himself to believe that they would be accompanied by a competent human.

When they had got to the fenceline and dismounted, he said to Nub, "I suppose your dad told you what we're doing here?"

"Well I *reckon!*"

But Shad, who was perhaps a competent human, still had not come. So far that was not necessarily a problem, for the line would have to be cleared and the old wire removed before the new materials would be needed.

Andy showed Nub everything he had shown his father. "Now you see what has to be done?"

"Well I *reckon!*"

By now Andy was conscientiously restraining his dislike for this slack-fleshed young man whose favorite three words bore invariably the whiff of intellectual superiority.

The two Juniors and Clay were unloading tools from the truck.

Andy had work of his own waiting on him that morning. He resolutely abandoned the fencing job to Nub and his crew and walked away. But he carried with him the insinuating small ache of his uneasiness, and his footing on the slope felt unsure as if he were walking on mud.

When he went back, Shad had come with the supplies, which had been unloaded, and he and the crew were finishing their lunch in the shade of a tree midway of the fencerow. From there all the results of their morning's work were revealed to Andy. The brush, instead of piling it neatly as he had asked, they had merely flung out of their way. The old wire too they had rolled up or wadded into handfuls and flung out of the way. And they had removed not only the old barbed wire, but beyond that also perhaps two hundred feet of still very good woven wire they had so mangled in tearing it out that it could not be put back. Had Nub, the all-reckoning one, started the others and forgotten to tell them to stop? Had he been asleep? Was he perhaps awake only when at the wheel of his magnificent pickup truck?

After he had succeeded in believing his eyes, Andy turned to look at Shad, who was with perfect candor looking at him. Needing very much to say something, Andy thought of nothing.

It was Nub, the master of subtlety, who first spoke. "It wasn't no sense in tearing out that good wire." His tone was corrective, even instructive.

So far as Andy could think in the moment, and he was a slow thinker, he was licked. They had, however clumsily, taken him hostage. His old fence now was gone, he needed it, and they were the ones most available to replace it. Further thoughts, as he knew and feared, would come later. But when he replied his voice was quiet.

"No. There was no sense in it. Don't tear out any more."

He looked at Shad. "You're going to be with these people until they're finished, I hope."

"Aw yeah. I'll be here."

"And you remember how to space the strands?"

Shad recited the measurements, which encouraged Andy a little.

He said, "Well. All right."

He went back a few times to see what they were doing and to signify his distrust, but his judgment of them had turned hard and he went near them only by forcing himself. He was looking forward now only to being rid of them.

The full wherewithal of speech having returned to him, he was cursing them in his thoughts for their ignorance, idiocy, laziness, violence, and haste. He saw that wherever there had been a choice, they had preferred the easiest way to the right way. He was filled with an exasperation that he recognized as his father's: "Barely, by God, sense enough to swallow." He knew that he would not outlive their bad work. And he felt with a sickness almost physical their insult to his place, to himself, and to the history, the legacy, of the good work of his forebears and friends. He reminded himself that there had been a time when he had known hired hands, black and white, who had never possessed a square foot of their own land, who out of the common sense of their culture and upbringing would have recognized the badness of this work for what it was, and would have resented it.

But he had also begun an agenda of self-reproach that would be with him for a while. Why had he not fired Nub on general principles and on suspicion before he even started? Why had he not stayed with Nub and the others to watch, to supervise, at least until Shad had come? He began the suffering of self-knowledge.

He knew well his inclination to trust people, a weakness perhaps that he had nevertheless made a principle, for he knew, and upon enough evidence, that without trust there can be no end to the expense and effort of distrust. But now that it had been so flagrantly abused, his trust looked foolish to him. He looked foolish to himself. Those who had brought him up, whose ghosts accompanied him now, had told him plenty about caution, about responsibility, about the importance of "seeing to things" and "tending to business." And he had once in fact gone so far himself as to fire a man who had come to replace a barn door, and whose work was so careless and slovenly as to be destructive. The man apparently had concluded, as apparently Nub and Company had done, that a place so obviously inferior, so far off the road and out of the modern world as this old Harford place, did not deserve his respect or his best work.

But firing the man, Andy's one exploit as a firer, had given him no pleasure, not even in his initial anger, and the lapse of more than enough time had not taken away his distaste. But now, as he accused himself of not having fired or supervised Nub when he should have done so, it came to him that on the farms he had known in his early life he remembered nothing at all of supervising and firing. His grandfather Catlett, for example, had one hired hand: Dick Watson, a black man, whom as a child Andy had looked up to and loved, whom he still loves. Andy spent hundreds of hours in the company of Grandpa Catlett and Dick Watson. Though the order of work was set of course by Grandpa, he never in Andy's hearing told Dick *how* to do anything or made a supervisory remark of any kind. Past work himself, Grandpa would often be watching, but he spoke of Dick's work to Andy only to commend it, to speak of Dick as an example for Andy to learn from. "Look yonder at how old Dick sets up and takes hold of his mules."

Thinking back, Andy can see that Grandpa Catlett trusted Dick Watson to work well because Dick was capable of working well, did so willingly, took pride in doing so, and trusted Grandpa to see that this was so. They were, to the extent of their mutual trust, free of each other—free, that is, to sit down together on upturned buckets in the doorway of the barn to talk and look out at the rain. In that trust and freedom, limited as it was, there was something of peace, maybe even a promise of peace, unregarded and bypassed as history wore on through its wars, beyond the deaths of those elders and their generation, to a time when no two men even of the same race would sit together in a barn door to talk and watch the rain.

During his first twenty or so years, Andy played and then worked in the company of a good many hands, black and white, who worked by the day, straight time or temporarily as through a harvest. They and their work varied a good deal in quality, but with few exceptions, they were more like Dick Watson than they were like Shad Harbison's fencing crew. Long ago the good ones, farm-raised and self-respecting, had either died or gone to jobs in industry. To replace them now were only the machines, the chemicals, and, in a pinch, the barely awake, the barely sober, the barely conscious, the incompetent, indifferent, and more or less accidently destructive.

At last, actually fairly soon, the Harbison crew messed and blundered its way to the completion of a usable fence, newer, shinier, and tighter at least than the old one. Andy wrote Shad a check for the too much that they had agreed on, that had now become much more than too much. Shad graciously accepted the check and hoped that Andy, if he ever had more fence to build, would just let him know.

"Thanks," Andy said, and he watched their vehicles go down the lane and out of sight, he hoped, forever.

III

And so he was left to submit his outrage to time, hoping, praying in fact, that before he died he would come to some manner of forgiveness both for the Offensive Fencers Incorporated and for himself.

Unignorably in the way of that lay the mess that the fencers had left behind: the scatters and tangles of brush and small logs, the randomly discarded rolls and wads and bits and pieces of old wire that now defaced and affronted the beautiful field that for fifty years he had lovingly housekept. There had been a time when in his strength he would have thought nothing of cleaning it up. He could have done it by himself in a few hours. Now he was depressed and diminished by it. It looked impossible.

He thought of calling his son to come and help him, but he rejected that thought as soon as it came. It was too late now to ask Marce. If he had asked when he should have, the two of them working together would have built a good fence with no mess or shortcutting. Moreover, they would have enjoyed working together.

Now, grieved by that loss and dismayed by the result, he was also embarrassed. He could not bear the thought that Marce might *see* the mess. He knew Marce would not say, but he dreaded that he would think: "Well. You oughtn't have dealt with those damned counterfeits in the first place."

Andy knew very well why he had dealt with them: He was ignorant and knew it and was in a hurry and went ahead anyhow. And so he didn't call Marce.

But there was one recourse he might still have. There was a good boy from down at Hargrave, Austin Page, a boy not farm-raised but interested in farming, who had asked to work for Andy while he was in high school, and Andy often had been glad to hire him, to have his help, and to have his company. He *liked* Austin, who was intelligent, eager to learn, willing to work, and humorous enough to put up with the correction he sometimes received. Andy had put him to the test a number of times, and Austin had always passed. By way of Andy's instruction, and sometimes his impatience, Austin had learned to work *with* Andy. Now more often than not he knew where to get, and more often than not he could anticipate what came next. Now he was in college, majoring in music, in which he was perhaps exceptionally gifted. As Andy had grown older and weaker, Austin had grown older and stronger. He was a big boy now, well-muscled, with freckles and tightly curled hair the color of a new penny. He was easily embarrassed and a radiant blusher, which made him especially valuable to Andy.

"I can turn that boy on and off like a light bulb," he said to Daisy

Page, Austin's mother. Daisy Page was a woman whom Andy somewhat excessively admired, and all the more when she replied, "Mister. Catlett. You are too near the drop-off to be a smartass."

She said that as a prelude to saying that Austin soon would be done with his summer courses and was wondering: Might Andy have work for him before he had to return for the fall semester? Andy said yes, he might.

And so it happened that about three days after the departure of Harbison and Crew, when Andy was sorely needing him, Austin called him up.

"Mr. Catlett, this is Austin. Do you need help?"

"Do you mean am I helpless?"

"Oh nosir. I mean, do you have something to do that I could help you with?"

"Yes, Mr. Austin, my friend, I do. Come in the morning."

Andy had a small, low-wheeled wagon that was easy to load. It was not often used, and he and Austin had to go to some trouble to get it out from among the other implements where it had been put away. When they had it unencumbered and in the clear, they brought out Andy's old team of horses, the white one and the black, and hitched them to the wagon. By then Andy felt that he too had come into the clear. The oppression of the fencers and their mess had lifted from him like a cloud.

In his new clarity he had a sort of vision of himself and Austin there with the team and wagon at the start of their morning's work: an old man full of an outdated pride and demand, counting his losses, still suffering his dream, two nights ago, of the handtools of all the tradesmen of Old Port William heaped up and auctioned off to "collectors" who did not know their uses—and, standing beside him, this vivid boy, his mind on fire, his hair burning his cap off, this Austin Page, fresh from his summer courses, clearly glad now to be with Andy, outdoors, going to work.

Andy handed the lines to Austin and was amused, also much pleased, that Austin took them as a matter of course into his own hands and spoke to the team.

They went up to the fence row. When they had come to their starting place Andy said "Whoa," and he and Austin stepped off the wagon.

Andy said, "You see what we've got to do. It's a mess."

And Austin, quoting and correcting, said, "A damned mess," and Andy laughed.

"We'll pick up the brush first," he said, "and we'll pile up the wire as we find it. It's scattered everywhere. We'll pick that up last. Finding all of it'll be the problem." In fact they would not find it all that day. As Andy expected, he would be finding the smaller pieces by surprise for a long time. Once, as he had feared, he found a fugitive hank of the heaviest of it by cutting into it with his mowing machine.

He picked up the first limb and laid it on the wagon. And then Austin picked up a somewhat larger one and, from a distance of perhaps a dozen feet, with a young athlete's depreciating nonchalance, tossed it over onto the one Andy had loaded.

"Hold on!" Andy said. "Wait a minute." He had spoken almost before he thought.

In his happiness at Austin's arrival to help him, Andy had seemed to himself to be both in the moment and outside it, watching. And now, his mind alerted in all the strata of its years, he was inhabiting also a moment much older. He was fourteen years old and had been formally hired, not at last by his father but by Elton Penn, to help in the tobacco harvest, and thus, small for his age as he was, had arrived at last at the status and dignity of a hand. But he had just handed Elton a stick of tobacco, turning loose his end as soon as Elton took hold of the other, greatly increasing the effort for Elton.

"Now *wait* a minute!" Elton had a transfixing grin, and Andy was transfixed, knowing well by then that his situation could get worse.

"You handed that stick to me *wrong*. Now I'm handing it to you *right*. Now you hand it back to me *right*. That's the way. That's the way I want you to hand it to me from now on."

Andy said, "Austin, my good boy, damn it, wait a minute. We ain't going to make a mess to clean up a mess. Do you want to put one load into three loads or into one load?"

He looked at Austin until Austin said, "Well. Obviously. I would rather put one load into one load."

Andy saw that Austin's ears were turning red, and he was amused, but he said fairly sternly, "Well, come and pick up that branch you just threw on and turn it over so it takes up less room. Now snug the butt up against the headboard of the wagon.

"That's right," he said. "That's the way we do it. We pick up every piece and look at it and put it on the load in the place where it belongs. We think of the shape of every limb and stem and chunk and pole, and that's the way we shape the load.

"It's the use of the mind," he said, "what they ought to be teaching you in school."

Andy and Henry, his brother, had gone to see Elton one day shortly after Old Jack Beechum had died and Elton had bought the old Beechum place. In Old Jack's declining years he had become dependent on hired hands and tenants, some of whom had not lived or worked up to Old Jack's standards. They had not stayed long, but they had each left a deposit of dooryard trash, broken toys, bits of furniture, things put down and left lying. Now Elton was cleaning it up, setting the place to rights, as in duty to the old man, to himself, and to their joint ownership. The Catlett brothers found nobody at home that day, but in the barn lot there was a wagon loaded with the debris of human carelessness as well as bits of old lumber and the scattered rocks that Elton had picked up as he went along. Henry stopped his car and he and Andy sat for a few minutes, admiring the load which was, of its kind, a masterwork. Every piece, every scrap conferred upon the whole load the happiness of its right placement.

"He couldn't make an ugly job of work to save his life," Henry said.

"*Now* you're shouting," Andy said to Austin. "Now you're doing it right.

"Now," he said, "we're practicing the art of loading brush. It is a fundamental art. An indispensible art. Now I know about your 'fine arts,' your music and literature and all that—I've been to school too—and I'm telling you they're *optional*. The art of loading brush is not optional."

"You talking about symphonies?" Austin had stopped and was standing still to signify the importance, to him, of symphonies.

"Symphonies! Hell yes!" Andy said. "You take a society of people who can write symphonies and conduct symphonies and play symphonies and can't put on a decent load of brush, they're going to be shit out of luck."

Austin's face, starting with his ears, had become almost astonishingly red, and Andy rejoiced. He was bearing joyfully now the burden of knowing better. Maybe in the passing on of his ghostly knowledge he was doing his duty to Austin. He was sure that a man hiring a boy had a duty to help him along if he could. But his thoughts were moved now by a parental fear for this Austin, this boy with his mind on fire, kindled by symphonies and God knows what. Andy was entirely familiar with that fire. Any sorry poor human having a mind, some time or another it would be on fire, with the old prospect of burning the mind's owner or burning the world, invoking always the old familial hope, for every grown boy anyhow, that the heat might be so contained as to warm a hearth or boil a kettle without burning down the house. So an old man, leaning toward a young one, would try to dampen a little the omnivorous blaze. But also he would be warming his hands. If he was helping Austin to get a start in life, he was also restarting his own. He felt a strange elation coming into his heart, so familiar now among the dead, so strange among the living. He wasn't going to say much more, but for the moment he was standing his ground.

"My dear Austin, my good boy, maybe it's possible to blow things up and burn things up and tear things down and throw things away and make music all at the same time. Some, it looks like, think you can. But: If you don't have people, a lot of people, whose hands can make order of *whatever* they pick up, you're going to be shit out of luck. And in my opinion, if the art of loading brush dies out, the art of making music finally will die out too. You tell your professors, when you go back, that you met an old provincial man, a leftover, who told you: No high culture without low culture, and when low culture is the scarcest *it* is the highest. Tell 'em that. And then tell me what they say."

Now instead of blushing Austin was thinking. His face, his posture, his movements all now bore the implication of thought.

He said finally, "I reckon you'd make brush-loading a required course for music majors."

Andy laughed, which he had been wanting to do for some time. "I probably would, if it was up to me. But listen, Austin. I'm serious."

"I know it."

"And I'm telling you all this because I'm your friend."

"I know it."

They finished the load. Andy took the lines himself this time. He stood to drive, and Austin made himself an uncomfortable place to perch.

"The art of *piling* brush begins and ends," Andy said, "with knowing where to pile it."

He drove some distance to where a grassy slope came down to a wooded bluff. They came to a swale in the pasture where once there had been a gulley, now long-healed and sodded over, "haired over" his father would say. But the gully was still open and raw where it steepened, going into the woods. Andy positioned the wagon just above that place.

He had a theory, two hundred years too late to prove, that gullies like this one had been opened by plowing and cropping the slopes. Before that, when the country still wore its deep, porous, rootbound original soil, the water draining through such places was more apt to seep than to flow. Where the slopes were not too steep they could be healed under grass. On the bluffs, even after the trees had returned, the healing would be slow, if it could happen, if it could happen in human time. Andy nonetheless loved the thought of the healing of the gullies. He knew they could not be healed from the bottom up, for there the flow had gathered too much force. But for a good while he had thought, experimentally, that by using brush to slow and divert the water a little just below the edge of the grass, he might start the healing from the top. He laid his thinking out for Austin, showed him what he had in mind, and then to the head of the gulley they applied the art of piling brush.

And so they worked through the morning. And so they worked to the end of their task in the middle of the afternoon. By then Andy was tired. By then Austin was doing most of the work, and all of the hardest of it. Andy was keeping out of his way, helping a little as he could, and watching, as Austin stepped with the happiness of his young strength into the work. About as far as it could be done in Andy's lifetime, they had undone the bad work of the fencers. Maybe they had helped a little the healing of the hurt world. And he was proud of the boy.

Epilogue

from Sabbaths 2016—VIII

What Passes, What Remains

Here the mingling of the waters
of Shade Branch, Sand Ripple,
the dishonored Kentucky River,
tells the history of our country
which is the history of our people.
Here the mind submits
itself to be shaped, and so
it shapes its thought, partly
of itself, partly of all
in time it has come to know.
Here in this passage of valley
hollowed by the passage of water,
great Life has come in passing

to inhabit every body
inhabiting this place,
giving desire and motion,
giving sight, light,
color, and form, giving
stories, songs, calls,
cries, outcries. How long?

This is the place in which
the living live in the absence
of all who once were here,
their stories kept a while
in memories soon to be gone
the way of the untongued stories
preceding ours, reduced
to graves mostly lost
and a few found strayed
artifacts of stone.

Of those now living here
already few recall
the names of the Rowanberrys
whose home this rough land was
that bears in presence only
their worn ways, some scars
their work made, the well
the early ones dug and walled
where their log house stood
and burned, the disassembled
chimneys, the sundered hearths.
Their numberless disappeared
footsteps are traceable now
only by the remaining few
who remember the last of them.

By love we keep them with us,
and so we have remembered
ourselves as members, gathered
in Love's household that stands
surpassingly in time: we few
remaining, who keep the stories.

"My lord, they worked hard
for every nickel and dime
they ever had. One crop
finished and gone to market,
they'd start clearing a patch
of hillside for the next crop.
If you look about, you'll find
their monuments that will last, I reckon,
clean to Judgment Day:
mounds or squared cairns
of rocks turned up by their plows,
dragged out of the furrows,
lifted and put down, and nothing
automatic into it, neither.
Here and there you'll find
their gullies too, mostly healed
under the young woods about
the age of an old man."

"I was grubbing bushes
and sprouts with an axe, setting
my own pace, but hard at it.
Art and Mart were felling
and logging up the trees
with a two-man crosscut saw.
After while Mart said, 'Pascal,
I'll rest you a little. Let me

run that axe, and you
get here on the saw with Art.'
So we traded, and good God!
I felt like I had a hold
of the tail of a stout big calf
and couldn't turn loose. Even
what they called rest was *work*.
And Mr. Early Rowanberry
—the old man, but not so old
then as I thought—he
would be working always, always
somewhere ahead of them."

"He come in there at Burgess's
one evening late, a bunch
of us loafing there, talking,
the way we'd do. He bought
a steel-beam rounder plow,
paid in cash, and then
did what not a one of us
foresaw. He'd come walking.
It was a *heavy* plow. Somebody
would have hauled it down there
for him in a day or two.
He picked it up by the beam of it
and laid it over his shoulder
like it wasn't more than a hoe,
hunched it into place,
and set off home on the path
down Shade Branch, a mile
to walk and it getting dark.
Lord amighty! Hurrying
to be ready to work in the morning,
I reckon. No time to lose."

"Oh, it hurts me to remember
how hard my daddy worked."

And she by then was old
after a life of her own
hard work, hers and Pascal's,
by which they bought, paid for,
and improved their farm, built
and paid for a good small house.
Theirs had been a time
kinder to them than her father's
had been to him. Their life
even so had been in its way
a triumph of work and thrift,
care and self-respect.
Whoever knew them knew
something inarguably good.

"A while after we got married
and set up housekeeping
over across the river,
knowing she missed her folks,
I brought Sudie back home
for a visit late that winter.
It sleeted during the night.
In the morning all outdoors
was coated with ice. They'd been
cleaning up another
hillside for another crop:
felling the trees, grubbing
out the bushes, closing in
on a great snarl of briars
still in the way. After
breakfast, Mr. Rowanberry

sent us boys to the barn,
slipping and sliding on the ice,
to do the chores. And he
took down his scythe from its nail
and went to the hillside to mow
that big blackberry patch
before the day warmed up
and melted off the ice
from the catclaws of the briars."

And so some days they were favored,
when place and work and weather
seemed to answer one another,
when what the world asked
and what they gave seemed
almost in rhyme, hour
after hour, daylight to dark,

days too when the world asked
for all they had to give
and more, when a boy, under
the demand of a father brittle
and driven, could wish to be
some place he could not go.

"My daddy remembered Art Rowanberry
disking ground with a team of mules
when he wasn't more than eight years old.
His feet didn't reach to the frame of the harrow,
and his daddy had tied him onto the seat
with a little piece of cotton rope.
He was all the help his daddy had.
I don't reckon Art remembered
when he didn't know how to drive a team."

"Art enlisted in the army in '42
when he was thirty-seven years old.
In basic training he rested up.
He said he gained a little weight."

"To stand around waiting to work,
that was something I had to *learn*.
One day they give us out some axes,
thick as your foot, dull as a froe.
I taken a file and whetted mine
to where it was some account. Them boys
just stood around and watched me chop."

"He was the oldest, the eldest son.
He thought if he went, the younger ones
would be spared. But they drafted two of them.
If he hadn't enlisted, Art might not
have had to go. But oh my!
He saw a world he'd never dreamed of,
and dreamed of, I reckon, the rest of his life."

"I stopped in Bastogne with a buddy of mine
and we bought us a big plate of potatoes.
We still were eating them when the Germans
cut us off. Before that was done with
we *needed* a big plate of potatoes.
We was hungry, down to just
one little pancake a day."

I said, "I reckon you all were glad
when they broke through and got you out."
And he said, seeming to look and see it
again through almost forty years,
"We was glad to see that day when it come."

"It was during the war, I reckon.
I don't remember why,
but I was mowing weeds
with an old machine we had
and my good team of mules.
The weeds was tall as the mules
and it was smothering hot,
punishing hot, the air
flying full of chaff
and biting flies. And that
old leftover machine,
you had to run it fast
to make it cut atall.
I hit a stump and broke
the cutter bar clean off.
I never was as glad
of anything in my life"
—Mart.

      Or any of them,
at work in the hot sun,
might have looked into the woods
at the trees standing in shade
at ease and quiet, and thought
again that man must earn
his bread by the sweat of his face.
Mart, who here stands
imperfect as he knew he was,
was rightly somewhat glad
that when the Reckoning came
and he stood before his Maker
he would at least have met
the terms of our condition, discharged
his debt, his account of sweat
and labor paid in full.

At last, when we'd worked together,
through the morning, and Flora
asked, as we came into the kitchen
for dinner, glad to see him
as she always was, "How're you,
Art?" Art said, "Well,
they say you're once a man
and twice a child, and I believe
I've been through just about
all them possibilities."

Now they and all their days
are gone into the silence
and invisibility that come
with an old man's gathered years
to hover over the home,
the known, land. None
like them will ever live
in such a time as theirs
in such a place as this
place was in their time.

Eternal in its passing, Life
came to them, offering its gifts,
making its demands, and they
answered by their work, their pleasure,
their enduring, knowing at times
a timelessness in which
they woke as living souls.

To one who has watched and remembered,
listened and remembered, in time
sharing the work and the weather,
the laughter and the grief, it seems
that Life is with us always

as a wide wind passing
through the woods, moving
every leaf. As it gives us
our lives and then, as we
have made them, takes them away,
a fitting care remains
as ever still and whole
in our great Taskmaster's eye.

Thanks

My debt to my family is acknowledged on the dedication page.

When I published *The Unsettling of America* forty years ago, I thanked Thomas Grissom for the help he had given me in the writing of that book. It is a pleasure to thank him even more for his help with this one. Many pages of this book are directly indebted to his long study of the history of The Burley Tobacco Growers Co-operative Association and the economic history of our region. I have benefited happily from his research and his conversation.

To David Charlton and Tanya Berry I owe more than thanks for typing and retyping my manuscript, and for putting up ever so generously with my many changes of mind.

And, as before, I offer my gratitude and praise to Julie Wrinn, whose copyediting I understand both as a practical necessity and as a work of friendship.

I thank my friends John Logan Brent and Mark Lawson for allowing me to quote portions of their letters.

For publishing parts of this book and for attendant help and encouragement, I thank Wendy Lesser of *The Threepenny Review* and Ruth Conniff of *The Progressive*.

For their willingness to keep me out of trouble, and for standing by me through many years, I am grateful to my dear allies, David Kline and Wes Jackson.

I wish, for their sake, that I were not so dependent on my friends. But my work as a writer has taught me, above everything else, that I cannot do it alone. For indispensable help I am indebted also to the following people, who have improved this book both by their editorial and other suggestions and by their influence: Charlie Sing, Tracy Sides, William H. Martin, Jim Powell, John Lukacs, Jason Rutledge, Ole Faergeman, Irene Eckstrand, Fred Kirschenmann, Ricardo Salvador, and Brian Donahue.

Finally I need to notice, because I cannot forget, that I have known Jack Shoemaker as a friend and editor for forty-five years. In that time we have had a number of business adventures, have written many letters, have talked for many hours face to face and on the phone. Our friendship has been, for me, an entertainment, a consolation, and, profoundly, a collaboration.

To Jack and to Counterpoint, again, my thanks.

None of the above, but only I, should be blamed for any errors of fact or flaws of thought that may be discovered herein.

WENDELL BERRY, an essayist, novelist, and poet, has been honored with the T. S. Eliot Prize, the Aiken Taylor Award for poetry, the John Hay Award of the Orion Society, and the Richard C. Holbrooke Distinguished Achievement Award of the Dayton Literary Peace Prize, among other honors. In 2010, he was awarded the National Humanities Medal by President Barack Obama, and in 2016, he was the recipient of the Ivan Sandrof Lifetime Achievement Award from the National Book Critics Circle. He is also a fellow of the Academy of Arts and Sciences. Berry lives with his wife, Tanya Berry, on their farm in Henry County, Kentucky.